Buying Time for Heritage

Buying Time for Heritage

HOW TO SAVE AN ENDANGERED HISTORIC PROPERTY

J. Myrick Howard

Preservation North Carolina | Raleigh, North Carolina

Sponsors

National Endowment for the Arts

The Mary Duke Biddle Foundation

Preservation North Carolina Publication Endowment *(created at the Community Foundation of Western North Carolina by Amy and Damon Averill)*

Federation of North Carolina Historical Societies

Design and production by Chris Crochetière, BW&A Books, Durham, North Carolina.
Printed by Jostens, Winston-Salem, North Carolina.

Distributed by
The University of North Carolina Press
116 S. Boundary St.
Chapel Hill, North Carolina 27514-3808
Additional copies of this publication may be ordered by calling 1-800-848-6224 *or from the Press's website,* www.uncpress.unc.edu.

Library of Congress Cataloging-in-Publication Data

Howard, J. Myrick, 1953–
   Buying time for heritage : how to save an endangered historic property / J. Myrick Howard.
      p. cm.
   Includes index.
   ISBN-13: 978-0-8078-5868-4 (pbk. : alk. paper)
   1. Historic buildings—Conservation and restoration—United States. 2. Historic preservation—United States.
   I. Title.
   NA111.H69   2007
   363.6'9—dc22
                          2007030212

Photo Credits
Photographs were taken by the staff, board, or volunteers of Preservation North Carolina, except for the following:

Coolmore Plantation (page 16, color insert), photos by Tim Buchman originally taken for *North Carolina Architecture* (1990)
William R. Davie House (page 102), photo courtesy of North Carolina Division of State Historic Sites
Glencoe streetscape (page 9, color insert), photo by Steve Cann
Kamphoefner House (page 92), photo by Bryan Hoffman
Moore-Gwyn House (page 68), photo by William H. Dodge
Rhode Island Mill (page 11, color insert), photo courtesy of Weaver Cooke Construction
Southern Living cover, March 1986 (page 12), courtesy of *Southern Living*
UNCG Chancellors House (page 38), photo by Chris English and courtesy of Chris English/UNCG
Union Tavern (page 40), photo by Ramsay Leimenstoll Architects
PNC is grateful for the use of these photographs.

Top photo on the front cover, and photo above: Patty Person Taylor House, Franklin County. Other photos on front cover (l. to r.): Dr. Victor McBreyer House, Shelby; the Shell Station, Winston-Salem; and Glencoe House #19 ("The Leaner"), Alamance County. Back cover: High Rock Farm, Rockingham County.

Contents

Acknowledgments

"You should write a book." I can't tell you how many people have told me that. Having worked with endangered historic properties at Preservation North Carolina (PNC) for nearly thirty years, I can tell innumerable stories of both "hurry-up" (agonizing cliffhangers) and "wait" (projects that seem to take forever). I've visited fascinating places down back roads throughout North Carolina and worked with a wide spectrum of humanity.

When a program officer for the National Endowment for the Arts (NEA) says "you should write a book," it takes on a different meaning. Having seen a presentation about PNC's property work, Mark Robbins encouraged me to apply for an NEA grant to help underwrite a publication that would aid other organizations seeking to work with historic properties. PNC applied, the award was granted, and the obligation became binding.

The stories that I tell in this book belong to many people. Through the years, I have been the (sometimes uncomfortable) beneficiary of the "ooohhhs" and "aaaahhhs" of audiences who see photos of properties that have been transformed from dilapidated wrecks to pristine jewels. I recognize that the praise is misplaced.

Historically speaking, we at Preservation North Carolina are in the picture for only a fleeting moment with each endangered property. It's a critical moment, when the property (and its stories) might otherwise be lost to posterity. The accolades should actually go to the local contact who let us know about the property, the purchaser who took the risk of buying and renovating it, the craftspeople who did the work, the lender who provided capital despite the building's condition, and a host of others. Early in the writing of this book, we decided that I should tell the stories without naming the participants. So once again, I'm not sharing the credit that's due others – with apology.

Like the properties we work with, this book has been an exercise in both urgency and patience; it was nearly a decade in the making. Numerous individuals have helped make it a reality – literally, too many to mention. I'm grateful to PNC staff and board members, property owners, donors, colleagues, interns, friends, and others who aided and abetted this venture. I have been very fortunate to be surrounded at PNC by wonderful people who care passionately about North Carolina and its future.

I'd like to especially thank the following people who individually spent many hours on this project: David Perry at UNC Press and Barbara Wishy, PNC's former director of the Endangered Properties Program, who both encouraged me from the beginning; Chris Crochetière at BW&A Books in Durham who took a manuscript and photos and turned them into a book; Kathy Adams at the National Trust for Historic Preservation who pushed me to think about an audience beyond the boundaries of North Carolina; Bynum Walter and Andrew Stewart, planning students at the University of North Carolina, who read and re-read the manuscript and gave sage input; Shannon Phillips at Preservation North Carolina, who helped raise the money to do the project, and the rest of the PNC staff who helped with photography, proofreading, fact-checking, and simply listening to me talk about it; and Brinkley Sugg, who gave me unlimited support at home.

Thanks, too, to the sponsors (listed on the back of the title page) who generously supported this project financially. They made it possible.

I've learned a lot in the process of writing this book. I hope you'll find it valuable, too.

Myrick Howard
Spring 2007

Buying Time for Heritage

ONE

Introduction

IN 1974, when Lee Adler of the Historic Savannah Foundation spoke to a gathering of the North Carolina Society for the Preservation of Antiquities about Savannah's pioneering preservation revolving fund, the thirty-five-year-old Antiquities Society was in generational crisis.

On the eve of the American Bicentennial, the old guard was of necessity passing the torch. The Antiquities Society had been founded in 1939, mainly by ladies of status or wealth, to encourage preservation of North Carolina's most prominent historic sites. Through its work the Antiquities Society had founded or assisted dozens of museums. So that North Carolina would no longer have to play second fiddle to neighboring Virginia and its revival of Williamsburg, the Antiquities Society had successfully led the effort to reconstruct Tryon Palace in New Bern, the state's colonial seat of government. While no one else seemed interested in historic preservation, the Antiquities Society persisted and persevered with its righteous message— with real achievements to show for its efforts.

But by 1974, the times had caught up with the Antiquities Society. Its founders were aging out; those still alive were in their seventies and eighties. The group had been no match for the federal urban renewal and interstate highway programs of the 1950s and 1960s. A well-intentioned decision to grant life memberships for $50 had decimated the budget; the group had hundreds of life members who felt no obligation to pay dues. The Antiquities Society was in deep trouble.

In 1974, a new generation was coming to the fore. Younger, more assertive, often male and professional, these preservationists were smitten by Lee Adler's tales of blocks of Savannah buildings being saved by an aggressive preservation organization. Museums were no longer the preservation solution of choice. These new preservationists talked of economic impact, community revitalization, revolving funds, tax laws, zoning, and even lawsuits.

Adler encouraged the group to consider creating a statewide revolving fund for historic preservation. No other state had done it, but the idea had unquestionable appeal. It might just work in North Carolina, a state of small cities and rural areas. Unlike Virginia (where Williamsburg and Richmond dominated preservation) and South Carolina (which had Charleston), North Carolina had no towering giant in preservation. For centuries the state had been called (sometimes with pride, sometimes with derision) the "vale of humility between two mountains of conceit." Its heritage was relatively modest and spread widely across the state.

But the banner of the Antiquities Society was too tattered to lead this bold new initiative to success. For starters, the Antiquities Society had a board with more than one hundred directors who

This booklet illustrates the disheartened spirit of preservationists in the 1970s when North Carolina's new statewide revolving fund was established. Nearly two decades later, the building on the cover, the Dodd-Hinsdale House in Raleigh, was sold with protective covenants by Preservation North Carolina.

of a new statewide revolving fund. Within a year the new fund, the first of its kind in the nation, was launched with a $35,000 grant from the Mary Reynolds Babcock Foundation to hire its first full-time director, Jim Gray of Winston-Salem, and get started.

Thirty years later, the accomplishment record of the succeeding organization, Preservation North Carolina (PNC), probably exceeds its founders' wildest dreams. The organization has worked with more than 600 endangered historic properties, many of which would otherwise have been lost. These properties represent at least $200 million in private investment for purchase and historic rehabilitation. Many of the saved properties have truly been community landmarks. They have ranged from small eighteenth-century houses to large twentieth-century schools, factories, and hospitals. Buyers have put these properties into a multitude of new uses, adding millions of dollars to local tax rolls and creating numerous jobs. Several of the larger properties have been adapted into affordable housing. More than 2,000 acres of open space have been placed under protective covenants, perpetually restricting their development. Today, the organization employs six full-time professionals who work exclusively on saving the state's endangered historic places.

This book attempts to explain why PNC's pioneering effort succeeded when others have failed and to provide insights from the organization's thirty years of direct preservation action. A few salient conclusions about Preservation North Carolina's work steer this book:

gathered once a year for a breakfast meeting during Culture Week. To work with property, such a board would be disaster. Further, the volunteer-driven, aging Antiquities Society would have a difficult time raising the funds necessary to launch the effort.

A series of organizational changes resolved the generational impasse. The Antiquities Society updated itself with a more modern name, the Historic Preservation Society of North Carolina; and it adopted a bundle of new initiatives, such as a regular newsletter, an annual conference, and a broadened awards program. A smaller executive committee would govern the organization. A separate organization was spun off to carry out the creation

- Unlike most preservation organizations, the "revolving fund" (a problematic term to be discussed later in chapter 4) of Preservation North Carolina was launched as a single-purpose preservation organization. Unencumbered initially by membership events, conferences, newsletters, and the like, in its early years the fund focused exclusively on saving endangered historic properties (i.e., real estate). That focus, which has endured despite broadened activities, has brought financial support, credibility, and an enviable record of tangible achievement.

• Preservation North Carolina has generally avoided the temptation to renovate its endangered properties or to make long-term loans to buyers. By using options and selling properties in as-is condition, PNC can work with more properties and perform more nimbly, since it has less money invested in any single property.

• Preservation North Carolina has achieved surprising continuity in its human resources. Many of its professional staff members have stayed with the organization for years, and its board is populated with a mix of "old-timers" and "newcomers." (The organization's bylaws contain term limits, so "old-timers" have returned to the board after breaks in their participation.) Continuity has provided institutional memory, enhanced donor confidence, and supplied political credibility.

• The organization has generally reached a workable balance between board responsibilities and staff empowerment. Working with real estate requires quick decisions. Without the capacity to act quickly and decisively, an organization working to save historic buildings is doomed.

• Preservation North Carolina has generally chosen to work with properties that offer a reasonable prospect for success. If economic, structural, or political analysis leads to the conclusion that a property will be well-nigh impossible to save, then PNC moves on to a candidate with better prospects for success. "Fighting," a frequent mantra for many preservationists, is seldom good for a real estate–oriented preservation organization.

Before a preservation organization launches into a program to work directly with endangered properties, it needs to reach a consensus about what it is trying to achieve. The goals vary; they may include downtown revitalization, neighborhood renewal, individual landmarks, landscape preservation, community building, or the preservation of a community's historical and architectural legacy. Each requires specialized tools and focused efforts.

The field of historic preservation is important for a veritable host of reasons. That's one of its joys— and one of its challenges.

TWO

Why Historic Preservation Matters

MAKING THE CASE FOR HISTORIC PRESERVATION

ISTORIC PRESERVATION makes for strange bedfellows. Under the same tent, one can find Colonial Dames, environmental activists, Civil War reenactors, downtown advocates, artists, city planners, African Americans, gays, ardent conservatives, and more. The reason they can fit under the same tent is that historic preservation signifies different values for different people.

Preservation can be about preserving a community's architectural legacy. Whether working to save a fine eighteenth-century Georgian courthouse, a flamboyant Victorian storefront, or an inventive 1950s Modernist home, many preservationists can articulate the value of architecture as the most public form of visual art. These buildings bring beauty, variety, continuity, identity, and richness to a community. Where historical value is added to architectural significance, preservationists can make their best case.

History certainly has its own credentials in preservation. But when historical significance has to stand on its own, making the case for preservation becomes more challenging. A different set of preservationists, often more academic in their interests, may be inspired by a modest or architecturally undistinguished home or school that is significant solely because of its connection to a person, event, or time. These preservationists convey quite a different message and must use different tools than

connoisseurs of historic architecture. Preserving a one-room schoolhouse is important for reasons other than economic development or community revitalization. Its suitability for adaptive use may be limited; its worth is as a communal artifact.

Years ago, preservation broadened beyond just individual buildings to historic districts and downtown areas. The numerous success stories about neighborhood and downtown revitalization have spawned a series of economic impact statements for

The conservation spirit that's prompted Americans to recycle billions of aluminum cans has not carried over to its older buildings. Mountains of demolition debris have needlessly been relegated to America's landfills, squandering embedded energy and excellent building materials.

historic preservation. Quantifiably, historic preservation is a good tool for encouraging community reinvestment. Now preservationists are invited into discussions about a wide gamut of community issues, from affordable housing to containing sprawl, from downtown revitalization to heritage tourism, from highway beautification to adaptive use. Political candidates have learned that historic preservation can be a powerful platform with the electorate.

Some preservationists come to the tent through environmental interests. "Reduce, Reuse, Recycle" (the mantra of environmentalists) would be a sensible tagline for preservationists. Preservation is "the ultimate recycling." The vast amount of energy and nonrenewable materials consumed in the construc-

tion of a new building, in addition to the loss of farmlands and forests as sprawl advances, should give any citizen pause. Preservation can rightfully be called "smarter growth," since it doesn't substitute one kind of suburban sprawl for another.

Others adhere to the old saying "They don't build them the way they used to"—and with good reason. Anyone who's owned a historic house for several years can attest to how quickly modern materials fail, especially in comparison with older materials. Modern additions to historic buildings often exhibit more structural and material failures than their historic counterparts. Our ancestors did not build with the idea that their structures would have a life expectancy of twenty or fewer years; they built with the expectation that their children and grandchil-

North Carolina's rural heritage is fragile, as small farms are consolidated into much larger agricultural holdings. Many important historic structures, such as Twin Oaks in Wayne County, have been lost during recent decades.

dren would continue to benefit from their efforts. A recent syndicated column recounted—without irony—the life expectancies for various building components: twenty years for roofs, fifteen for windows, ten for certain siding products and mechanical systems, and much shorter durations for electronic gadgetry. It was downright depressing.

When all is said and done, rehabilitating a building that's in good structural condition is generally going to be less expensive than constructing a new building of similar size and quality. Reduced efficiencies of use with a renovated historic building are often offset by lower construction costs, better materials, and more character. Project after project demonstrates that a judicious full renovation of a building costs less than a similar-sized replacement.

When I'm told that rehabilitation is more expensive, I respond with pointed questions. Are the contractor and architect experienced in renovation? Just as you wouldn't want a brain surgeon to do open-heart surgery, you don't want to entrust a historic rehabilitation project to professionals whose primary business is new construction. It's a different set of skills. Is plaster being torn out for replacement with drywall? If so, is it necessary? Or is the contractor being "lazy" by not finding craftspeople who can repair the plaster at a much lower expense? Anyone who has lived with both plaster and drywall will probably confirm that plaster is the superior building material. Are the windows and doors being replaced? If so, why? Is replacement a good investment? How long is the replacement apt to function properly? North Carolina has numerous buildings with double-glazed windows whose vacuum seals have failed after less than a decade, thereby eliminating any energy advantage over historic windows simply retrofitted with storm windows. Usually excess expense is a sign that too much is being done to the building, often stripping the historic building of its integrity and character.

Many preservationists eventually conclude that preservation is most powerful as a tool for building community. Preservation brings a diverse crowd together under the same tent, at a time when our society is increasingly segmented. Preservation is common ground. African Americans and conservative whites can come together in the preservation of a landmark that tells powerful stories about both cultures. Gays and straights can work side by side to preserve a neighborhood. Management and labor can advocate for the preservation of a factory where their parents worked. Wealthy and poor both can benefit from living in historic environs.

Despite these many attributes, preservation has not thrived as much as some veterans in the field would have liked and expected. Why? In part, as a generalist field that appeals broadly to many, historic preservationists have found it hard to reach consensus among themselves when difficult issues arise. With so many people bringing such diverse values to the table, unanimity of thought may sometimes be impossible. That's where our preservation organizations must exert leadership, trying to solve preservation problems creatively. And often those solutions are grounded in real estate.

If you save a historic resource, its stories can still be told. The cultural and economic benefits of preservation can be enjoyed. But if the resource is destroyed, its place in history will eventually be lost. Its value as a trigger for economic development and community revitalization will have been squandered. Where historic buildings survive, so does a community's sense of history and identity. One might even say that these buildings constitute the heart and soul of a community. A capable preservation organization, skilled in real estate, can help guide a community away from the Faustian dilemma of having to sell one's soul for short-term profit.

THREE

Real Estate Is the Name of the Game

*F*OR MORE than a decade, year after year the National Trust for Historic Preservation repeated an educational session at its annual conference—same four speakers, same format. As any conference planner knows, reruns don't work at conferences. Yet each year the room was full, and people came back for more. At least half of the attendees were veterans.

The session: "Real Estate Is the Name of the Game." Its purpose was to encourage nonprofit preservation organizations to become actively engaged in real estate. These sessions haven't been the only efforts by the National Trust to encourage organizations to take the plunge into active involvement with buildings and sites. There have been specialized conferences, publications, grant funds for consultants, low-interest loans, and more. Yet preservation still has a disappointing paucity of organizations that have actually taken up the challenge. Involvement in real estate helps build long-term strength for a preservation organization, and the roster of the nation's most successful preservation organizations attests to this success.

Fundamentally, successful historic preservation is an exercise in dealing with real estate. Usually when a building or site is endangered, the problem relates to its owners or its use, not to the building itself. The building would be fine if someone would just take it and invest in its continuation. Its problem may be that its owners want too much money (often because its land is too valuable for the welfare of the building). Or its owners may not be sympathetic to good preservation standards. Perhaps its owners don't know what to do with it, or the building is being used for the wrong purpose. "Crack houses" are a glaring example. No one wants drug dealers or users in the house next door. The problem is the use, not the building, and demolition doesn't solve the problem. A house freed of the drug scourge can once again be used as a good home without being torn down.

Preservation North Carolina is an animal shelter for endangered buildings and sites. We are working with the "poor dogs" that don't have a good home. Shelter dogs are sweet, good animals, worthy of love and affection. They may need a bath and grooming, and they may need their shots. In some cases, they also need some medical attention. What these dogs have in common is an owner who can't or won't take care of them. It's not the dogs' fault; nor is it the buildings' fault.

In our work with endangered historic properties, we are trying to buy time for fine buildings— buildings that need love and affection. The problems are usually external to the buildings. If a building is on destruction's doorstep because of genuine structural problems, then a preservation group should deliberate carefully whether investing in its survival is appropriate. If such a property is truly of special significance, investment in its revival may be the right course, and the community will contribute to the effort. Alternatively, recognizing a lost cause and walking away is sometimes the right decision. Overinvesting in a property that is truly "too far gone" without having an explicit strategy for subsidizing its preservation can be deadly for an organization.

Is a nonprofit group involved in real estate competing with the mainline real estate community? No. Animal shelters don't compete with pet shops. They cater to different markets, and their work can be mutually supportive. Our preservation work to save "poor dogs" encourages others to visit the pet shop. Many people who have looked at buying an uninhabitable house from Preservation North Carolina have gone on to buy a habitable home through a local real estate agent. Some folks are "animal shelter people"; others aren't.

So why should a preservation organization get actively involved in real estate? Here are ten reasons. Many have positive financial ramifications for the organization.

1. Saving historic buildings is at the heart of a preservation organization's mission. Instead of just talking about preservation on the sidelines, nonprofits involved in real estate are doing preservation. They are fulfilling their mission in the most direct way. In many cases, if a private nonprofit organization can't find a way to save an endangered property, it will be lost. Public regulatory tools (such as the National Register of Historic Places or local historic designation) are vitally important for buying time and providing financial incentives. However, if its owner is determined to destroy it, regulation often can't save that property from eventual destruction. Sometimes only the acquisition of a property by a sympathetic party will succeed.

2. Active engagement in real estate energizes an organization's existing members, donors, the staff, board, and volunteers with tangible successes. The sale of an important property or the successful relocation of a threatened building to a new site provides a recurring opportunity for celebration and renewal. There aren't many jobs or volunteer opportunities that can

give such routine affirmation. Members are pleased to be associated with an organization that makes a tangible difference in their community as a direct result of their support. Preservation North Carolina, as an example, has a surprisingly high average for individual gifts and a strong membership retention rate. Every time we have surveyed our members, we've found that support for our endangered properties work outstrips the next most important program by a margin of more than ten to one.

3. Real estate work can be a tool for recruiting new members. When an organization is actively marketing its properties (as well as its mission), it has a natural tool for membership recruitment. Every person who responds to a property ad or visits the website for more information about property available for restoration is a prospect for membership. Instead of the expensive (and often depressing) proposition of having to buy lists of names and trolling for members through direct mail solicitations, the organization has interested prospects calling it. The challenge is to convert that interest into financial support. After their restoration, the preserved sites are excellent locations for membership development events, tangibly making the case for preservation.

4. Working directly with historic properties increases the organization's technical capacity to save endangered buildings. The organization and its staff better understand the complexities of preserving a building and are therefore more competent at successfully resolving preservation crises. Through experience its personnel learn how to solve a multitude of preservation problems, whether in design, planning, rehabilitation, or finance. The organization's staff members truly become the experts in preservation problem-solving. Once gained, this experience is then the organization's most valuable asset in promoting further preservation activity. The organization truly becomes a technical resource for preservation.

5. In turn, the technical expertise gained through direct real estate involvement lends the organization credibility in the community. The credibility that experience confers is considerable. When involved in real estate transactions, a preservation organization

Property work confers special credibility on preservation organizations. Preservation North Carolina can speak with authority about how to reuse school buildings because it has purchased and resold more than two dozen schools (such as the old Lenoir High School).

and its staff have firsthand experience with the issues that make or break successful preservation ventures, whether public or private. Because the organization has experience with complex issues such as adaptive use, rehabilitation costs, preservation incentives, zoning and code requirements, and so on, it can work credibly with property owners, buyers, and neighbors.

6. Real estate experience also bestows credibility for educational and advocacy efforts in the public arena. An endangered properties program indirectly serves important educational roles: raising the public's awareness about landmarks, debunking misconceptions about preservation, and advocating sensitive and sensible rehabilitation. When our organization tells a local school board that its bids for renovating an old school are inflated, we have added authority from experience. Over the past two decades we have owned more than twenty old schools, so we know something about school rehabilitation costs. When we testify in the legislature about the need for rehabilitation tax credits, we understand what kinds of problems older buildings pose and what kinds of incentives will stimulate investment. When a jour-

nalist asks us whether a deteriorated building is salvageable, our opinion carries credence, since we have worked with troubled properties for years.

7. Real estate work strengthens the network of practitioners in historic preservation. The organization learns who to turn to for assistance and builds an invaluable network of allied preservation partners. Close relationships are forged with developers, contractors, lenders, professionals (such as architects and lawyers), craftspeople, and investors because preservation business is being generated directly through the organization's property work. These relationships generate numerous mutual benefits. For example, when Preservation North Carolina is working to save an endangered school building, we will contact a list of capable developers who might be interested in acquiring the property. These developers are grateful to PNC for being directed to potential projects. In turn, many are generous financial contributors and regularly give us pro bono advice and advocacy support. Testimony from successful developers is invaluable in a public hearing; they combine knowledge about historic buildings with the mystique of being successful businesspeople.

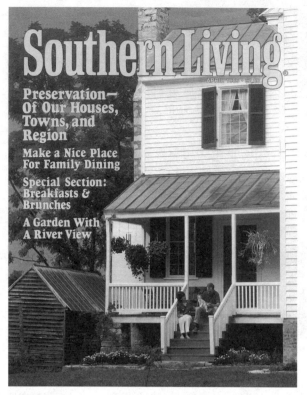

Working directly with historic properties offers preservation organizations many opportunities to benefit from favorable publicity. The home featured on this cover of Southern Living *(Woodleaf Plantation in Franklin County) had long been vacant when it was sold for rehabilitation by Preservation North Carolina.*

8. *Working with property provides numerous opportunities for the organization to obtain beneficial publicity.* Working with property keeps an organization in the public eye. Nothing in historic preservation catches the interest of the media and the public more than an important property that is imminently threatened with destruction. The fate of an endangered building will receive more sustained media attention than a conference or a special event, no matter how successful. Through the years, Preservation North Carolina has received hundreds of thousands of dollars' worth of free and routinely favorable publicity about its property work: articles, interviews, editorials, photographs, public service announcements, and so on. One recent national magazine article resulted in more than 250,000 additional hits on our website. Each successful endangered property transaction can be a veritable mill for publicity. We often get coverage when we gain control of the property, while we're marketing it, when we sell it, and again after it has been renovated. In addition to media exposure, marketing a property draws attention to the work of the organization; for example, just a sign in the yard of a property available for restoration will generate conversation and interest.

9. *Real estate expertise lends itself to obtaining gifts of real estate for the organization.* Donations of historic real estate become a natural source of major financial support for an organization in the real estate business. These gifts allow the organization to serve its mission while making money. Properties donated to PNC have ranged from large mills and mill villages to small rural houses, from school buildings to downtown commercial buildings. In some cases, their sales have been worth hundreds of thousands of dollars for the organization—in addition to advancing the mission. At PNC, income from property work, especially from sales of donated properties, routinely exceeds the combined income from membership, corporate, and foundation contributions.

10. *An organization's active involvement in real estate may motivate planned giving.* Donors can be encouraged to contribute historic properties through bequests and other planned giving instruments. Planned gifts of this kind can be invaluable in building endowment funds and providing long-term stability for the organization. When prospective donors witness the organization's thoughtful stewardship of donated properties, they are confident that their gift will be appreciated.

The basic premise of this book is that involvement in real estate can help build a successful preservation organization. Look at the roster of the nation's most distinguished preservation organizations. Many, if not all, of the preservation nonprofit organizations that have excelled in the United States for a sustained period of time are those that have been directly involved in real estate. In their communities, the tangible impact of these organizations can be seen on the ground. In cities where preservation has long thrived, such as Charleston,

Savannah, Providence, Newport, Pittsburgh, and Galveston (and, in North Carolina, Salisbury and New Bern), there has been a gutsy nonprofit organization that engaged directly in real estate work for a sustained period of time. In some cases, these organizations have evolved into new stewardship roles, but their real estate impact will be felt for decades.

Conversely, in many cases the real estate work has built the organizations themselves into sustainable entities with professional staff and financial depth. These organizations have benefited financially from their involvement in real estate.

So why haven't more preservation organizations become involved in real estate? Why do people keep coming back to the "Real Estate Is the Name of the Game" session at the National Trust conference without going home and implementing the message? Why have land trusts flourished during the last decade, using many tools perfected by preservationists, while preservation groups have not? Perhaps answers to those questions include lack of capital, fear of failure, risk aversion, and shortage of expertise.

This book will attempt to address these impediments, starting with the perception that you must have a big pot of money to work with real estate. You don't.

FOUR

Working with Endangered Properties

HOW PRESERVATION NORTH CAROLINA
WORKS WITH PROPERTY

W E USED to say that Preservation North Carolina operates a revolving fund; now we say that PNC operates an endangered properties program.

What's in a name, and why does it matter? The classic definition of a "preservation revolving fund" (a pool of capital created and reserved for preservation, with the condition that the money be returned to the fund to be reused for similar activities) no longer reflects the breadth of nonprofit preservation property work. Instead, organization use options, lines of credit, program-related investments, block grant funds, fees for services, donations of property, bargain sales, and other sources of flexible funding. Organizations rarely come up with their own funds from a reserved pool of capital.

When contemplating getting involved in real estate, preservation organizations too often get fixated on how much money they have to have in a revolving fund before they can successfully start working with property. They view a revolving fund as a pot of money rather than a program. They conclude that until they have a massive supply of money, they can't have an endangered properties program. To make matters worse, some funding sources confuse revolving funds with endowment funds. So in the end, nothing happens, and important buildings are lost.

Preservation expertise is much more important than available capital in working to save endangered properties. Working with endangered properties is a program, not a bank account. Part—and only part—of saving a property from destruction is figuring out where the money will come from. Many property transactions can be accomplished by a nonprofit group without having available capital.

There's confusion in the field about what it means to operate a revolving fund. "Revolving fund" and "revolving loan fund" have become synonymous terms, even though there are fundamental differences between an organization that buys and sells historic properties (an acquisition fund) and one that make loans to other preservationists to undertake preservation projects (a loan fund). The skill sets, sources of funding, and operating models are all completely different.

Preservation North Carolina operates an acquisition fund. It is routinely referred to as a "revolving loan fund," even though it almost never makes loans. A fine example of a true loan fund is the Providence Revolving Fund, Inc. It makes loans for exterior rehabilitation in target areas, prepares plans and specs, does construction administration, makes "gap" loans in the downtown, develops affordable housing, and provides technical services on a fee-for-service basis. Its income comes from contract grants with the City of Providence, loan interest income, capital fund investment income, development fees, and fees for services. Its Neighborhood Loan Fund consists of five funds, each with its own lending requirements. The sources of the funds have been Community Development Block Grants, loans from the state historic preservation office, Providence Bond Funds, bank loans, and its own revolving fund capital. Its larger Downtown Fund is a program-related investment from the Rhode Island Foundation. This organization has had a substantial impact in Providence; in terms of what it does and how it does it, though, it is decidedly different from Preservation North Carolina. To lump them together as "revolving funds" illustrates the imprecision of the term.

So how does an active real estate program for a nonprofit preservation organization work?

Throughout this book, I will be drawing on the work of Preservation North Carolina. Many other preservation organizations are doing good work with property, and their experiences are equally valuable. However, property work with PNC is the basis of my experience.

Since 1977, Preservation North Carolina has operated a singularly successful statewide endangered properties program in North Carolina. The premise is simple: Preservation NC acquires endangered historic properties and then finds purchasers willing and able to rehabilitate them. In every case, as a condition of purchase, covenants are placed on the property to ensure its protection in the future. Acquisition does not necessarily mean that we purchase the property at full market value before we have a buyer in place.

What kinds of historic properties are we working with?

We typically work with "problem properties." Usually they are long vacant; often they are in the state's poorest counties. Sometimes the properties have had fires or been vandalized. Often the properties are in estates or owned by a number of heirs, requiring the agreement of numerous parties. The traditional real estate market is not interested in working with these properties because of their poor condition, their low market value (resulting in a minuscule commission), or their complexity. Unless Preservation North Carolina works with these properties, they will usually disappear from the landscape.

Our properties have ranged widely in age, size, acreage, condition, original use, and environs. They have been put to a multitude of new uses. Each has presented its own set of challenges.

PNC uses five criteria for selecting the properties with which to work. Preservationists who seek precise rules won't find them in our criteria. These guidelines are applied flexibly and often on site under pressure.

1. Is the property endangered? Properties threatened with immediate demolition are certainly endangered. So are seriously deteriorated or vacant properties. You don't have to wait until demolition is imminent to know that without new ownership, new use, or new investment, their loss will be inevitable.

If the land value is proportionally too high for the historic structure, we would consider the property endangered. Examples would include a small building in a downtown district, a small house in a highly desirable neighborhood, or a historic property with acreage in a strong real estate market. Properties likely to be subdivided (or otherwise likely to lose their integrity) are at risk, even if the historic structure itself is in good condition.

2. Is the property significant? As a statewide organization, Preservation North Carolina has adopted a policy of working with properties that are on or eligible for the National Register of Historic Places. Often we don't get a formal determination of significance by the National Park Service or the North Carolina Historic Preservation Office. Our staff routinely has to evaluate a property's significance in the field, based on our own experience. We wouldn't market a property as eligible for the National Register without consultation, but often time is of the essence in saving a threatened property. Frequently with real estate, you have to make quick decisions and not look back. In some cases, a building could be lost while a discussion is going on about whether it is sufficiently significant.

A statewide entity needs to be more selective about property than a local or neighborhood organization. The level of the bar for significance should be adjusted according to the mission and the resources of the organization. When you look through the roster of properties on which Preservation North Carolina has protective covenants or preservation easements, superlatives come to mind: the finest Queen Anne house in the county; the last plantation house along the river; one of the best bungalows in the state; the home of a prominent nineteenth-century craftsman; the commercial building on the corner of the downtown square; the most intact mill village in the region. A local or neighborhood group might consider its own superlatives in considering significance: a prominent corner property in the neighborhood; the best bungalow in the block; the home of a noted longtime neighborhood figure; or, perhaps, a structure important to the rhythm of the streetscape.

3. Can the property be bought? If a property owner is unwilling to sell his or her property, PNC can do little through its Endangered Properties Program. Alternative strategies for preservation (such as public regulatory measures or adverse publicity) must then be considered. These strategies should be undertaken in a way that doesn't burn bridges with owners, since they might change their minds at a later date.

4. Can the property be sold? We work in a very narrow niche market. Our idea of a marketable property is very different than that of many real estate agents, since we're accustomed to working with problem properties. Most of our buildings are structurally sound, but they may have no bathrooms, no usable wiring, no heating/cooling systems, and so on. We will sometimes describe a building as being in good condition despite having no modern mechanical systems at all. Sometimes buildings that haven't been modernized are preferred by preservation-minded buyers. At least they don't have to remove poorly installed systems. Unfortunately, the forms used by lending institutions don't recognize these advantages of untouched buildings!

We once had an amusing phone call from an interested potential purchaser who wanted details about the kitchen appliances in a house for sale with fifteen acres for $30,000. Appliances? Ha. The house didn't have running water! Our properties clearly don't fit into the traditional real estate market.

And then there are the properties with structural problems, such as major roof leaks, fire damage, significant termite damage, walls filled with bat guano, structural elements that have been removed by salvagers, and the like. Once again, the standards of the traditional real estate market would deem these structures losers—or, at least, requiring too much time and energy for a profit likely to be made. What realtor wants to show a damaged house to dozens, if not hundreds, of clients in order to make only a small commission? But to us, these problems may present only modest impediments to preservation.

Despite our atypical perspective about what's marketable, even we have limits. We can't save everything. If the property has extensive structural damage, or if its site has unsuitable surroundings (for example, strip development, hog farms, or mobile homes) that aren't conducive to the kind of financial investment that the property will require, or if the land value is simply too high, the property may not be marketable without finding a creative

Seen here seeping through the openings, bat guano in the walls of the early-nineteenth-century Smithwick-Green-Clark House didn't render the rural Martin County house unworthy of renovation. Special instructions were provided to potential purchasers about how to safely remove the bats and their droppings.

solution. Might there be an adaptive use that would save the building? Can we buy additional land to solve a problem? Is it appropriate (or necessary) to consider moving the building? Is there a way to find a financial subsidy for the property? These kinds of questions will be addressed in more detail in later chapters.

5. Is there local assistance, or will there be local spin-offs? As a statewide group, it is imperative that we have local volunteers to help with showing the property, keeping it presentable, securing it, and other similar tasks. Many of the properties we work with are several hours away from our closest office. (Even when distance isn't an issue, a preservation organization might well want to use volunteers to help show property.) When a prospect has seen a property and appears to be serious about purchasing it, our paid staff will meet with him or her to discuss the property and the process of purchasing it in more detail.

If saving a property is likely to have a significant impact on the preservation of other historic properties locally, we will give it special consideration. Sometimes saving a pivotal individual property can result in several others being renovated.

How does Preservation North Carolina find out about endangered properties?

We usually hear through our extensive network of local preservationists (including members, advisers, and directors), the staff of the North Carolina Historic Preservation Office, professional associates, and local preservation commissions. Since we routinely advertise properties available for restoration throughout the state, we often hear from interested citizens who have no institutional affiliation. In any given month, we learn of several troubled properties. We ask the person contacting us to provide more information about the property (such as contact information for the owners, the property's location, its significance, and the nature of the threat). We use the historical and architectural inventories published by the State Historic Preservation Office for further information about the property's significance. We try to learn more about

the owners, their financial circumstances, and their temperament before contacting them.

We have not been systematic in identifying the most significant and endangered properties. We don't maintain a formal list of the properties that we want to save—though perhaps we should. Many preservation organizations have followed the example of the National Trust for Historic Preservation to develop a list of the most endangered properties in their locales. Such a list would be invaluable in setting priorities for an endangered properties program. Two perceived risks have stopped Preservation North Carolina from developing such a list for publication: (1) a fear that the list might alienate property owners with whom we would need to work, and (2) acknowledgment that Preservation North Carolina itself owns some of the state's most endangered properties. Someday we'll do our list, but we may not publish it.

How do we approach the owners?

Once we have the needed information about a property and its owner, we approach the owner about taking a look at it. If we know someone who has a good relationship with the owner, we ask him or her to accompany us. We visit the property and make some judgments about its significance, the nature of the threat, and its marketability.

Wherever possible, we try to get the owner to give us an option on his or her property rather than purchasing it outright. An option gives PNC a specified length of time during which it can purchase the property at an established price. Once we have found a buyer during the option period, then we purchase the property and resell it on the same day. Working with options necessitates a much smaller capital outlay than outright purchases. Unless there are unusual circumstances, our staff doesn't need board input to get an option. However, if the property owner is unwilling to grant an option, we'll consider whether to purchase the property outright, after evaluating the property's significance and the organization's financial ability to purchase and retain it until a buyer can be found. More on that later.

Sometimes an owner's motivation for working with Preservation North Carolina is financial; in other cases it's emotional. It's important to recognize the difference.

If the seller's motivation is financial, then we must persuade the owner that he or she will benefit most from letting us find a buyer for his or her historic property. We might make the case that our national marketing effort and our extensive network of potential purchasers will help maximize the selling price for the property. In a small town with a slow and limited real estate market or in a declining neighborhood, that argument is easy to make. Who else but PNC will be marketing the property nationally? Or we might be able to combine a variety of preservation tools and nonprofit tax incentives for the owner to maximize his or her return. If the owner's family has long owned the property, capital gains taxes may present a problem, and a sale at less than full market value might be advantageous.

The approach to an owner who has emotional motivations for working with Preservation North Carolina is much different. Many of the properties we've worked with have been in the owner's family for decades. They have been long vacant because their owners are attached to them and can't bring themselves to sell. These owners are struggling to do the right thing, and often they have been avoiding an inevitable dilemma: if they don't invest in their properties soon, it will be too late. There, Preservation North Carolina can provide a sympathetic solution: let us sell the family heirloom with preservation covenants to a buyer who will love it too. The pitch to this kind of owner plays to the owner's love of the property and doing the responsible thing for it. These transactions require patience and lots of handholding. Asking for the property to be donated may meet with success.

A business might be persuaded to dispose of unused property in a quest for positive community relations. For example, a merger of two banks may result in historic bank buildings becoming surplus. A gift of a redundant bank building to a preservation organization for resale with protective covenants may be a public relations coup. It may have additional benefits for the bank, such as obtaining a significant tax deduction, attaining compliance under the Community Reinvestment Act, and reducing the time and expense spent on disposition. The preservation organization can sweeten the deal by agreeing to place the proceeds from the sale in an endowment to be deposited in or managed by the bank. Other examples might include the gifts or sales of closed factories or stores, the transfers of vacated public buildings, and the disposition of foreclosed properties. In these cases, the preservation organization may be doing a service to the owner by taking the unused historic property off its hands. And in those glorious cases, good preservation work results in organizational income.

How do you determine the price?

A good starting point is to ask the property owner what he or she thinks the property is worth. Their opinions may be so strongly held or so inflated that further discussion is not fruitful. Then take a look at the property's tax assessment. The owner may have the assessed value readily available, and often assessment information is available online. Local real estate agents can give you some guidance about whether an area's assessments are generally too high or too low. Check the date of the last assessment to see how recent it is. If the owner's expectations and tax assessment are close, then further appraisals may not be warranted.

When we are working with a property on an option basis, we often have more flexibility in trying to determine the appropriate price. We can market the property at the higher end of its likely range of value and see what the response is. If the general response is that it's a great property but too expensive, then we may be able to go back to the owner and suggest a lower price. Since we are bringing in potential buyers from all over the country, that suggestion may well be heeded. When signing a purchase contract rather than an option, you don't have the same opportunity to renegotiate price after testing the market.

In the early days of the Endangered Properties Program, we frequently obtained a value opinion from a real estate appraiser to give us guidance on a property's value. A value opinion is less detailed (and less expensive) than a full appraisal. Getting a professional appraiser's opinion on value can be helpful by providing an objective starting point for discussing price with an owner, especially if the owner has unrealistically high expectations. It can also be helpful when a buyer needs to find financing.

At best, appraising historic properties is an inexact science. Due to their distinctiveness, many historic properties are indeed unique. You often can't find truly comparable sales in the same market. It's difficult to compare historic properties with non-historic properties, and the value of historic properties varies significantly from town to town. So determining the market value for a vacant rural house with great woodwork but no mechanical systems or for a vacant textile mill in a small town is a challenge for both a professional appraiser and an experienced staff member of Preservation North Carolina.

After working with historic properties for several years, we found that appraisers were coming to us for our opinion about property values. We had an ample record of comparable sales of historic properties in our own files. Now we are usually able to come up with our own educated estimate of value, taking into consideration what the owner thinks the property is worth, what the local market is doing, and how similar properties that we are working on are selling. Still, sometimes a professional appraiser's value opinion can be helpful in negotiations.

With a few years of experience, you develop a pretty good sense of value. For example, right now in North Carolina, a vacant textile mill is likely to sell for $0.50 to $3.00 per square foot. The price will be at the higher end of the range if the property is in a good location or in especially good condition, lower if there are environmental problems or the mill has long been vacant. If an owner won't sell a mill for less than $10 per square foot, we know that a sale is likely to be an exercise in futility. We can decide whether the mill is so important that we'll try to find a buyer anyway.

Any option or contract to purchase a property should allow the organization to have the property inspected and tested for environmental hazards before a purchase is completed, and it should allow for the option or contract to be cancelled without penalty if unexpected hazards are found. Nearly all historic properties will have lead paint, and most will have at least some asbestos. Those hazards can usually be abated within a reasonable budget. Other hazards, such as underground storage tanks, drums of unknown substances, and spills, may require such expensive mitigation measures that the price of the property must be reestablished. Direct experience in real estate can help a nonprofit provide better information about when these hazards are truly problems and when they are not.

Does PNC rehabilitate properties before selling them?

No. If anything, we will usually do only minimal stabilization work to secure the property, such as plug a roof leak or, where appropriate, secure window openings with plywood. We leave the rehabilitation up to the buyer. Rehabilitating a property prior to its resale greatly increases the organization's investment and its risk, increases the likelihood that money will be lost, and complicates the use of some preservation incentives. It may even harm its resale, if buyers don't agree with the location of bathrooms or the detailing of a kitchen. If you are working with a property under option, doing rehab work is not really an alternative (unless the option is unusually long). In a few instances, Preservation North Carolina has partially renovated buildings before their resale in order to help create a market for other buildings. More on that later.

Who are the buyers for these properties?

Our purchasers are an interesting and diverse mix of people. We have people come to North Carolina from all over the country to look at the properties that are available for restoration through PNC. Sometimes they have North Carolina connections, such as family or friends; often they don't. About half of the buyers are North Carolinians. Occa-

The eighteenth-century Old Town Plantation in Edgecombe County had to be moved in order to save it from eventual loss. A large corporate hog operation was established on the adjacent property, making the house unfit for habitation on its original site.

sionally our buyers have family associations with the properties. About three-fourths of the buyers of houses use them for their own primary residences.

Our buyers are rarely "wealthy." Usually they expect to do some of the work themselves. The houses that we work with usually aren't suitable for "affordable housing," unless the buyers have access to favorable financing and plan to put in extensive sweat equity. Because our properties are often uninhabitable, they require extensive work. Plenty of more affordable historic buildings are available through the traditional real estate market. Rarely do buyers of our houses have small children; raising children while restoring a historic house would require exceptional energy, and the potential safety hazards would necessitate caution.

Generally speaking, our buyers are community-oriented people. They are taking on projects that will require a great investment of time and money. Our properties are not usually candidates for flipping for a quick profit. The buyers' greatest rewards will likely be more personal than financial: personal satisfaction, participation in house tours, and commendation from the community, such as a feature article in the local paper or a local award. In time, the financial rewards will often follow. Find-

ing ways to bolster buyers' pleasure, such as including them on house tours or nominating them for awards, should be considered an integral part of a properties program.

Along with their financial commitment to their own properties, these new buyers become advocates for their new communities and for further preservation efforts therein. They become members of community boards (whether religious, civic, social, or charitable), participate in local preservation activities, and help build social capital in their new hometowns.

Are financial incentives available for purchasing and renovating historic properties in North Carolina?

Yes, a wide variety of incentives are available. For many years, preservation tax incentives have driven many of the sales of larger commercial and industrial historic properties. Now homeowners in North Carolina can benefit from the addition of state rehabilitation tax credits.

By marketing these incentives to potential purchasers, the organization is promoting preservation in a broader educational realm. The preservationist's toolbox contains many different financial tools, and a preservation organization can encourage the purchase and successful rehabilitation of historic properties by developing expertise in the use of those incentives. Are there state financial incentives for rehabilitation? Local property tax incentives? Is the property eligible for the rehab tax credits? How might a preservation easement be used to enable a project? Are affordable housing incentives available? Who are potential equity partners for the use of tax credits? Are there local incentives for first-time home buyers? Do local banks have loan products that make rehab financing easier? Unfortunately, too few preservation professionals can answer these basic questions, because they are not actively engaged in property work.

Does PNC make money on its properties?

Because of the distressed nature of these properties, it is very difficult to make a "profit" on them unless a property has been donated. If someone could have made a profit, they would already have done so. Recouping expenses is usually the goal. With optioned properties, Preservation North Carolina tries to mark up the price of the property sufficiently to recoup its costs. However, when PNC has to purchase a property and hold it for more than a year, we will seldom be able to fully recoup our expenses. The costs of securing and insuring a vacant property can be expensive, and those costs are difficult to recover. Chapter 6 will consider when outright acquisition is necessary.

So how much money do you need to start an endangered properties program?

Preservation North Carolina has saved more than 500 endangered historic properties, generating an estimated $200 million or more in private investment. This scale of investment wrongly implies that PNC has a large "revolving fund." It doesn't. Our "fund" has never exceeded $500,000, even in the most prosperous times. By using options, we have had to purchase and hold fewer than 5 percent of our properties. When we have had to buy a property, many times we have used someone else's money.

Our leverage ratio, when the generated investment is compared with the size of the "fund," is monumental. A $500,000 fund that generates $200 million in private investment—wow! But if you view endangered properties work as a program, you realize that the comparison, though impressive, is wrong. In recent years, our organization annually spends more than $500,000 in operating expenses to carry out its endangered properties work. We have six full-time professional staff who only work with endangered property, plus support staff. In a typical year, we might sell $1.5 million worth of real estate, which in turn might require an additional investment of $5 million in rehabilitation. Leveraging $6.5 million from a $500,000 program is still very impressive. Some years, because of a large project, the investment may reach $10 million or substantially more. Even better!

In contemplating the operation of a new properties program, would an organization be better off with $100,000 for operating costs for the program, or $100,000 in capital? (Pick your number: $100,000? $250,000? $500,000? The number doesn't really matter.) I'd vote for having the funds to start up the operation of the program, despite the well-known axiom that operating funds for an ongoing program are the hardest to raise. With the Endangered Properties Program, the ongoing revenue will come from "earned income" and from increased donor support. Unlike many other preservation programs, spending $100,000 for an established endangered properties program may generate $100,000 or more in additional revenue (from fees, sales proceeds, enhanced membership support, gifts of real estate, etc.), thereby allowing the program to carry on year after year. Preservation North Carolina, despite having put less emphasis on "resource development" than it might have, operated in the black for fifteen consecutive years—a rare feat for a business, whether nonprofit or for-profit. Our net worth has grown steadily, because of the property work (not because of grants).

In the late 1970s and into the early 1980s, Preservation North Carolina launched its Endangered

Properties Program with funding from startup grants from major North Carolina corporations and foundations and from special appropriations from the North Carolina General Assembly. The board and staff found it increasingly difficult to segregate the organization's capital fund from its program expenses. (For example, is insurance a program expense or a property expense?) Our auditors routinely remarked on the complexity of the organization's finances, as funds were spent and recouped and spent again. We were learning that working with endangered properties is a program, not a bank balance or capital account. Whether property expenses should be classified as operating expenses or as capital expenditures was a difficult accounting question.

In the end, we defined the Endangered Properties Fund as the "available net worth" for the purchase of properties. That figure varies wildly—from month to month, from year to year. Immediately after the sale of a major donated property, significant funds might be available for capital expenditures. At other times borrowed funds exceed PNC's own funds (but not the cumulative market value of properties). Though PNC would relish having sufficient capital to acquire and stabilize numerous endangered historic properties at any given time, that dream has proven elusive thus far. Nevertheless, we've usually been able to find an available source of capital when needed.

When dealing with real estate, whether as a nonprofit organization or as a for-profit developer, the fundamental challenge is cash flow. Finding the money to pay the staff on time can be far harder than finding the capital to work with property. This perennial challenge reinforces the premise that a revolving fund is a program rather than a pool of capital.

When contemplating getting directly involved with saving historic properties, an organization needs to ask the right question: does it have the real estate and preservation expertise available to save the property? Most endangered properties can be saved without the organization's having significant capital in hand. The next chapter will explore alternatives to outright purchase as a means of saving an endangered property.

FIVE

Creative Alternatives to Acquisition

USING OTHERS' MONEY AND TIME TO DO YOUR WORK

WHEN a historic property is threatened with destruction, buying time to find a preservation solution is of the essence. Delaying demolition isn't enough; delay alone prolongs the inevitable. Delay can also ruin relationships with property owners and disillusion the public.

To be successful, preservationists often must find a way to gain control over the property for long enough to find a real preservation solution. If a preservation organization doesn't have a large properties fund (and we at Preservation North Carolina don't), its challenge is to gain control with minimal expense or, alternatively, with someone else's money.

One of the oft-repeated lines during discussions about revolving funds is "The best way to control the fate of a historic property is to own it." That's partially true. But there are numerous ways to gain interim or permanent control over a property that are less expensive and less risky than buying it outright at full market value.

PNC's Endangered Properties Program has been able to save endangered historic properties far beyond the scope of its modest Endangered Properties Fund by successfully using a variety of legal or financing tools to buy time for endangered properties until a preservation solution can be found. With less than $500,000 in available capital, PNC is usually working with more than $5 million of historic property at a time. It may own as many

as thirty historic properties for sale, but most have been acquired through donations, bargain sales, or other creative arrangements.

In setting up a new endangered properties program for a nonprofit organization, if I had to choose between having the operating income for a creative entrepreneurial staff with real estate expertise and having a large fund for capital (i.e., a revolving fund account), I would readily choose the former. Usually creative staff can find a preservation solution that does not necessitate having all of the money in hand. Here are some alternatives to using an organization's resources for outright acquisition.

OPTIONS ON PROPERTY

Most often, PNC obtains options on endangered properties and works to find purchasers during the option period. PNC asks the owner for an option at little or no cost for six to twelve months, offering the owner an alternative way to sell a problematic historic property. PNC then markets the property. When a purchaser is found, PNC acquires the property and resells it with protective covenants in the same transaction.

An option buys time—often very inexpensively. Through the option, the purchase price is set. During the option period, the owner may not sell or

The antebellum Ravenscroft School for Boys in downtown Asheville was being demolished when Preservation North Carolina purchased a six-month option for $5,000, with an option to renew for an additional $5,000. (Usually PNC obtains its options for $1.) After its sale to a private purchaser, its rehabilitation was one of the first in downtown Asheville.

transfer the property to others, and if we commit to exercising the option at the stated purchase price, then the owner is legally obligated to sell it to PNC.

Usually PNC can work with the closing attorney so that the organization does not have to provide any cash at the property closing. The buyer's purchase money is placed in the attorney's trust account, and the original owner is paid from the sales proceeds. So, in effect, PNC purchases the property using funds advanced by the buyer.

Why would an owner give PNC an option at no charge? PNC has expertise in working with difficult properties, so it is able to market a troubled property to a much broader market than most local real estate agents. As a nonprofit group with a mission of saving endangered historic properties, PNC typically works with properties that the standard real estate market has passed by. It's unrealistic to expect a real estate agent to spend innumerable hours and underwrite expensive advertising in order to sell a property whose value is substantially less than other properties in the market. Additionally, if the owner has sentimental attachments to the property, PNC can offer reassurance that the property will be marketed with respect and protected through PNC's covenants after the sale.

An option is a good tool to use for a property

that is sitting vacant and lacking attention. The problem with the property may be that the owner doesn't know what to do with it or hasn't given it much thought. Asking the owner for an option so that the property may be marketed and sold with covenants may be doing the owner a favor.

An option is less useful if demolition is imminent and the owner is hostile. It won't work if the owner is unwilling to sell the land on which the building sits. (If the building can be moved, then an option on the building alone becomes a possibility.) If a property is under a public preservation commission's demolition delay (or prohibition) or if a property has been condemned for code violations, the property owner may have an added incentive to grant an option to a preservation organization.

Options account for a substantial percentage of PNC's real estate activity. Using an option to buy time has saved several hundred properties in North Carolina. An option minimizes the organization's capital outlay. During the option period, the risk of damage or loss is on the owner, and the owner is responsible for holding costs, such as insurance, mortgage interest, taxes, and so on. Our nonprofit organization will obtain liability insurance (which is not expensive) in order to protect itself from accidents on the premises. In some circumstances, PNC will undertake minor temporary repairs (such as stop-

The antebellum Walnut Hill Cotton Gin in Wake County was donated to Preservation North Carolina. Its highest value for appraisal purposes was for salvage and vacant land. PNC's covenants significantly reduced the value of the property for resale. It has been creatively converted into a residence.

ping leaks) or clean the property up (sometimes using volunteers) in order to buy additional time for the property or to make it more marketable.

An option can also be a useful tool when a property may be donated or when it must be moved. If a property owner might be interested in donating a troubled property but the organization is not sure whether to accept the donation, the organization might obtain an option to purchase the property for $1 as a way to learn more about the property and test the market before accepting ownership. Then, when the organization is ready to take ownership, the property owner can donate the house and take the tax deduction. Similarly, obtaining an option on a structure that must be moved allows the organization a chance to see whether the move is feasible before taking full responsibility for the structure.

An option places the organization in a flexible position. If after marketing the property for several months we realize that the property really is not marketable at the option price, then we can explore alternative strategies while the property is still under PNC's control. Alternatives might include doing stabilization work on the property, commissioning appropriate studies of the property (for example, having an engineer evaluate a structural flaw or having an architect propose design solutions for a property's idiosyncrasies), raising money to subsidize the purchase price, or considering a public use. Another legitimate alternative, though it's sad, may be calling it quits and moving on to another property.

Once a property has been purchased by the organization, turning back is not an option.

DONATIONS OF REAL ESTATE

Sometimes it works out very favorably for an owner to donate a historic property to a 501(c)(3) nonprofit preservation organization, especially if the property has problems. The owner can take a tax deduction for the value of the donation, whether the donation is in whole or in part. If the property has appreciated substantially while in his or her ownership, he or she has the added benefit of reduced capital gains taxes. The gift may relieve the owner of a headache and provide community recognition.

Additionally, the sale of a donated property will usually generate proceeds that PNC can use to further its mission. Properties donated to PNC have ranged from large mills and mill villages to small rural houses, from school buildings to downtown commercial buildings. Some have been outright donations; others have been bargain sales (discussed later), where the donor is selling the property at less than fair market value and taking a deduction for a partial donation. In a handful of transactions, PNC has netted between $250,000 and $1 million from the sale of properties acquired through donations or bargain sales. In other circumstances, PNC has cleared little or no profit, but through the gift we have solved a preservation problem with only modest expense.

Don't accept every property that comes your way. Check the gift horse's mouth. Before accepting a gift of real estate, do your due diligence, just as you would with any property you would buy. Inspect it. If appropriate, commission a Phase 1 environmental survey to be undertaken. Have a lawyer do a title search, and purchase title insurance. One of the hazards of accepting donated properties is that some owners might try to unload properties with tax liens, structural problems, environmental issues, and other maladies. As long as the preservation organization is aware in advance of the problems associated with the donation, it can sometimes still take advantage of the donation to solve the problem and preserve the property.

Several years ago, Preservation North Carolina was offered the gift of a vacant downtown property in a Main Street community. The handsome late-nineteenth-century building was clearly significant, and its many roof leaks assured its status of being endangered. If we had not had a title search done before accepting the gift, we would not have known that the property had nearly $20,000 of tax liens filed against it. The owner had not paid his property taxes in several years. Before accepting the property, we were able to negotiate a payment plan with the local government. We also were able to evaluate the financial risk of accepting the gift; we knew that if we couldn't sell the building for more than the liens, then the donation would cost us money. Without the title search before accepting the gift, we would have had an expensive surprise when we sold the property. Fortunately, we were quickly able to find a buyer, sell the property for a little more than the tax liens, and guarantee the rehabilitation of a problem downtown property.

One of the trickiest issues in accepting a gift of real estate is determining the value of the deduction for the owner. Be clear: the owner, not the charity, is responsible for establishing the value of the donation. The nonprofit organization might suggest qualified appraisers and, if asked, provide input to the appraiser. But the nonprofit needs to be unequivocal that the appraised value for the donation is between the owner, the appraiser, and the Internal Revenue Service. The appraiser and the donor must each sign an IRS Form 8283 that reports the property's value. The nonprofit must also sign the form, but only for the purpose of certifying that it has accepted the donation. If Preservation North Carolina's auditor didn't require us to record the value of the donation for our own financial reporting, we would sometimes have no idea what value the owner has attributed to the property.

Often someone will ask us for an appraiser who will place a high value on the property. Don't be tempted to do this. The penalties for overstating the value of a donation can be costly for both the owner and the appraiser. If the nonprofit group participates in putting together a fraudulent appraisal, it runs the risk of severe penalties and loss of tax-exempt status. The nonprofit group is far safer to distance itself from the appraisal process. Provide the names of qualified appraisers and supply the appraiser with any requested information; otherwise, keep your hands off!

Despite those caveats, the appraiser can be simultaneously legitimate and creative. Preservation North Carolina received the donation of a remarkably intact antebellum cotton gin on a developable piece of land. What is the economic "highest and best use" of a cotton gin? What would it be worth if it were placed on the market with no restrictions? After some brainstorming, the appraiser concluded that the gin's highest market appraisal might be for disassembly and salvage for its timbers. Salvaging the gin's timbers would have been easy because it was constructed with huge heart-pine timbers (in order to bear the weight of the cotton) and wood pegs (its lack of nails would make disassembling the structure and resawing the timbers into new flooring much easier). So the appraiser legitimately appraised the structure for its salvage value and the land for its development value, and the donor appropriately deducted that amount. After accepting the gift, Preservation North Carolina placed protective covenants on the property, greatly diminishing its economic "highest and best use." The property came on to Preservation North Carolina's financial books at its appraised value, and then our accountant reduced the property's value on our balance sheet as a mission-related diminution of value. Clearly, selling a historic cotton gin for salvage would have been contrary to our mission. The cotton gin was ultimately sold to a purchaser at a price much lower than its salvage value, and buyers have creatively adapted it as a private residence.

Where the economic "highest and best use" for an unrestricted piece of real estate is demolition for redevelopment, a donation might be particularly attractive to its property owner. Though it may pain preservationists to contemplate demolition as the highest economic value, that market condition may be a boon for the nonprofit preservation organization where an owner is exploring his or her financial options—especially where the owner is a community-sensitive business. For example, a bank that owns a small historic downtown building that's been deemed surplus may be highly motivated to donate (or bargain-sell) it to a preservation organization. It's both good community relations and good financial strategy.

Bridgestone/Firestone donated the huge historic Loray Mill in Gastonia to Preservation North Carolina in 1998. Whether the corporation's motivations were community-based or financial, the decision was wise. Rather than spending hundreds of thousands of dollars for demolition and ending up with a vacant lot with limited market appeal, Bridgestone/Firestone chose to donate the property and thus received public acclaim and a substantial charitable deduction.

Gifts of real estate are wonderful! They can be very profitable for the nonprofit group, whether the property is in great or poor condition. They can provide a multitude of benefits for the owner. And they may permit the nonprofit group to explore creative preservation solutions that might not otherwise be considered. Let's consider two different alternatives.

When a property is donated, the nonprofit organization may have additional financial tools at its disposal to ensure that a good preservation solution is attained. When a property in poor condition is donated to Preservation North Carolina, we will often offer it for sale with advantageous owner-financing, giving potential buyers an extra incentive. For example, we might offer it for sale to a buyer with only a modest down payment, a reduced interest rate for the loan, and a balloon payment due in three or four years. These incentives help entice a buyer and encourage a quicker rehabilitation, since the buyer can focus his or her financial resources on rehabilitation expenditures rather than purchase. Sometimes we will offer the buyer a generous financial incentive to complete the renovation by a certain date, in order to get the property back into

A feasibility study for the Egyptian Revival–style Masonic Temple Building in Shelby suggested that the property could be renovated for a mixed use of offices and residences. One of the first downtown buildings in North Carolina in modern times to be renovated for apartments, its quick lease-up surprised many and inspired others.

good shape quickly. By the time the balloon payment is due and the buyer has to refinance with a traditional lending source, the property is in much better condition, and the terms for the buyer's permanent mortgage will be better. And when the balloon payment is paid, Preservation North Carolina has benefited handsomely—both financially and in its mission.

The donation of a property also allows the nonprofit group to borrow against the property for funds to stabilize it, prepare it for marketing, and pay associated operating expenses. The property itself serves as collateral. When Preservation North Carolina was given the Edenton Cotton Mill and mill village (57 houses) by Unifi, a textile manufacturer, we set up a line of credit with a sympathetic bank (BB&T) from which we paid for project planning, necessary infrastructure improvements (water/sewer, electrical, and road repairs), the renovation of a "model house," staff to manage the property, and all operating expenses associated with the project. After the sales of the first several houses, we repaid the loan. The next few sales helped pay ongoing operating expenses for the project. Then, as additional sales progressed, we were able to dedicate significant resources to a regional office for additional endangered properties work and an endowment to help sustain it.

The gift of the Edenton property worked out beautifully for all involved. Unifi shed a problem property and a potential public relations debacle. Preservation North Carolina preserved an important industrial property and opened a regional office for continued work in the area. However, it is important to recognize that the acceptance of this generous donation caused plenty of heartburn for the board and staff of Preservation North Carolina. We had to decide quickly whether to accept the donation, because of the timing of Unifi's tax needs. We had to rely on Unifi's environmental assessments; as part of our due diligence, we had environmental consultants quickly review the available information and provide an opinion about its adequacy. We knew that we would face many thousands of dollars in expenses before the project would break even. But we also knew that the gift of the prop-

erty would provide us sufficient collateral to obtain the loans necessary to pay those expenses. Our risk: what if the property didn't sell? We were confident that our preservation vision could be communicated successfully to enough preservation-minded buyers to bail us out of the debt. But what if we were wrong? The property ultimately had ample financial value as raw land to cover our expenses, if we failed to find a preservation solution. (You can learn more about the Edenton project and other industrial projects in chapter 14.)

BARGAIN SALES OF REAL ESTATE

Preservation North Carolina has frequently used bargain sales to acquire properties at a reduced price, allowing it more latitude in finding a preservation solution for troubled historic real estate. And in many cases a bargain sale has allowed PNC to make a substantial profit on the property's resale.

A bargain sale is a sale to a 501(c)(3) nonprofit organization at less than fair market value. The donor receives some compensation from the sale and is able to take a deduction for a partial charitable donation. A bargain sale functions much like an outright donation. A qualified appraiser must establish the value of the property. The charity must sign off on the donor's IRS Form 8283, acknowledging receipt of the donation. The value of the gift is the difference between the appraised value and the actual sale price. The donor may benefit from reduced capital gains taxes and community goodwill.

Bargain sales are a good alternative when a property owner has charitable inclinations but cannot afford to make an outright donation of real estate. Another variation of bargain sale is when a property has multiple owners, some of whom are willing to donate their share and some of whom aren't.

A bargain sale is also valuable where a historic property has strong development potential and the owner wants to sell the property but doesn't want to see its integrity damaged by demolition or new development. The owner can sell the property at a value commensurate with its current use and take a deduction for any additional development value.

The Piedmont Leaf Tobacco Company in Winston-Salem was sold to Preservation North Carolina in a bargain sale. The reduced sales price helped the owner with capital gains issues and aided its revival as urban condominiums.

Then the nonprofit organization can sell the property with protective covenants at its reduced price. A bargain sale may be a more suitable alternative to a preservation easement when the property owner is seeking to sell an unrestricted property. With a bargain sale, only one appraisal is required (whereas easements require a "before" and "after" analysis), and the owner and the organization can negotiate the sale price, thereby determining the size of the owner's deduction.

When Preservation North Carolina's Endangered Properties Program staff members meet with property owners about trying to help preserve their properties, they will routinely ask owners to consider donations or bargain sales as well as options to purchase. More than once, we have been pleasantly surprised!

TRANSFERS OF PUBLICLY OWNED PROPERTY AT REDUCED PRICES

A good day's work at Preservation North Carolina was in 1979, when we got North Carolina's General Assembly to enact a statute allowing local governments to sell surplus historic properties to nonprofit preservation organizations at a negotiated price. Typically, local governments must dispose of publicly owned property through a cumbersome bid process. When historic property is placed on the auction block without protective covenants, it runs the risk of being sold to a buyer that doesn't respect its value and integrity. If the price goes too high, then demolition may be inevitable.

Taking advantage of this statute, Preservation North Carolina has worked with innumerable local governments to find sympathetic buyers for important historic buildings, such as old schools, city halls, hospitals, and recreational facilities. These sales can be structured using options to purchase or contracts for services, so that the nonprofit organization doesn't have to take title until a purchaser is found. On occasion, the governmental unit may choose to sell the property for $1 in order to get rid of it or to encourage community revitalization. Working with public institutions will be discussed in more detail in chapter 13.

As with privately owned properties, working with surplus governmental properties doesn't necessarily require a large pool of money. But it does require real estate expertise and community credibility.

LEASES

In a few circumstances, when a property owner won't part with a property, PNC has acquired a long-term lease on the property. A lease can buy time for the property and attract an investor more interested in rehabilitation than in acquisition. If the lease is long enough, rehabilitation tax credits may be used for the property's renovation by a private lessor. (Generally the lease must be at least 30–35 years to use the tax credits.)

PNC's own rehabilitation of the Bishop's House

in Raleigh as its Headquarters Office shows how a lease can save a historic property. In 1989, when its owner, Saint Mary's School, announced plans for demolition, the school had no need for the 1902 house, and it didn't have the financial resources to mothball the house for future use. However, many of the school's alumnae were upset about the planned demolition. Selling the house, which anchored the front corner of the campus, was not a realistic alternative, so PNC persuaded the school to lease it to the nonprofit group for $1 a year for twenty-five years. PNC renovated the house at its expense and moved its headquarters there. Having an office in a beautiful Queen Anne house in a parklike campus setting was a treat. The house became a valuable revenue source for PNC as a place for weddings, receptions, and other special events.

Twelve years later, Saint Mary's needed the house back for faculty housing. The school agreed to buy out the remainder of PNC's lease, and it invested in further renovations. PNC used the buyout money for the renovation of another endangered building as its headquarters. All parties gained advantage, and the house now serves as faculty housing.

Knowing how close the Bishop's House came to being demolished, it is particularly gratifying to walk by the house on a summer night and see its residents enjoying its wonderful porches—or, in winter, to see a Christmas tree in the window. The lease gave PNC enough control over the real estate to save an important Raleigh landmark. And in the end, we did its owner a great favor by buying time for a valuable asset and helping it avoid a public relations debacle.

BORROWING MONEY FOR ACQUISITION

Too often preservationists believe that nonprofit preservation groups must have a revolving fund large enough to acquire significant properties. In the first place, raising sufficient capital for such a fund, especially without a track record in real estate, is in itself an overwhelming goal. Second, why do we expect a nonprofit group to have sufficient cash on hand to handle its real estate purchases? Most individuals don't purchase property with cash; they get mortgages. Businesses don't either; they have lines of credit or they rent space. And, for that matter, governments don't; they issue bonds.

PNC is no different from people who can't buy their homes with cash and businesses that don't maintain sufficient cash to undertake their real estate transactions. Through judicious borrowing

The Hayes House in Blowing Rock was saved at the eleventh hour by creative financing made possible by several interested individuals. The house had to be moved to a new site.

PNC has been able to exponentially increase the reach of its endangered properties work.

Borrowing money is unnerving for a nonprofit board of directors. All too often, a nonprofit's board tends to want to put money into savings rather than spend it. Some may consider a nonprofit's borrowing money to be a sign of weakness or poor fiscal management. PNC's board has shown a remarkable willingness to take risks, a characteristic that is rare for a nonprofit group. At the beginning of 2003, PNC had outstanding loans for more than $2 million for real estate acquisition and development. Daunting? Yes. Wise? In light of nearly $7 million in accumulated real estate value, the borrowing was prudent, and it was essential for PNC to accomplish its mission.

Some of PNC's most exhilarating property rescues have involved creative borrowing, often in combination with donations of property and/or services. For example, when the Hayes House in Blowing Rock, the resort town's most flamboyant Victorian house, was inexorably threatened with demolition, the only preservation alternative was relocation. A firm deadline was imposed. Numerous relocation sites were considered and rejected for a variety of reasons. Less than forty-eight hours before the deadline, the deal came together, thanks to several community-minded citizens. The house was donated to PNC; a private preservationist loaned the funds for the relocation with no interest to be paid for two years; and the new site was sold to PNC with no down payment and no interest for two years. PNC was able to move the house with no initial cash investment, though it incurred more than $75,000 in debt. Fortunately the house sold in less than two years, so all lenders were repaid before interest clocks started running. The house has been sympathetically renovated, and the angst of the pending deadline and the impending debt are now vague memories.

In 1997, Raleigh's most important historic commercial building, the 1874 Briggs Building, was sitting vacant, and its roof was leaking badly. Located in the middle of the second block of an unsuccessful pedestrian mall, the building was quickly heading toward being "too far gone." Regardless of the availability of various preservation tax incentives, the private real estate market showed only limited interest in the building, because of the building's long and narrow footprint, the pedestrian mall's lack of activity, a weak downtown office market, and the projected cost of renovation. A longtime friend, the executive director of the A. J. Fletcher Foundation, a private foundation focused on the arts and social needs in the community, called me to ask, "What are we going to do about the Briggs Building?" I turned the question back on him: "What are *we* going to do?" A few months later, a partnership of Preservation North Carolina and the Fletcher Foundation was purchasing the building for $500,000 and starting a $2.7 million renovation project. The project required a courageous leap of faith by both partners. Would nonprofit tenants be found for a renovated historic building in a "dead" area of the downtown? Would the partners be able to get their money out of the building? Both the Fletcher Foundation and PNC agreed to move their own offices into the building. Other nonprofit groups responded to the publicity about the building, and it quickly filled up. By the completion of renovation, the building was 100 percent occupied. The Fletcher Foundation financed its own interest in the building, and it loaned Preservation North Carolina $1.2 million as a program-related investment. After four years, PNC was able to refinance its interest in the building through conventional financing from a sympathetic bank (BB&T). With $300,000 of its own equity (proceeds from its previous headquarters and additional contributions), Preservation North Carolina was cooperatively able to help leverage a $3.2 million downtown project.

The results have been spectacular. The Briggs Building looks great—so good that the City of Raleigh frequently features it on the masthead of its website. Several other historic buildings in the same block as the Briggs Building have since been renovated, including another project initiated by the Fletcher Foundation. The city has removed the pedestrian mall and reopened the city's historic main street. A new downtown National Register historic district is being listed. Several large private construction and renovation projects are under way nearby, and scores of new residential units are planned for downtown. The Briggs Building served as a catalyst for downtown revitalization. As with many preservation projects, the Briggs Building alone did not turn the key, but it certainly encouraged other projects, which in turn encouraged still more.

And by inspiring a community-oriented entrepreneur, the Briggs project also indirectly served as the catalyst for a major renovation project in another city. The chairman of the board of the Fletcher Foundation, inspired in part by the Briggs Building, has undertaken the largest historic rehabilitation project in North Carolina's history: the American Tobacco complex in Durham. One could boast—without exaggeration—that our initial investment of $300,000 in the Briggs project ultimately helped to leverage more than $200 million in additional historic rehabilitation in Raleigh and Durham.

In other, more typical cases, Preservation North Carolina has purchased imminently threatened properties with private financing. Often, if asked, owners of troubled properties will agree to sell them with 90 to 120 days to close (providing time to find a buyer) and financing arrangements featuring a minimal down payment, annual or semi-annual interest-only payments (again, buying time), and a balloon payment due after a few years. These owners are often anxious to get rid of the properties, and the nonprofit can get control of them with relatively little cash outlay. The challenge is to sell the property quickly enough that holding costs don't accumulate excessively and the balloon payment doesn't come due. If the organization can't sell the property before the balloon payment is due, it needs to have a friendly lending institution or a line of credit ready to pay off the private financing.

When the organization borrows, it must be highly disciplined. Time is truly money. Many times we have recognized that we are better off accepting a lower offer from a potential buyer early in the process than holding out for a better price. A nonprofit organization dealing with real estate, especially when funds have been borrowed, needs to have an expedited decision-making process (i.e., the staff or the executive committee need to be authorized to make such decisions) so that it can take advantages of timely opportunities rather than waiting for the ideal. If we lose only a few thousand dollars in order to save a highly endangered and significant property, we can usually declare victory. Such transactions make great stories for membership solicitation letters!

As mentioned earlier, PNC has acquired properties by donation or bargain sale and then borrowed against them to get the funds necessary to make the properties marketable. Sympathetic lenders have provided lines of credit so that PNC could hire staff to market the properties, make critical repairs, install needed infrastructure, and even pay interest.

Without the board's resolve to borrow funds, Preservation North Carolina's most prominent projects could not have happened. Some of those projects have generated significant new revenue for operations and endowment, as well as publicity, membership, and acclaim. One might call the borrowed funds "venture capital."

USING CONTRACT PROVISIONS TO BUY TIME

When you recognize the value of buying time in saving a building, you start realizing that there are many ways to pick up months or years.

Some are very simple. In contracts to purchase, asking for 90 or 120 days to close the transaction is usually reasonable. Under some circumstances, one can ask for 180 days or more to close without seeming unreasonable. Using these simple techniques (techniques used by developers all the time), you can get a head start on finding a buyer before the clock starts running on holding costs.

ACQUIRING PROPERTY SUBJECT TO A LIFE ESTATE

Buying a property subject to a life estate may be worth considering at times. Such a purchase might be advantageous where the current owner is sym-

The McBreyer House in Shelby was maintained by Preservation North Carolina during the final years of its elderly owner, who was in poor health. She agreed to place the property under easement and to have her estate reimburse PNC for any money it spent on maintenance.

pathetic to preservation, but his or her heirs are not (or where they may be openly hostile). The organization buys the property, but the current owner (or owners) retains the right to live there for his or her lifetime. Though the organization owns the property, the owner is responsible for continuing to fulfill all maintenance requirements, pay taxes and insurance, and discharge other obligations typical of property ownership. The price is typically set by determining its current value and discounting the price by a percentage that's obtained from actuarial tables (readily available through attorneys, insurance agents, or accountants). The owner of the property may be willing to sell the property with private financing in order to assure its preservation. This option is explored in more detail in the next chapter.

Even better is when the organization can get the property donated subject to a life estate. It may be many years before the organization receives the full benefit of the gift, but the donor can benefit from a current income tax deduction and possible estate tax savings by removing the property from his or her ownership. Promoting gifts of real estate subject to life estates may be an excellent way to launch a planned giving program and build an endowment for the organization's long-term future.

PRESERVATION EASEMENTS

A preservation easement can be an invaluable tool in efforts to save an endangered historic property. Indeed, the current owner of a historic property can use an easement to ensure that his or her property will not become endangered in the future.

A preservation easement is similar to protective covenants. Both apply permanent restrictions to a property. Covenants are placed in the deed of a property when it is sold or otherwise transferred to a new owner. In contrast, an easement is placed on a property voluntarily by its current owner. Under certain circumstances, the owner may be able to take an income tax deduction for the easement's imposition. Further, the incentives for placing an easement on a property may include estate tax reductions and reduced property tax assessments.

Preservation North Carolina has found preservation easements invaluable in securing the future for historic properties that are in good shape when they are for sale through the conventional real estate market. Easements can remove future uncertainty by prohibiting unsympathetic subdivision and the loss of historic integrity. In these cases, PNC has found that the easement needs to be placed on the property in advance of its being listed by a real estate agent, so that all potential buyers and all agents are fully informed of the obligations contained in the easement. Having the easement recorded in advance of marketing the property eliminates the possibility of having to compromise its protections at the demand of an unsympathetic purchaser.

A preservation easement may be a vital component in the financial strategy for saving a historic property, and easements and the rules governing their deductibility are complex tools. A historic preservation nonprofit organization needs staff or available counsel who understands how easements work. In order to properly advise a property owner, one needs to know how preservation easements are appraised, when a property is a good candidate for a deductible easement, what language must be incorporated into an easement in order for the owner to take a charitable deduction, what needs to be in place before the deduction can be taken, how easements can be used to reduce a property's basis (and when that is advantageous), and many more technical issues. Easements are discussed in greater detail in chapter 13.

Once again, real estate expertise may be more important than capital in saving historic properties.

CONDUCTING FEASIBILITY STUDIES

Sometimes all it has taken to save an important historic property is a study to assess its feasibility for reuse. Although not part of a revolving fund's traditional purview, occasional expenditures have been made from Preservation North Carolina's Endangered Properties Fund for engineering, architectural, or marketing studies, especially under circumstances where the purchase or sale of a property is implausible (such as in a campus setting).

All too often, consultants and vendors without rehabilitation expertise misinform institutional property owners about the cost of renovation. For example, an architect who makes his or her living designing new school buildings may tell a school board that renovating an existing older school will be financially infeasible or structurally impossible, when indeed its renovation is likely to be less expensive than new construction. In such cases, which have been all too frequent, PNC has asked the school board to allow it to find the funding to undertake an alternative study of the building by preservation-minded professionals. Many school boards and local governments have allowed PNC the time necessary to reassess the building, resulting in the successful preservation of a number of important public historic buildings. In these cases, PNC has usually worked in coordination with the National Trust for Historic Preservation's Preservation Services Fund, a source for small grants for planning and feasibility studies.

In its work to save public school buildings, Preservation North Carolina has sometimes gained disturbing insights. On more than one occasion, PNC has learned that architects have given school boards erroneous (if not fabricated) estimates for the cost of renovating existing buildings. With no serious evaluation of the existing school building, they have provided inflated rehabilitation estimates. And in some cases, the school board knows that the estimates are not valid. A feasibility study sponsored by PNC may reveal that no information about the existing building was gathered for even a cursory evaluation. In such circumstances, it is important to consider how much to say publicly. A private discussion with the local school superintendent may be more fruitful than public disclosure. Public accusations of deception create ill will and embarrassment and often turn the discussion away from the true subject at hand: how much will it cost to save the threatened building? Emotions will prevail over facts. Additionally, any opportunity for future collaboration is likely lost. Preservation North Carolina may want to go back to the same school board later to try to acquire a vacated school building. Having a well-documented study about the costs of renovation authored by credible and experienced professionals may be the most influential and productive approach.

Our organization's real estate expertise and its credibility for knowing the economics of preservation have been essential to its ability to engage in such public discussions. Since Preservation North Carolina has sold more than two dozen school buildings for private rehabilitation and reuse, it brings more to a debate about a school than just general preservation enthusiasm. Its staff knows about how much it costs to renovate a school building or how to make a school building accessible to the handicapped. It is well acquainted with architects, engineers, and contractors who can provide information. The organization's direct experience with real estate, including surplus public properties, has opened many doors with public agencies—and, with feasibility studies in hand, has led to a number of high-profile preservation successes.

FUNDRAISING TO SAVE A BUILDING

The best way to save a building may well be to own it and thereby control its destiny. But what happens when you can't buy it under any circumstances? You may have to find the money necessary for its stabilization or renovation while the property stays in its current ownership.

In a few instances, where historic homes owned by elderly residents have been in dire need of work, PNC has gathered teams of volunteers to work on their homes. Additional stabilization or rehabilitation work has been initiated and paid for by Preservation North Carolina in exchange for an agreement that PNC would be reimbursed from their estates. These agreements have also contained provisions allowing PNC to market the home subject to a preservation easement after the death of the current owner.

PNC raised $1.5 million in private funds to relocate and renovate the historic Chancellor's House, which was slated for demolition, as the new admissions center on the campus of the University of North Carolina at Greensboro. Far from the typical revolving fund transaction, the effort is firmly rooted in the tradition of finding solutions for the preservation of troubled properties. And without PNC's real estate expertise, the project would have failed. Preservation North Carolina leased the house and its new campus site from the university, moved the house, and undertook its complete renovation. At the end of the lease, the house was returned to the university for institutional use. The relocation and renovation were administered privately by PNC. The project cost several hundred thousand dollars less than the university's estimates, which were obtained under public construction rules (confirming the notion that public construction projects pay a premium). However, raising the funds for the project was extremely time-consuming for PNC. Though it garnered exceptional publicity, the prolonged project (and the university's tacit resistance to it) was wearisome for PNC and its supporters. In the end, the house turned out

With private donations from alumni and friends, Preservation North Carolina moved and rehabilitated the historic Chancellor's House at the University of North Carolina at Greensboro. Instead of being demolished, the house now serves as the university's admissions and visitors center.

beautifully, works well, and appears to be cherished. Unpleasant memories have receded.

On other occasions, fundraising has been part of the solution for more traditional endangered properties transactions. How can PNC save a building if a property is worth more without the historic building than with it? By going to the local community for financial support to fill the gap. PNC acquires the property at its unrestricted market value and then, with charitable contributions in hand to close the gap, sells it with covenants at its reduced value. In other cases, especially where you must relocate a building to save it, financial support has been invaluable in offsetting the costs, which generally must be borne upfront. These circumstances, which lead to outright acquisition, are discussed in later chapters.

CONCLUSION

Buying time is usually the most important thing that a preservation organization can do to save an endangered historic property. Generally the more time that it can attain, the more likely a preservation solution can be found. There are several different tools for buying time. Many of them cost little or nothing, or allow the organization to acquire property using others' money. Using them creatively—sometimes using more than one tool at once—is the challenge.

A key to success in saving an endangered property is to focus first on the strategy: how can the property be saved? Then, after seeing whether the strategy will work, figure out where the money is going to come from. With a good project and a smart strategy, you can usually find the money.

SIX

Going to the Mat for a Property

WHEN PURCHASE IS THE ONLY ALTERNATIVE

SOMETIMES THE BEST—and only—way to save an endangered historic property from destruction is to buy it. Owning a property bestows control over its future.

Ownership has its downside too, especially for a nonprofit group: ownership is expensive. First, the group has to come up with the purchase price plus other closing costs. Then, carrying costs, such as interest costs (direct or indirect), insurance, and upkeep, can quickly become expensive, and any hope of recouping those expenses is often ephemeral.

PNC generally purchases property only when acquisition is the *only* alternative to certain loss of the historic resource. Before proceeding with an outright acquisition, PNC's staff and board of directors will evaluate the property's significance, the nature of the threat, and the organization's financial ability to purchase and carry the property until a buyer can be found.

PNC seldom breaks even on the properties it has to buy at full value and hold during an extended period of marketing. Intuitively, that makes sense. Last-minute rescues involve properties that are significantly distressed, whether because of their poor condition, their unsympathetic ownership, or their development value. If someone could have made a profit, they would already have done so. Having to hold the property adds costs that generally can't be

recouped. Most carrying costs add no value to the property, and usually a deteriorating property is not an appreciating property.

Before purchasing a highly endangered property outright, a preservation organization needs to determine how much it can afford (or is willing) to lose on the property—and how much of that loss can be recovered through contributions.

In 1991, PNC bought Union Tavern in Milton, home of the famed antebellum free black cabinetmaker Thomas Day. The National Historic Landmark had been devastated by fire in late 1989, making it a risky purchase. The board of directors recognized that we could lose tens of thousands of dollars, but it concluded that the property was so important and so visible that we had to take the risk. This property exemplifies why PNC has an Endangered Property Fund. We concluded that our donors would support our effort even if it resulted in a financial loss. Indeed, if we took no action, a more significant loss of community respect and credibility might ensue. Fortunately for PNC, a group of local citizens soon joined together to create a nonprofit group to buy the property from PNC with a goal of opening it as a museum honoring the work of Thomas Day. PNC helped get the group going and was able to minimize its losses. As a result of the risky purchase, an extremely impor-

A 1989 fire nearly destroyed Union Tavern in Milton (Caswell County), the home and workshop of the famed free black cabinetmaker, Thomas Day. PNC purchased the National Historic Landmark and held it while a local nonprofit group was organized to restore it as a museum.

tant historic resource was saved, and a new institution memorializing an exceptional African American craftsman was born.

Weeks after North Carolina's Main Street Program was created (one of the nation's original six) and the first Main Street communities were selected, PNC bought a fire-damaged commercial building in the fully intact 100 block of Salisbury's main street. Demolition work was already under way at its rear. Immediately, PNC halted demolition and braced the front façade. In order to market the "building and a half," as we jokingly called it, we commissioned an architect to produce schematic drawings to show how it might be successfully renovated. Fortunately, within a year we found a local buyer who renovated it for his own business, leaving a courtyard where the fire had occurred. This kind of eleventh-hour "save" is both invigorating and risky. The press loves a down-to-the-wire cliffhanger, so the publicity that accompanied this purchase was significant. We were risking not just our funds, but our reputation. If we had failed, it would have been a high-profile failure, and the new Main Street program would have been tarnished as well. We lost about $15,000, but our reason for initially taking the risk—supporting the nascent Main Street effort in Salisbury—paid off. Downtown Salisbury is now a real gem, emulated by many other communities.

Several times PNC has acquired imminently endangered properties and held them while local preservation or historical organizations were incorporated to take them over. The L. P. Best House in Warsaw, the turn-of-the-century home of a prominent North Carolina family, was in awful condition and had been condemned by the town. A wealthy member of the adjacent church had acquired the property from its sympathetic owner subject to a written agreement that neither he nor any future purchaser would destroy the house. He then donated the property to the church for a parking lot. How could that be considered legal? Since the church acquired the property through donation, no "purchaser" would be demolishing it. A lawsuit against the buyer and the church brought by local activists and political maneuvering within the congregation temporarily deterred the church from destroying the house. The church agreed to offer the house for sale for a limited time. Using lapsed grant funds from the State of North Carolina, a donation from a descendant of the original owner, and a bank loan, PNC bought the property only hours before demolition was slated to begin. The activists who had united to forestall demolition established a

Rosedale Plantation in Charlotte sits on eight acres of prime land on the Queen City's main street. PNC purchased the property, a rare reminder of Charlotte's early history, to make sure that it wouldn't be destroyed and sold it with protective covenants to a nonprofit group that has restored it as a museum.

nonprofit organization to raise the funds to buy and restore the house as a museum to commemorate American veterans. (The town of Warsaw is noted for its long-standing Veterans Day celebrations.) The house has been handsomely rehabilitated and has been the site of numerous receptions for weddings held at the adjacent church. The descendant who helped finance its purchase endowed its future upkeep. As is often the case, now that the house is a beautiful community asset, the controversy that surrounded the condemned house's preservation has become a distant memory.

If Rosedale in Charlotte, an important Federal-style plantation house sited on eight acres along a major highway thoroughfare, had ever gone on the conventional real estate market without limitations, it would almost certainly have been destroyed. Its owner, an elderly lady whose family had long owned it, had been a remarkable steward of the property as fast food joints and motels popped up around her. We had been cultivating a relationship with her because of the house's significance and its precarious setting, and when she decided that she needed to move to a retirement facility, she approached Preservation North Carolina. She allowed PNC adequate time to explore a number of preservation alternatives for restoring the house and its site. The purchase price, however, had to reflect the property's development value because it represented her primary financial asset. PNC worked with a local chapter of Colonial Dames, a women's patriotic society, to bring together the resources, both human and financial, to create a new nonprofit organization, buy the property, and start restoration of the house as a decorative arts center. PNC bought the property, held it for a year, and then sold it subject to protective covenants to the new organization after it obtained 501(c)(3) status from the Internal Revenue Service. During that year, PNC acted as fiscal agent for the project, accepting contributions on behalf of the new organization. The transaction was far from risk-free for PNC. The new organization could have stumbled, leaving PNC saddled with ownership of a property that would be difficult to market. But things worked out very well. Rosedale is now a green oasis along the highway corridor between downtown Charlotte and UNC-Charlotte, and the restored house contains exceptionally fine decorative highlights, such as early wallpaper found intact beneath later wall coverings. Its surroundings have experienced a remarkable revival.

In Eden, it was clear that if PNC bought and resold the historic D. F. King House, we would lose at least $20,000 because of the land's value for development. The town's most outstanding Victorian home was prominently sited, overlooking the textile mill, on a large piece of land zoned for commercial use. The land appraised for more without the house than with it, and the owner wanted maximum value. So PNC obtained a one-year option at the higher value and set out to find a buyer at a reduced value. Meanwhile, instead of venturing to buy the house as a museum, the Eden Preservation Society successfully raised $20,000 to offset the anticipated losses that PNC would incur upon resale with protective covenants. To purchase and restore the house for museum purposes would have cost several hundred thousand dollars, and its annual upkeep would have entailed many thousands more. Contributing $20,000 to underwrite the rescue of a landmark through a private sale with protective covenants was probably a financial bargain for the citizens of Eden, cheaper in the long run than establishing a small-town house museum that would likely struggle with ongoing operating and maintenance costs. Now restored, the privately owned King House sits on its bluff overlooking downtown Eden.

The most Preservation North Carolina has lost on an individual property was $60,000, early in the Endangered Properties Program's existence. The loss occurred because the property, Clarendon Hall in Yanceyville, had more than 200 acres, and the soaring interest rates of the 1980s had deflated land values throughout the state. The loss was certainly painful, but we never regretted having purchased the property. An elegant brick Greek Revival house, Clarendon Hall is extremely significant architecturally and is prominently sited in an important historic district. The before-and-after images of its restoration were used repeatedly in fundraising materials in the early days of the program, and its owners have proven to be steadfast friends, opening their home many times to tour groups and journalists.

When the organization has been faced with the choice of moving a building or losing it, the preservation and financial decisions have been all the more difficult. Sometimes there is enough time to market the building and find a buyer who will bear the cost of buying the new lot and moving the building; sometimes there is not. Where time is limited and inflexible, if you miss the deadline, the building is gone. Estimates can be obtained for the cost of the move and a new foundation, but it is invariably difficult to envision how a relocated building will look on the new site. Will the building look at home, or will the site look raw? The potential for damage during the move, though unlikely with a qualified mover, is yet another uncertainty that might discourage buyers or require further investment to repair.

After a move, a house may look like an overwhelming project to most home buyers, even though a knowledgeable contractor might view it as a straightforward rehabilitation job. The organization may have to spend money to reinstall porches, invest in a new roof, repair plaster, and landscape the property so that it is marketable. This work takes time, as does finding a willing buyer. The organization will lose significant money if holding costs accumulate for more than a couple of years. (For more about relocating buildings, see chapter 9.)

Where the community supports saving a property, losing money may be acceptable. Regrets about property purchases and subsequent losses have occurred only with properties of lesser significance. Losing money to save a fine house from destruction may be palatable; taking a big loss to save a mediocre house may not. When a quick decision is required about whether or not to save a property from demolition, there are two important criteria to consider: Is the property truly significant? Or will it be a significant catalyst for additional preservation efforts? Unless the property is very important or is going to catalyze other projects, buying it at the eleventh hour may be a mistake. Since moving buildings inherently encompasses more uncertainties, when evaluating whether it will undertake the relocation of a structure, PNC's policies now require the building to hold a higher standard for significance than it otherwise would.

Buying a property at the moment of crisis doesn't always result in a loss. A group of five neighbors in Lakewood Park in Durham went in together to buy a troubled house at a pivotal location in their neighborhood to keep it out of the hands of slumlords. Before buying the small Victorian cottage, they concluded that even if each partner lost a couple thousand dollars, the benefits would outweigh the loss in terms of their property values and their quality of life. They bought the house and were able to recoup all of their costs upon resale. The house is now a handsomely renovated, owner-occupied home under protective covenants held by Preservation Durham. Its revival has sparked additional neighborhood investment and energy. The neighborhood residents have gone on to buy other problem properties in the neighborhood and put them into good hands.

Sometimes buying a property offers a nonprofit group a chance to be entrepreneurial, while serving its preservation mission. Several years ago, a fine but badly deteriorated Federal house in a rural area near Madison was sitting vacant, its interior trim having been removed by a decorative arts museum. The house was truly a pitiful sight, though originally it had contained a remarkable amount of early decorative painting. The museum readily agreed

Clarendon Hall in Yanceyville illustrates one of the hazards of purchasing endangered historic properties outright. Preservation North Carolina bought the vacant Federal-style house with 180 acres in 1981 shortly before interest rates soared to more than 20 percent, causing agricultural land values to plummet. PNC lost more than $60,000 but saved an important historic property.

that if the house could be saved, its interior would be returned at cost. The museum had paid little for the salvage rights and had invested in the labor to carefully retrieve and store it. Meanwhile, the estate that owned the house put the property up for auction. Since the house had been stripped and looked awful, the only bidders for the property were farmers (interested only in the land) and Preservation North Carolina. As is often the case when buying a property at auction, we strategically waited until after the auction to submit an upset bid rather than actively engaging in bidding. We were able to buy the property at land value only, reacquire the woodwork, and market the property as restorable. Upon resale of the property with covenants, we recouped our costs plus a little and saved a wonderful property. Under different circumstances, Preservation North Carolina might have marked up the price and made some money, but in this case being able to sell the house at a very reasonable price expedited its restoration.

One of the riskiest purchases that Preservation North Carolina ever made was High Rock Farm in Rockingham County. High Rock, one of the state's most important Federal-style structures, had been purchased in the early 1940s as a wedding present for a preservation pioneer, Tempie Prince (known fondly by many as "Miss Tempie"), and lovingly restored. By the late 1980s, Miss Tempie was elderly and in poor health, and High Rock was beset with significant deferred maintenance. The fate of High Rock weighed heavily on the mind of Miss Tempie; she feared that her heirs would not be sympathetic to the property after her death. Placing a preservation easement on the property would have been an ideal solution, but we were concerned that after her death, her legal competence to grant an easement might be challenged. So Preservation North Carolina bought the property, subject to a life estate. As with most purchases subject to a life estate, the property's price was discounted to reflect the value of the life estate, based on actuarial tables. Resolving the fate of her beloved High Rock seemed to be a great relief for Miss Tempie, and she died only weeks later. Preservation North Carolina quickly found excellent purchasers who have beautifully revived the property. The purchase was a gamble. If Miss Tempie had lived for many years, PNC would have had to tie up significant capital in the property. We knew that and took the risk anyway.

Our work to save a pair of twin historic houses in Goldsboro led to state legislation allowing nonprofit preservation groups to buy property from local governments without bid. The Weil Houses, a pair of Victorian houses owned by a Jewish family prominent in Wayne County's business and political circles, had been acquired by the county for demolition during the days of urban renewal. The plan was for the houses to be torn down and replaced by parking lots for then-dead downtown Goldsboro (as if parking would save downtown!). Bowing to political pressure from a group of young activists, the county gave Preservation North Carolina six months to find a buyer for one of the houses, the Henry Weil House. The commissioners probably felt confident that no buyer would be found and figured that they could then proceed with demolition with clean hands and a clear conscience. When, to their surprise, we found a buyer, the county commissioners by a 4-3 vote rescinded their earlier agreement to sell the property. The Weil Houses hit the front page of the local newspaper day after day; editorials blistered the opposing commissioners. Preservationists, stunned by the board's action, called for the commission to reconsider. Even an emotional appeal from a dearly loved longtime local legislator couldn't change the vote. But an ensuing election did. Opponents of the sale lost their seats, and the new board voted to sell the Henry Weil House to Preservation North Carolina for resale with covenants.

The commissioners who opposed the sale justified their change of heart by noting that the sale of property would still have to go through a public bidding process. Permitting the sale of the Henry Weil House wouldn't necessarily guarantee that Preservation North Carolina would end up as its owner. After all, in the bidding process the house might be purchased by a third party for demolition. So we went to work to get legislation that makes it possible for a local government to sell surplus historic properties to nonprofit preservation groups at a negotiated price without bid, so long as the properties are placed under preservation covenants. That legislation helped save the neighboring Solomon Weil House three years (and another election) later. Both Weil Houses have been lovingly restored, and downtown Goldsboro is experiencing a revival under the aegis of the Main Street Program.

The legislation has been used over and over by Preservation North Carolina and other local preservation organizations to acquire unused publicly owned historic properties. Occasionally, Preservation North Carolina has been able to profit substantially in reselling these surplus local properties. Local governments have sometimes been so happy to get rid of the properties—and the problems they represent (whether in perception or in reality)—that they have sold important properties to PNC for as little as $1. These sales have taken place in full public view without objection, and the local governments have benefited significantly from the increases in tax base.

The City of Sanford sold Preservation North Carolina its former city hall, sitting vacant and pigeon-infested, for $1. In turn, we sold it two years later for $85,000. Certainly there was anxiety for PNC during those two years. Buyers would look at the building and conclude that they couldn't recoup the investment that the building would require. The building was on the "wrong side" of the railroad tracks, which cut through the downtown. The other side of downtown was where revitalization activity was taking place. We wondered whether we had indeed been given the proverbial "white elephant." But then Progressive Contracting Company entered the picture. A Maryland-based company specializing in historic rehabilitation, Progressive was looking for a place to expand into North Carolina. The old city hall would suit its needs beautifully. Sanford is centrally located. The building had room for both offices and equipment, and the building's street-front offices lent themselves to commercial rental spaces. PNC was able to finance the sale favorably on a short-term basis, since the building had in essence been given to it.

The result is a classic case of economic develop-

Battles to save the 1875 Henry Weil House in Goldsboro (shown before and after renovation) and its matching twin house, the Solomon Weil House, led to statewide legislation that allows nonprofit preservation groups to acquire surplus property from local governments at a negotiated price, rather than through sealed bids. Bidding could lead to a historic property's destruction for its land value.

ment. Progressive Contracting bought the building from PNC and undertook a signature renovation. Because of the building, Progressive brought its specialty business and a number of employees to Sanford. Progressive has bought the neighboring

The old Sanford City Hall was sold to Preservation North Carolina for $1. Its resale with covenants to Progressive Contracting Company netted needed funds for PNC, while bringing a new business and jobs to downtown Sanford.

historic buildings and renovated them for expansion. Both sides of downtown Sanford have benefited. Banners for Downtown Sanford now boast an image of the old City Hall, a building until recently considered valueless. The local visitors' center is a tenant in the building. Financially the City of Sanford has done very well with its $1 sale, and so has PNC.

When buying a property (even for $1!), an organization needs to consider a variety of scenarios. What if the organization has to hold the property for several years? Will the value of the property increase or decrease over time? The worst-case scenario is holding the property for several years while the building deteriorates and its value decreases.

There are ways to reduce the carrying costs of ownership. For example, rather than paying cash for the property, can the nonprofit get a loan at less than market rate? Sometimes an individual, a group of individuals, or a community-minded bank will lend money to the nonprofit at a lower or zero interest rate. (Here's an alternative to a no-interest loan: in one North Carolina community, a local bank lends the nonprofit organization the money to buy property with a conventional loan, and when the property sells, the bank donates back all interest paid by the nonprofit during the life of the loan.) Cautious board members may resist taking on debt. Yet in reality it is usually much easier—and quicker—for a nonprofit to come up with the interest costs for holding the property for two years (say, $16,000 for a $100,000 purchase) than to come up with cash ($100,000) for the purchase price. And when time is of the essence, borrowing may be the only way to save the property.

Borrowing makes sense when the prospects for

quickly selling the property are strong. The interest money can be escrowed to give the lender greater security. Borrowing gets dicey when the property hasn't sold after the first two years, and second thoughts start circulating about having bought it. That's when we start asking questions like "Whose idea was this purchase, anyway?"

If the property is worth more without the building than with it (often the case when the property's development value is the threat), the nonprofit may opt not to obtain fire and casualty insurance. Liability insurance, relatively cheap, is a must. Fire and casualty insurance, on the other hand, is difficult to obtain and prohibitively expensive if the building is vacant. Why would a group choose not to insure the property for fire and casualty? If the building burns down, its historic value is gone, and the best strategy may be to clean up the site and sell the property for compatible new construction. At that point, the nonprofit probably wouldn't reconstruct the historic structure, even if funds were available. More tricky is the situation where the building is partially damaged by calamity. Will donors consider the group irresponsible for not insuring the property, or will they help out financially with the needed repairs? Although a depressing topic for discussion, it's worth asking: if the building ever catches on fire, what's the likelihood of irreparable damage? Is the building likely to be totally destroyed before the firefighters arrive and get the blaze under control? Alternatively, are there firewalls that will contain a blaze to a limited area? In many cases, answering these questions realistically will lead the group to at least consider not insuring the property.

Even these ways of reducing carrying expenses may not be enough to offset the high cost of buying a property for resale and having to hold it for an extended period. However, buying an endangered property and reselling it to a private purchaser with deed restrictions is almost always going to be much less expensive than the preservation alternative of buying and restoring it for public use (such as museum use). Gaining the community's financial support for a few years of expenses may be easier than generating long-term support for a museum. The challenge is how to craft that fundraising message effectively.

For a nonprofit preservation group, losing money is not necessarily a failure, but losing an important historic structure is. Although no nonprofit organization wants to routinely lose money, its board, membership, and staff should evaluate what an endangered property is worth to the community . . . and then take action.

SEVEN

The Architectural Animal Shelter

MARKETING ENDANGERED PROPERTIES

*W*ORKING TO FIND buyers for endangered historic properties may be akin to finding a home for a dog at the local animal shelter. You are taking what one person has cast off and looking for someone else to take it and love it. We are the animal shelter; the conventional real estate market is the pet shop. Our way of marketing is going to be very different. Often we will be appealing to the heart rather than the head or wallet to find someone to acquire the property. It's a somewhat different market from the conventional real estate market. Add in a limited advertising budget, and the need for creative and savvy marketing becomes obvious.

So now that your organization has an option on an endangered historic property, or you've purchased it, how do you find a buyer willing and able to preserve? And how do you guarantee that the property will be preserved?

The private, behind-the-scenes part of saving an endangered property (that is, getting an owner to work with you so that you can find a new buyer) is only half the battle. The public part (finding the buyer and closing the deal) is where a preservationist's knowledge, skills, imagination, and powers of persuasion can be used to bring about a successful conclusion. Again, an organization must rely on the abilities of its personnel (paid and volunteer) more than on its financial strength.

MARKETING THE PROPERTY

Marketing a historic property to the public is tantamount to marketing the cause of historic preservation and marketing your organization. That's one of the great benefits for a preservation organization that is involved directly with real estate: you have the opportunity to tell the world why your community's historic resources are important by focusing on one tangible piece of real estate.

In your marketing, you have a story to tell, not just a set of facts. The story has drama: this building is endangered, and you are trying to save it. Through that story, you can tell the world about the historical or architectural importance of the historic resource that's for sale. You can highlight the financial incentives for historic preservation. You can promote the good work of your organization. And since you have a story, you can get a reporter's attention. Anyone who has ever tried to pitch a generic story about the good work of an organization has probably been disappointed. The media is looking for stories, personalities, and drama, not a recounting of institutional good deeds or social events.

So before you put the property up for sale, determine a media and marketing strategy. Your organization could be the beneficiary of lots of free publicity. In your media strategy, consider: does your property have any particularly interesting stories in its history? Details about unusual or prominent people, love stories, murders or other crimes, controversial events, or ghosts will engage the media and potential buyers. Romance the property, since many purchasers respond emotionally to a property's significance rather than following their purely rational or economic judgment. Animal shelters publish compelling photographs and stories of animals awaiting adoption; preservation organizations should do the same for their properties!

If you think that talking about a property's ghosts is going too far, think again. What is your goal? You are trying to find a buyer. The wider you cast the net, the more likely that you will find that buyer. A property's ghost stories will generate much more media attention than its architectural features! Efforts to preserve a ghost-inhabited building will be broadcast far and wide.

Give thought to who will be a good spokesman for the organization and its property. The spokesman needs to be enthusiastic, knowledgeable, and articulate about the project. With television, the spokesman needs to be comfortable in front of a camera. If an on-camera interview goes badly, it won't be used. Consider who can best tell the story of the property or who can reach an important target market. For example, select a train buff to talk about a railroad-related building. Have an African American woman advocate for a property that has significant historical connections with African American women. Or consider having a gay spokesman for a property when your best prospects for purchase may be gay. Having a gay spokesman doesn't mean that you are marketing the property exclusively or even explicitly to gays, but it does send a subtle message that your organization will welcome a gay buyer. After all, this is marketing!

Who's the voice of preservation in your community? If that person is admired and considered to be moderate and reasonable, then he or she may be your best advocate. If that person is on your organization's staff or board, all the better. That ties the story of the property to your organization. Beware of using a hard-core preservationist as your spokesman. If the community views him or her as strident or uncompromising, then potential buyers may be turned off. Perhaps you could team your spokesman for the story of the property with a person who can articulate the preservation incentives. One sentence in an article or interview about rehabilitation tax credits or local tax incentives may spark interest in the property by the right person.

The media is looking for current news. If you have obtained an option on an important and endangered property, it's news when it happens. It's not news a few weeks later, unless no one else knows about it. Take advantage of events that may constitute news: a cleanup day, for example, or the installation of a new roof on a building long thought to be a goner, or a sale.

Is the preservation of the property going to be a cliffhanger? Or is it going to be controversial? Those elements of suspense will guarantee media coverage. Play on them. If it's true, be emphatic that unless you find a buyer for this building, it will be lost.

Working with endangered properties truly opens lots of doors with the media. That publicity will attract potential buyers, members, and donors. Recognize that once you have contacted the media, you will not have control over what they say. There will be errors and omissions. There will be opposing points of view. However, if your organization is doing good work, its profile in the community will rise.

Learn to distinguish between good publicity poorly written, and bad press. If a newspaper reporter botches the details of the story but writes a generally positive article, that may be just fine. The article may send dozens of potential buyers to the organization's website, despite its inaccuracies. I find it helpful to send a reporter a note of thanks when his or her work has been well written and is accurate. That reporter is now my friend. If the article has a few inaccuracies, I still say thanks; glaring inaccuracies, if not critical to the story, can be rectified in the reporter's next work. To me, bad press is when the article will set back your efforts to preserve the building because of its tone, inaccurate presentation, or omission of crucial information.

Only then do I consider sending (or getting someone else to send) a letter to the editor that supplements what has already been published. A critical letter to the editor about an article may satisfy your frustration with bad coverage, but it is apt to alienate the reporter—probably the very same reporter who will be assigned to write the next article about your project.

How do you generate publicity for your property? A well-written press release sent by e-mail is a good start, especially for smaller newspapers and radio stations. There are numerous sources for information about writing good press releases.

With larger newspapers and television stations, a telephone call to the appropriate reporter will be better. When you read a newspaper or watch television news, be aware of which reporters tend to do articles about history, architecture, or human interest. For commercial properties, note who writes about real estate in the business section, then call the appropriate reporter about your story. Pitch your story by telling the reporter about its interesting and timely aspects. Offer to give the reporter the names and phone numbers of others who might be good contacts for the story (for example, former residents, neighbors, preservation professionals, even opponents of the building's preservation), making his or her job a little easier. Offer to send archival newspaper articles or architectural inventory listings that will provide accurate historical information. In this context, a press release might enable the reporter to easily recheck the facts of the transaction, such as the price, acreage, and so on, but a reporter will seldom rely on a press release for the telling of the story. Be honest about the project; if it's going to be a tough one, say so. Make your best case for the property without lapsing into fantasy. If you need to tell the reporter something in confidence, ask to go off the record in advance. Most reporters will honor that request. However, don't place your entire conversation off the record unless you can send the reporter to sources who will talk freely. Choose your words carefully, because unless you are off the record, everything you say is fair game for use. Anyone who has ever been interviewed frequently will have his or her horror stories about being misquoted or taken out of context. On the other hand, don't be so circumspect that you never say anything of interest!

After the article is complete, try to view it in the context of meeting your ultimate goal: finding a buyer for the property. You may be embarrassed by a quote that you think makes you sound like an idiot, but the rest of the world may not even have noticed! Here's the bottom line: did the article send interested buyers, members, or donors to your organization's website or phone? Preservation articles often end up with excellent placement in a newspaper or magazine, and the value of the publicity can be inestimable. Don't let little problems get in the way of the big picture.

Once you have worked with a reporter, you may become a good resource for that person when he or she is doing other preservation articles. Try to return a reporter's calls promptly, since he or she is working under deadline. Help guide the reporter to good contacts for other articles. Sometimes one good preservation-oriented quote can turn an article from negative to positive. If you prove to be a ready and reliable resource for a reporter, you may get a little extra attention for your projects when you need it.

For preservation to receive strong television placement, the project generally needs human activity: a cleanup day, a building being moved or renovated, and so on. Unless the story or the spokesman is outstanding, it's hard to make compelling television stories out of static buildings. We preservationists may get a shot of adrenaline from a fine Federal mantel, but the public at large may not! A house with a ghost story, though—that's a different matter! So the challenge is to get human interest out of an inanimate object.

One of Preservation North Carolina's most successful mechanisms for obtaining property publicity on television and in newspapers is having a volunteer cleanup day at an endangered property on a Saturday morning, followed by a Sunday afternoon open house. At Preservation North Carolina, we call our cleanup volunteers a SWAT team: Saving

A team of volunteers help secure and clean out Rosedale Plantation in Beaufort County. Long vacant, the house had a leaky roof and was full of trash. The work of the SWAT ("Saving Worn-out Architectural Treasures") team enabled PNC to successfully market the house for relocation and restoration.

Worn-out Architectural Treasures. Our SWAT teams undertake a wide variety of tasks, reflecting the skills of the participants. Old vacant buildings are often piled high with trash inside and out. Volunteers clear out the trash, cut back vegetation, and sweep the property. Often we will have a Dumpster (ideally provided at no cost, of course!) filled with debris by the end of the day. Volunteers with specific skills will undertake carpentry repairs, remove poorly built intrusions (such as cheap paneling or intrusive closets or bathrooms), or carry out stabilization projects (boarding up windows, fixing roof leaks, etc.). These SWAT events serve three distinctly different purposes for Preservation North Carolina: (1) the marketability of the property is greatly improved, with its instantaneous transformation from trashy to tidy; (2) the events get great publicity; (3) the events engage volunteers and members in projects with tangible and satisfying results.

Since weekends tend to be slow news days, a community cleanup event can make good news material. The television crew will film workers in action and interview sweaty participants. The news about the workday then shows up Sunday in time to promote the open house, guaranteeing a substantial turnout. If Sunday too is a slow news day, the media may show up again to film the open house. Having on the front of the available building a banner that lists the organization's website will encourage television viewers or newspaper readers (if a photo is included with the article), as well as passersby, to visit the website. Several SWAT events have resulted in quick sales for PNC after the event, sometimes to volunteers who participated in the cleanup!

Newspaper, magazine, and television features can be even more valuable if they include the organization's website. We specifically ask reporters to include the website in articles. An article about Preservation North Carolina in the February 2002 issue of *Country Living* brought more than 300,000 additional hits to the PNC website in ensuing months.

The Internet has changed how you advertise a historic property for sale. To reach a national market, you no longer have to rely solely on expensive national advertising. Thousands of potential buyers will find you on the Web if your site can be easily found through search engines. Links through other websites such as the National Trust for Historic Preservation can direct thousands more to your site. Several national websites market only historic properties, and they may offer your organization a discounted price. When you garner publicity and develop helpful links on the Web, your organization's website needs to be ready to market your endangered property. It's a missed opportunity to get great publicity about a property in the newspaper or on television and then have no current information about it on the organization's website.

In today's market, an organization's website is the most important piece of a media and marketing plan. A successful website is easy to find; the address should be intuitive to anyone who knows the name of the organization. Links from and to community sites, such as the local newspaper, will increase traffic. Once visitors reach your website, you want them to quickly find the property and information they are seeking. Property listings should include enticing photographs, floor plans, available financial incentives, and community information and should generally emphasize the property's best attributes. All too often an ad for a property will fail to tout its best selling point: the community. Proximity to the beach or the availability of cultural or educational institutions are more important to most buyers than nice dentils. website visitors come from all over, and they may not know Salisbury from New Bern from Asheville. So educate them, and promote your community's assets, and make it clear that the buyer will be welcomed as a hero.

The website should explain the next step for additional information about the property. Details about how to set up an appointment to inspect the property, what kind of protective covenants will be placed on the property, and the procedure for making an offer to purchase the property should be included.

A website marketing properties is also marketing the preservation cause and the organization itself. Don't lose sight of the fact that once you have attracted visitors to your website, you have an opportunity to convert them into card-carrying preservationists. Tell them about your community and your organization. Inform them about preservation incentives. Provide tips for good rehabilitation. Promote the virtues of preservation. Give them a chance to join your organization online and get involved, even if they don't buy the property.

A media strategy looks for creative ways to drive prospects to the organization's website. A sign or banner in front of a property for sale might prominently display a website instead of a name and phone number. Ads and press releases may be used strategically to send visitors to the website. E-mails and electronic newsletters may be used to direct members and other interested parties to the website to learn about properties that are newly available for rehabilitation. A postcard may have more impact than a magazine for encouraging visitors to take a look at the website. An organization might consider developing a Web-based event, such as a virtual auction, in order to increase Web traffic for the benefit of the properties. Some national or regional publications will provide nonprofit groups working with endangered historic properties with free advertising; use your ad to send people to your website.

Try to get your property into the local Multiple Listing Service. Sometimes to do this, you may have to list the property with a Realtor, which typically means settling on a commission for the Realtor and other agents in the event of a sale. Since the nonprofit group is also advertising and showing the property, a friendly Realtor may be willing to arrange for a reduced commission if the organization finds the buyer without the Realtor's services. Too often, nonprofit groups are shortsighted about paying for professional services. Paying a Realtor 3–6 percent to get a property into the Multiple Listing Service may be a bargain. When the property is imminently endangered or when the interest clock is running, it may even be the urgently needed solution. Paying a commission will probably be cheaper than an extra year of holding costs.

Be creative with mailings about properties. Postcards about a property are easy to produce and cheap to mail. They also may serve a second purpose as a ready handout to distribute in local coffee shops and other businesses. A simple and clever postcard can catch people's attention and refer them to a website or phone number for additional information.

Does the organization have a storefront, or access to nearby empty storefronts? A postcard can inexpensively be enlarged and turned into a poster for storefront display, held by an easel or by suction cups on the glass. Other brochures can be put on display, letting the public know of available properties and the organization's work with property. It's gratifying to watch people checking out available properties from the sidewalk.

When people inquire generally about property, we send them a magazine listing all of the properties that we have available for restoration. The magazine also includes information about properties that are being offered by other North Carolina preservation organizations (which pay a minimal fee) and by private property owners and Realtors (who pay a modest charge for the advertising). We want to encourage sympathetic acquisition of historic properties, whether ours or others', and our members appreciate receiving a publication with dozens of properties available for purchase, rather than just a few. We consider the inclusion of other properties in addition to our own as a service to the mission and our members. We have applied the same inclusive approach to Preservation North Carolina's website.

When people inquire about a specific property PNC is making available for restoration, we send them attractive brochures for each property with historical and architectural information, a frank description of building conditions, photographs, floor plans, area information, and a summary of available incentives for rehabilitation. The brochures are also available for downloading from the website. Where appropriate, we include information about lead paint, asbestos, and other environmental hazards, as well as guidance about their remediation.

And we always point out, of course, that Preservation North Carolina is a nonprofit organization supported by donor contributions!

Preservation North Carolina uses its properties work as a tool for building and maintaining donor support. Watching people thumb through PNC's magazine for the first time, you can always tell when they reach the properties available for restoration. They quit thumbing and start reading. For many, it's like looking at a mail-order catalog. Inquiries about property are by far Preservation North Carolina's best source of members.

We send our magazine out whenever we receive an inquiry about property. However, we will send it only once. If a person is unwilling to join the organization after receiving their complimentary magazine, we don't believe that they are sufficiently serious about buying property to continue getting free copies. Access to our website, on the other hand, is unlimited.

SHOWING THE PROPERTY

If your marketing is successful, you will not lack for people who want to see the property. Open houses provide an easy way to handle large numbers of lookers. They also provide a way to get good publicity—and face-to-face contact with the organization's members. Postcards, signs, e-mails, and Web notices can boost turnout. Have marketing materials about the property (and other properties) at the open house, including information about financial incentives. Develop posters or presentations with before-and-after photographs of other properties in the area to build confidence and excitement among lookers. Demonstrate that equally deteriorated buildings have indeed been renovated. Make sure that the property is safe for inspection; rope off unsafe areas. Have light refreshments so that you have an opportunity to talk about the property and your organization to visitors. Your ultimate buyer may not be at the open house, but he or she may receive materials the next morning from a casual attendee.

Consider ways to highlight the property's features and to address its problems so that the potential buyers can learn about the property on his or her own tour. Many buyers don't want to be followed around the house. Set out stand-up signs (for example, using freestanding acrylic frames) that draw attention to features such as marbleizing or original paint. If the property has a structural problem and the organization has had an engineering study to address the problem, set out a sign that lets lookers know about the availability of the study. If floor plans have been done, tape them to the walls, and have them available as handouts too. Make it easy for the potential buyers to learn about the property without being trailed through the tour. You don't want to lose the sale because the prospects are uncomfortable with the person who's showing them the house.

Volunteers may be most helpful in showing properties to first-time lookers, saving the paid staff time for other purposes. We have had properties that re-

quired more than 100 showings before finding a buyer. Volunteers need to be educated about the property and trained to represent the organization. If a prospect shows continued interest and seeks to visit the property for a second or third time, the staff should meet with the prospects. Volunteers should be instructed to let the staff know of prospects who show special interest in the property so that the staff can follow up with them. A volunteer should also be coached to defer more difficult questions to the staff.

At any showing of the property, sample preservation covenants and purchase contracts ready to be filled in should be available. The organization needs to make it easy for an interested and qualified buyer to purchase the property. The process of buying a historic property from a preservation organization is probably going to be intimidating for many people, and having information about the process readily available can dispel some of the mystery.

And, of course, have plenty of membership information available. Even if the visitors don't buy the property, they should be actively encouraged to support the organization. Your marketing of real estate can be the portal for building financial support.

EIGHT

Closing the Deal While Protecting the Property

THE DELICATE BALANCE BETWEEN
THE IDEAL AND THE ACHIEVABLE

ONE OF the hardest lessons in real estate is that "until a property is sold, it's not sold." However earnestly submitted, many offers (whether verbal or in writing) don't result in actual purchases. Buying real estate already seems complex and incomprehensible to most folks. When you add such intricacies as the special financing challenges of older buildings, appraisal uncertainties, unfamiliar covenants, the limited availability of skilled craftsmen, environmental issues, and buying from an organization rather than an individual, buying one of our properties may be a recipe for heartburn for all but the most intrepid. The preservation organization once again needs skilled and patient personnel (paid or volunteer) to work through the issues with a prospective buyer.

When a potential purchaser is serious about buying a property, send him or her a partially completed offer to purchase. You are going to want to control the form and substance of the sales contract. The purchase agreement needs to address such unusual provisions as the inclusion of protective covenants, the as-is condition of the property, the terms for property inspection and evaluation during the contract period, and the exclusion of standard language relating to termite damage or the condition of mechanical systems. By providing clients with sample forms to use, you are making it easier for them to submit an offer and easier for the parties to reach agreement. A sample purchase contract is contained in appendix A.

The contract should require the buyer to provide an adequate earnest money deposit to indicate that he or she is serious and to reimburse the organization for out-of-pocket expenses in case of default. The size of the required deposit is subject to negotiation; it might be as small as $500 or as large as 10–20 percent of the purchase price. In setting the size of the deposit, the organization should consider its comfort level with the buyer (is the buyer almost certain to perform?), the length of the contract (if closing is to occur quickly, less earnest money might be required), and the urgency of the situation (if the property will be lost should the buyer back out, then a larger deposit is justified).

Before signing any purchase contract, the organization must make legal decisions about how to handle earnest money deposits. If appropriate, the organization may seek to set up its own separate escrow bank account, following the local rules for escrow accounts. Many states and municipalities have stringent rules governing escrow accounts. Alternatively, the organization might choose to place earnest money deposits in the escrow accounts of an associated attorney or real estate agent. The penalties for mishandling earnest money deposits can be severe.

The purchase agreement with the buyer should

address how mutually acceptable protective covenants and a rehabilitation agreement will be developed prior to the consummation of the contract at closing. The organization might attach its sample covenants and rehabilitation agreement to the purchase agreement and indicate that the final documents will be "substantially similar" to the samples. If possible (and especially if the organization is not completely comfortable with the buyer), it is best to work out the covenants and rehab agreement prior to signing a purchase agreement. In that case, the documents are attached to the purchase agreement and incorporated therein.

PROTECTIVE COVENANTS AND REHABILITATION AGREEMENTS

Every property sold by Preservation North Carolina is sold subject to protective covenants and, if rehabilitation is needed, a rehabilitation agreement. These two tools can be employed by any nonprofit preservation organization and afford substantial protection of historic structures and their environments. The covenants are more general and are intended to protect the property for the long term. The rehabilitation agreement provides specific guidance and deadlines during the rehabilitation process. We try to keep the short-term needs and specifications out of the long-term covenants, since after the property is rehabilitated, those immediate concerns will be moot. The specifications about fixing the sagging southwest wall will not be of concern to a buyer looking at the covenants fifty years from now.

The protective covenants are attached to the deed conveying the property to the buyer and are incorporated into the deed by reference. They are recorded with the register of deeds in the county where the property is located, and they become a part of the chain of title for the property. Properly drafted, they will be enforceable against all future property owners.

When drafting protective covenants, try to determine in advance what's important about the property for long-term preservation. Is it the building's architectural features? What about interior features?

Is it the building's relationship to the streetscape? Is it the site? Would the cutting of trees substantially diminish the property's historic value? Should subdivision of the property be prohibited? Are new additions or additional structures to be permitted?

Your protective covenants give your organization its opportunity to control the future of the property. Alternatively, the covenants may provide an impediment to reasonable buyers. The challenge is to develop covenants that clearly address long-term concerns and demonstrate balance between preservation and ongoing utilitarian needs. One hundred years ago, today's kitchen, bathroom, and heating/cooling needs could not have been predicted. Even twenty years ago, wiring requirements for computers and media equipment would not have been projected. Conversely, twenty years from now, our current requirements will be viewed as antiquated. The covenants need to protect what's important, while providing latitude for the property to be used according to future needs.

When reading drafts of covenants, try to project yourself fifty or one hundred years forward. Will your covenants be understandable (and therefore enforceable) if you aren't specific about the property features to be protected? Instead of saying that the covenants protect "all mantels," isn't it more useful to specify that they protect "three Greek Revival–style mantels"? Even better, the covenants should indicate the specific locations of the three mantels being protected. Don't require someone to read your mind one hundred years from now.

Before selling the first property, try to articulate your organization's philosophy about its covenants. Is the organization more interested in "restoration" or in "rehabilitation"? In a museum village, architectural purity may be the goal. In the revival of a historic district, the ideal may be attracting an owner-occupant who will rehabilitate a problem house in the neighborhood. With a forlorn former industrial factory, the goal may be economic development. What are your goals, and do your covenants articulate them? Your buyers will be keenly interested in the organization's expectations, and the covenants will make or break sales.

Not having protective covenants is unacceptable.

If a buyer indicates that he or she is not willing to accept at least minimal covenants (for example, provisions prohibiting demolition and requiring a minimal standard of rehabilitation and maintenance), then the organization should reject any offer from that person. "Trust me" is not a valid legal agreement. A local North Carolina preservation organization sold one of its first properties, a fine but vacant Victorian house, to a buyer who told the group that he would rehabilitate it for a restaurant. However, he was unwilling to accept covenants. The group relented, and within twenty-four hours after the closing, the house was demolished to make way for a new steak house. The preservation organization had no legal standing to do anything. (Ironically, the restaurant eventually failed.)

Covenants typically run with the land, making them enforceable as to future owners. They may be created to run in perpetuity (if state law permits) or for a specific number of years. The covenants can protect as much or as little as the parties agree to. Covenants might control rehabilitation, long-term maintenance, demolition, new construction, exterior alterations, interior features, landscape features, tree cutting, archaeology, property subdivision, use, public access, and numerous other matters. The covenants will typically also contain provisions to govern their administration (for example, a right to inspect the property) and enforcement. A sample set of covenants is included as appendix B.

In the covenants, the organization may retain a right of first refusal, giving it a limited opportunity to repurchase the property in the event of a future sale. The right of first refusal provides a chance for the organization to make sure that future buyers know about the covenants and acknowledge their validity and enforceability. Preservation North Carolina has developed a recordable release of the right of first refusal that it will execute and provide to a closing attorney in a future sale of the property. We sign the release only after having a conversation with the new buyers, and the document requires the signatures of the buyers to indicate their acquiescence with the covenants. (See a sample release document in appendix D.) If the buyers were to indicate an unwillingness to comply with the covenants,

Representative Transaction Timeline

THE ELIZUR PATTON HOUSE, TRANSYLVANIA COUNTY

2006

April	PNC first contacted about the house (by owner)
May	Option to PNC signed by owners
June	First ads for Patton House on the PNC website and other property-oriented websites
Summer	Numerous inquiries and showings of the property; most prospects are intimidated by the house's condition
September	SWAT team clean-up (25 volunteers) with publicity
October	Ad in *North Carolina Preservation*
November	Ads placed in *Preservation* and *Old-House Journal* for January 2007
Late November	Contract signed with buyer
December	Development of draft covenants and rehabilitation agreement

2007

January	First lender bows out over concerns about the condition of the property; second lender is found
February	Buyer's attorney raises questions about the structure of the sale, due to new "anti-flipping" rules from HUD
March	Contract extended to accommodate financing delay
June	Property sold with covenants

Preservation North Carolina would first ask their attorney to stress to his or her clients their validity and the potential penalties for ignoring them. If that did not work, Preservation North Carolina would consider repurchasing the property to make sure that its preservation was ensured. Fortunately, we've never had to do that.

Preservation North Carolina uses the Secretary of the Interior's Standards for Rehabilitation as the guideline in its covenants. Just using the word "rehabilitation" rather than "restoration" is reassuring to purchasers. Chapter 9 contains more about our philosophy for the properties we sell and the enforcement of covenants and easements.

The covenants need to contain information about how they will be enforced. What kind of notice will the property owner get in the event of a violation? What penalties will be available for enforcement? How substantial must the violation be in order to pursue enforcement? The buyer—and the buyer's buyer—will want to know in advance.

Preservation North Carolina's covenants also contain a provision that calls for a modest covenant monitoring fee to be charged to future buyers of the property. The fee doesn't apply to the sale of the property by the original buyer, only in sales thereafter. Transfers to relatives or related parties are exempted from the fee. Far in the future, when renovated properties sell for handsome sums, the organization will garner guaranteed financial support for its obligation to track the properties.

The rehabilitation agreement used by Preservation North Carolina is a contractual agreement that addresses immediate rehabilitation needs and deadlines. Referred to in the protective covenants, this agreement is not usually recorded. It personally binds the buyers, but not future purchasers. If the work outlined in the rehabilitation agreement is not completed by the buyers before they dispose of the property, the buyers may technically be in default, and the organization may be in a position to negotiate a new agreement with the new buyers. The rehabilitation agreement is no longer enforceable after the rehabilitation is completed.

The rehabilitation agreement sets out interim benchmarks as well as deadlines for completion of exterior and interior rehab. For example, the agreement might stipulate that the roof and windows must be repaired within one year, though the project as a whole may be given a four-year deadline. These interim benchmarks aid the organization in making sure that work starts quickly and the property is stabilized and secured from the elements. If the buyers don't meet the interim deadlines, the organization can intervene and ultimately force a sale of the property. Without the interim benchmarks, the organization may be unable to act until the final deadline has passed.

We encourage buyers to outline their own plans and propose their own deadlines. If we are in agreement about their plans and timetable, then we develop our rehabilitation agreement to reflect those areas of agreement. In essence, we commit the buyers' plans into writing as the rehabilitation agreement, as long as their plans don't violate our guidelines. We often will allow more time for buyers who plan to do the work themselves, but we will add more interim benchmarks to ensure that work progresses steadily.

We will consult with the local State Historic Preservation Office or other preservation professionals if we have any concerns about what the buyer is proposing, either in the process of developing the rehabilitation agreement or while approving later revisions or submissions. If a buyer is planning to use the rehabilitation tax credits, we advise them about the process and assure them that state or federal approvals of tax-credit projects will suffice for our approvals, except in those rare cases where our requirements are more stringent than the Secretary's Standards. For example, we might prohibit new construction on a particular parcel, whereas the Secretary's Standards would only provide general guidance for the design and placement of new construction. Our covenants would prevail.

One of the requirements in all of our rehabilitation agreements is that the purchaser photograph the property thoroughly in its existing condition. This requirement serves two purposes: (1) In the event of a dispute, the owner has his or her own evidence of the property's condition at purchase (we have our own as well), and (2) on completing their work, many rehabilitators have later regretted not having taken as-is photographs. "Before" photographs are invaluable for bragging rights.

A sample rehabilitation agreement is included in appendix C.

HEADING FOR CLOSING

It's still not over once you've signed the purchase contract. Usually the buyer must find financing in order to purchase the property. In addition, the purchase contract may give the buyer the right to back out if specific environmental or structural conditions are found.

At this point, it's critical that the organization and the purchaser work cooperatively. Having the contract fail may be the death knell for the property, because time might run out for the property or the contract's failure may taint the property for future buyers. If a rumor circulates that a sale failed because the property has environmental or structural issues, then the organization will have an even more difficult time finding a new buyer.

The organization can often provide a buyer with invaluable information about sympathetic appraisers, lenders, inspectors, architects, contractors, and other professionals. This advice may be critical to selling the property. For example, an appraisal can make or break a bank's willingness to finance a property, and we have seen a wide range of appraised values established by appraisers. An appraiser with experience in evaluating older buildings is accustomed to seeing properties where the building looks bad but is in prime condition for rehabilitation. An appraiser unfamiliar with older buildings may view the same building as worthless and assign it no value, and this bad appraisal can kill the deal. The same result can occur from bad advice from other professionals involved in the purchase process, such as architects, engineers, and contractors. Here the organization's preservation expertise is crucial to a successful outcome.

The organization should try to remain objective throughout this process and not allow its interest in preserving the property to get in the way of the need for accurate and reliable information. In its dealings with a lender, the organization can be a good source of reliable information about the property, its condition, its potential resale value, and so on, but not necessarily about the buyer's ability to undertake the project. The lender will need to do its own assessment of the buyer's creditworthiness, and the organization needs to respect that. Beware of the temptation to underestimate the cost of rehabilitation in order to get the property sold. You want your buyer to succeed, and full disclosure is a key ingredient to that future success.

One of the organizational advantages of being directly involved with real estate is that the organization develops direct ties to preservation professionals, lenders, and others and can encourage clients to patronize them. In addition, these professionals may become donors.

THE CLOSING

Usually by the time of closing, the issues have all been worked out. Often even the signatures have all been obtained in advance and the attorney works through the paperwork alone.

If the organization has an option on the property to be sold, two closings must take place. The organization buys the property from the current owner under the option, and the organization in turn sells it to the new buyer. If the parties are in agreement, one attorney may be used for both transactions. Where no conflict of interest is found, having one attorney involved greatly simplifies the process. The organization's staff doesn't have to explain the process twice. Only one title opinion is necessary, and the parties may conclude that only one title insurance policy is needed. (The buyer's title insurance policy may suffice, since the organization owned the property only for minutes and the same attorney prepared the closing materials for both parties. If something goes wrong, the title insurance company

The Costs of Working with a "Typical" Residential Property Under Option

Obtaining Option *If money is paid for an option,* *it is recouped upon sale.*	No cost
Liability insurance	$ 45
Advertising	$ 800
Legal charges and fees at closing	$ 600
Title insurance	$ 120
Estimated staff time and expenses (such as telephone, mileage, etc.) *for arranging the option, showing* *the property, and negotiating a sale*	$ 5,000
Acquisition by PNC	$60,000
Sale by PNC	$ 65,000

Every property transaction is different. In this example, out-of-pocket expenses are recouped. However, PNC would lose about $500, once staff time and expenses are calculated. If a real estate agent brought the buyer to PNC, payment of a $1,950 (3%) commission would be appropriate. The loss is offset by donor support for the program. Alternatively, when PNC is working with a donated property, the gain upon sale may be substantial. Illustrative of the main premise of this book, the biggest expense for PNC's involvement with this property is staff time.

will go back to the closing attorney to rectify the error.) Property boundaries have to be typed only once. Funds can pass through the attorney's trust account in a way that precludes the organization from having to have its own financing to purchase the property. The buyer's financing pays off the current owner. The organization takes title primarily to place the protective covenants in the deed. Usually we try to build in a modest reimbursement for our work by selling the property for slightly more than our option price from the original owner. That margin, reduced by our share of the attorney's fees and other costs, is paid to us from the sales proceeds by the closing attorney. We typically arrive at the closing with no money in hand (unless we have held escrow funds), and we receive a check after the documents are recorded at the courthouse.

But if all the details haven't been worked out in advance, a closing can be nerve-racking. The organization should try diligently to go into the closing with everything worked out and all the necessary documents executed. If a buyer has not signed off on the covenants and the rehabilitation agreement prior to closing, the opportunity exists for the buyer to threaten to back out if the restrictions contained in the documents aren't weakened. The organization can be put in an awkward position: do you risk losing the buyer at the very last minute, or do you stick to your preservation principles? Waiting until the last moment to work out the details can wreak havoc.

Even though the typical closing may be little more than ceremonial, the organization can use the occasion as an opportunity to cement long-term relationships with both the sellers and the buyers. The closing (and immediately thereafter) provides a perfect photo opportunity: a major preservation event has occurred; the building is saved! New investment will be forthcoming, and great things will be happening. So make the closing a special occasion. At the closing or at the property after the closing, take photographs of the parties showing the transfer of ownership, break out the champagne or sparkling cider, introduce the buyers to local neighbors and fellow preservationists, and invite the local media to attend.

Unlike in the typical market transaction, the seller (i.e., the organization) and the buyer now have entered a long-term relationship. They have signed documents that bind their preservation interests together. The organization should consider ways of celebrating that relationship. Give the buyer a complimentary membership in the organization or an autographed copy of one of its publications. Consider presenting the buyer with a useful book about rehabilitation or an appropriate magazine subscription. Welcome the buyers into the preservation family. They will need all the help and support that can be mustered as they embark on this new challenge.

NINE

Doing the Right Thing and Staying True to the Building

FINDING A BALANCE BETWEEN PURITY AND FLEXIBILITY

*A*T LEAST once a week, I hear someone say something like: "I couldn't buy a historic house, because I'd want to have a good kitchen and add bathrooms." Or, "I'm not sure that I could live with these covenants because I'd need to build an addition." Or, "I'd rather not use the tax credits because they'll stop me from making any changes." From my perspective, these are scary words for preservationists. Much of the public is persuaded that we don't want anything to change; and because people think that change is not permitted, fine historic buildings go unused.

Sometimes preservationists (me included) will lament that a vacant, forlorn building was more charming and picturesque before it was renovated. That's a romantic folly. The charm will eventually decay into ruin if a suitable use and sympathetic owner aren't found. Poverty has had its place in preserving buildings in our country up to a certain point, but eventually lack of investment is a killer.

Part of the work of a preservation organization that's engaged directly with real estate is to monitor the properties subject to preservation covenants or easements and to evaluate proposed alterations to those protected properties. A balance must be achieved between architectural and historical authenticity and the need for sustainable use. My personal approach is derived from the Hippocratic Oath: "First, do no harm."

Through the years, as the person identified in covenants and easements for approving plans for alterations and new additions, I have had to review literally thousands of proposed changes to historic buildings. Many approvals have been easy; others difficult. Some of our decisions would not receive universal accolades. Occasionally we have permitted changes that other preservationists might not, and the results have been less than architecturally or historically ideal. But I still believe we've taken the right overall approach.

Most of the properties with which PNC has worked are "down and out." They are threatened with demolition, deterioration, loss of integrity of site, and so on. Often it is such a relief to have a buyer willing to take on such a substantial preservation project that more flexibility is permitted. If the new owner really doesn't like the historic colors for the house, that's okay. Paint is ephemeral; the next owner can paint it authentically. (Paint color is the least of our worries. In many cases, if someone doesn't put on a new roof pretty darn quick, the building will be lost!) If the buyer can't afford to (or doesn't want to) put a historically correct new roof on the house, modern alternatives can be considered. Installation of a new roof that will give the house at least twenty more years of life, regardless of its architectural purity, is something to be thankful for. Maybe the next roof will be historically accurate.

Most historic buildings have evolved through the years anyway. Rarely have they survived unaltered. Sometimes buildings are more interesting precisely because of their evolution. The juxtaposition of two or three distinct styles in one structure can be intriguing. The purpose of the covenants is not to stop the evolution process, but simply to monitor further changes. Hopefully, fifty years from now no one will say, "Why in the world did they allow *that*?"

Not all buyers will be able, financially or temperamentally, to achieve the ideal restoration, especially considering the derelict condition of most of our buildings. When you're the "animal shelter" for historic buildings, striving for perfection will result in disappointment. I'm generally happy with a grade of 90 out of 100 for any given rehabilitation of a "poor dog." Most of our buyers share our values and do better than that.

We seek to achieve good "rehabilitations" of our properties rather than true "restorations." We use the Secretary of the Interior's Standards for Rehabilitation as our criteria. Rehabilitation implies taking the existing building fabric (including more recent additions) and fixing it up for modern use. In contrast, restoration entails taking the building back to a specific point in time. (Unfortunately, the word "rehabilitation" is more widely associated with drugs and alcoholism than with preservation.)

Unless you have a museum, "restoration" may be an impossible goal. Modern use involves kitchens and bathrooms, electrical wiring, security systems, computers, cars, and every other component of today's living. It may also involve the use of materials that aren't historically accurate, such as latex paints and laminates. For buildings that have evolved through the years, rehabilitation would tend to leave those changes intact, while restoration would probably not.

If a historic building is going to be used for modern life, it must necessarily change. And if it can't be used well by its owners or tenants, the problem of disinvestment is simply delayed.

So am I saying that anything goes? Absolutely not. The "do no harm" standard implies that the changes by a new owner should not damage significant original fabric. A key element in the application of a "do no harm" philosophy is reversibility: alterations must be done without permanent harm to the building's basic integrity. We have approved innumerable additions to historic buildings. We generally have encouraged owners to build their additions at the rear of the main structure, check for archaeological resources, and generally do minimal damage to historic resources. We have often encouraged new additions to be connected to the historic building by breezeways or hyphens so that the rear elevation remains intact and visible. Sometimes I haven't personally liked the design of a new addition. Still, when the owners are firm in what they want, we have approved additions if they will do no lasting harm to the original buildings. A subsequent owner can "correct" the alterations. The bottom line: the historic building is still whole, and the owner has the benefit of a usable building that suits his or her personal needs and wishes.

"Do no harm" necessitates evaluating what is important about a building and balancing the building's future usefulness with its integrity. Here are some examples of tough decisions PNC has faced:

- A fine vacant and endangered brick Federal/ Greek Revival house in a small town had an elaborate late-Victorian front porch in poor condition. A sympathetic purchaser made an offer conditioned on our approving the removal of the Victorian porch and the reconstruction of an earlier-style porch. The option on the threatened property was running out, and there were no other likely prospects for purchase. Removal of the Victorian porch was conceded, but only under the condition that its decorative elements be stored in the attic and documentary photographs be taken for our files. Saving the house trumped the value of the later porch. The Victorian porch may eventually be restored by a future owner; the pieces are there. In my opinion, it's a more interesting porch than the reproduction. But the house is still there and is now in good condition.

• We were working to find someone to save a rural, early-nineteenth-century plantation house in poor condition. The Federal house had some surviving original faux-painted marbleizing on the baseboards of the parlor. The marbleizing was crude and in poor condition, making it interesting for study but less than attractive for many potential buyers. An offer was made on the property from a buyer who did not want to keep the marbleizing. So we worked out a compromise. The restoration experts at the State Historic Preservation Office gave us directions for how the owner could clean and seal the original marbleizing before painting over it. This procedure would make it easy to remove the modern paint in the future and reveal the original marbleizing. We again asked the buyer to provide us with photographs for our files.

• We were looking for a buyer for a small and highly significant brick Federal-style house on large acreage in a poor rural area. Because of the land, the price was high relative to the house's small size. The plan for the house and its high level of architectural detail did not lend itself to the introduction of new bathrooms, kitchen, and heating/air conditioning without either doing significant damage to woodwork or building an addition. Designing a sympathetic addition would be exceptionally challenging because the front and the rear elevations of the historic house were equally important, and the house's footprint was tight and symmetrical. We found our ideal buyers, and before they purchased the house, we agreed in principle that the best solution was a pair of additions, one to each side of the house. We recommended an architect and participated in numerous design discussions with the purchasers to reach a solution acceptable to all parties. We all agreed that the house could not suit modern needs without

an addition, and we also agreed that there really wasn't an easy design solution for adding on. Trying to incorporate new bathrooms, kitchen, and HVAC systems into the original house would result in extensive damage to its fine fabric. Fine Federal woodwork would have to be cut, and nicely proportioned rooms would have to be degraded. Further, the livability of the house would be severely compromised. An addition at the rear would destroy a primary façade. An addition to one side would destroy the house's careful symmetry. So we all agreed to the addition of flanking wings on each side. But, rather than trying to design wings that looked like original appendages (which would have been confusing to most onlookers and difficult to execute), the architect worked to achieve the look of a pair of flanking wooden outbuildings connected to the brick house with glass breezeways. From a distance the glass breezeways disappear, so the effect works. Nearly all of the house's mechanical systems are located in the new construction, so the interior of the historic house remains pure. Some preservationists have legitimately complained that the additions are too big for the house, but I believe that we reached a carefully balanced decision that "does no harm" and allows the house to work for continued habitation for years to come.

• We sold a fine rural Federal/Greek Revival plantation house that had been vacant for years. The house had significant woodwork and major termite damage. Going into the house with potential buyers made me nervous because of the pronounced "bounce" in the floors. We found our buyer, who proceeded to do a nice job with the renovation. A few months later, during a visit, we found to our chagrin that the owner had added a freestanding garage to the right side of the house without approval. The freestanding garage was connected to the house by an extension of the front porch. It was quite a letdown, especially

A Federal house of modest size with equally fine front and rear facades, the Moore–Gwyn House in Caswell County needed additional space to accommodate a modern kitchen, bathrooms, and mechanical equipment. Flanking wings connected by conservatory-like hyphens were approved after numerous design discussions. From a distance, the wings look like a pair of outbuildings.

since the renovation of the house had gone so well. If approval had been sought in advance as required by the covenants, we would have lobbied for the placement of the garage in a less conspicuous location. Even moving it back a few feet would have helped. But we learned from the owner that he had considered other alternatives and had concluded that the chosen location did the least harm to mature trees surrounding the house. Moving the garage even a few feet would have resulted in losing a tree. So, although technically we could have required the owner to remove the garage, we thanked him for his stewardship and urged him to let us know in advance next time. We also encouraged him to add a few plant-

ings in front of the garage. The garage is now inconspicuous, and the owners are taking good care of a house that was nearly lost. No harm done.

• We have approved our fair share of new bathrooms and kitchens—to a point where we can suggest some preliminary recommendations for new buyers. For example, how do you add bathrooms and closets to the second floor of a house with a central hall and two rooms on each side? We encourage buyers to "sacrifice" one of the four rooms (ideally the one above the kitchen or other bathrooms) and cut it in half, creating two bathrooms (plus closets), one oriented to the hall and one private to the adjacent bedroom. Architectural elements such as existing doors, mantel, and woodwork are to be preserved in place, creating distinctive bathrooms. With care, these bathrooms can be constructed with minimal damage to the original building fabric, thereby allowing a future owner the option of returning the room to its original configuration, if they want.

• Perhaps our most difficult design decision involved an endangered house that had been purchased by a grandson of the original builder. The new owner needed the addition of an indoor swimming pool and other athletic facilities for legitimate medical reasons. We agreed to a large barnlike addition that normally we would not have approved. The fact that the house was back in the original family of the builder somehow made the decision easier to justify. Many preservationists might disagree with the approval. But when all is said and done, the original house, though diminished by a large addition, is in great shape and is much loved. The next generation can decide whether to remove the medically necessary addition.

Sometimes, building a new addition is an affirmative benefit. A modest addition to accommodate the heavy load of a modern kitchen, additional bathrooms, and storage is often the best strategy for a historic house. The result is that less damage is done to the historic house.

Additions should be at least slightly differentiated from the original house rather than being a seamless copy. Differentiation clarifies the evolution of the house for keen observers, and it is often more affordable and interesting. However, when a buyer states a strong preference that her addition precisely match the original structure, we relent. (If the buyer is using the federal or state rehabilitation tax credits, we encourage her to get plan approval in advance, since the Secretary's Standards call for differentiated additions.)

In our work with two mill villages, where every house is essentially identical to others in the village, we chose to be particularly rigorous in our approval of design changes. This rigor may seem ironic, since individually these houses are not of great significance. Their significance is contextual, namely, their relationship to each other in the streetscape. In our design standards for the mill villages, we have dictated some design decisions inflexibly. In the Edenton Mill Village, owners have one choice for their roofs: standing-seam metal roofs painted silver. The only approved porch lights are recessed. Additions may not exceed sizes determined by mathematical formulas. The rules are very specific. After all, when the significance of the district is based on streetscapes with fourteen identical houses, then the goal is to assure the continuity of that homogeneity. An added challenge in these mill villages has been the need for consistency of approvals and enforcement for neighbors who are scrutinizing every decision. Personality disputes loom large. For example, we had a property owner complain that a neighbor used "buff"-colored mortar in constructing his new chimney rather than the approved "sand"-colored mortar. The two colors are almost indistinguishable, especially in mortar joints for a new chimney. The complaint wasn't motivated by aesthetics. The property owner was testing Preservation North Carolina to see how literally covenants would be enforced. Furthermore, he didn't like his neighbor!

In both mill villages, we built the first new addition on an existing house, and we hired designers to draw up plans for new houses to be constructed on vacant lots. Developing a "model house" helped buyers to understand what we are trying to achieve. The model new houses also expedited sales of vacant lots by saving buyers time and money.

Now that I have listed a number of circumstances where we have approved changes that many preservationists might disdain, let me assure readers that there certainly are many alterations to historic houses and their sites that we would not approve— changes where permanent harm would indeed be done.

When we receive applications for potentially problematic changes, we will consult with preservation experts from the State Historic Preservation Office (SHPO), as well as with private practitioners who routinely offer us advice and counsel. We try to offer property owners ways to solve problems and meet their needs. We guide them to experienced architects, contractors, and other professionals for advice. We try to use honey rather than vinegar. But when we must say no, we will.

The state's historic rehabilitation tax credits have been most helpful in achieving good preservation projects. The tax credits give buyers a financial incentive to do a good rehabilitation. If the State Historic Preservation Office or the National Park Service signs off on plans for rehabilitation in the tax credit program, in most cases PNC will automatically concur. (In some cases, we will also do that with local historic district commissions.) Rather than requiring buyers to negotiate two or three sets of design approvals, we will acquiesce to the professional judgment of the SHPO and the National Park Service.

Design review, whether in the public or the private sector, is fraught with difficulties. Maintaining a positive relationship with a property owner while combing through his or her property plans requires care and discretion. In the end, it's important to evaluate what really matters about the historic property and then "do no harm."

TEN

The Functional Nonprofit Preservation Organization

THE NEED FOR A STRONG STAFF AND A SUPPORTIVE BOARD

DURING the last several years I have participated monthly in what I call, with tongue in cheek, "group therapy." Chief executive officers from twelve nonprofit organizations in Wake County gather once a month for lunch and confidential discussions about reading assignments and current activities. These nonprofit directors come from a variety of disciplines, but we share many similar issues and concerns. Successfully running a nonprofit organization is quite a challenge—whether in historic preservation, the arts, social services, the environment, or education.

Repeatedly our group returns to two subjects: (1) the relationship between the board and staff, and (2) personnel matters. Not surprisingly, those two matters must be carefully considered by a preservation organization that wants to work with real estate.

To make an endangered properties program work successfully, the organization must have (1) savvy personnel dedicated to the program's success and authorized to act, and (2) a board of directors that is judiciously monitoring the program's activities. Before going further, I must qualify that statement. "Personnel" in preservation organizations that are working with real estate are usually paid staff, but "personnel" may also be highly dedicated board members or volunteers who have sufficient time or available human resources to keep such a program going. "Judicious monitoring" implies a balance between having sufficient information to be legally responsible and having confidence in the competence of the organization's paid staff. I'll explain both.

A preservation real estate program shouldn't be undertaken without sufficient human resources. As I have asserted in several previous chapters, expertise is essential for a successful real estate program, even more important than capital. If you have a good project and sufficient expertise, you can generally find the money to undertake it.

A real estate program requires constant attention. Phone calls and e-mails from potential buyers must be answered. Maintenance and security issues often can't wait. An offer to purchase must be responded to quickly, or it risks being withdrawn. I have seen several properties programs successfully operated by volunteer personnel, and I have great admiration for them. They have usually been led by one or two individuals with special real estate interest or expertise. These volunteers have often been retired, self-employed, or in a position where they are able to make use of their own staff. The bottom line: they have time and flexibility. Whether volunteer or paid personnel, someone must be available on a near-daily basis and authorized to act when needed.

For a real estate program to work successfully, the board must be willing to delegate sufficient and clearly defined authority to the program's personnel. The terms of accountability should be made clear. The board should insist on being kept informed, but in many instances it must also know when to stay out of the way. Imagine negotiating a real estate contract by committee: what a nightmare! Even worse, imagine being the potential buyer who has to negotiate a real estate contract with a committee.

An individual (whether the CEO, the director of the real estate program, or a volunteer) needs to be delegated the ultimate responsibility for dealing with a property and authorized to proceed within clear boundaries. Board and staff members who bring expertise to the table are invaluable and certainly should be consulted, and the authorized property person, whether staff or volunteer, is wise to solicit and value the advice of other professionals in the field. But having a board or committee manage all the details of a property transaction generally won't work. Authority needs to be delegated, and the authorized person should be held to an appropriate level of accountability.

Not only should the board delegate authority to an individual; it should also authorize a committee to work with that person and make quick decisions, where needed, within clear limits. That committee might be the executive committee or a property committee; in any case, committee members must be well informed about real estate matters and available for quick decisions.

What kind of boundaries should be established for a delegation of authority from the board? Some requirements will be clear and unequivocal: "We will require protective covenants." "We will accept an offer from a qualified buyer within a certain price range without further consultation." "We will authorize expenditures up to an established amount to be spent on options, repairs, insurance and other financial outlays." To put these in context: if the authorized person can obtain an option on a significant endangered property at minimal cost to the organization, he or she should be authorized to act immediately, with no board consultation. If the owner is ready to work with the organization, delay

serves no purpose. In another example, if the authorized person receives an offer at asking price from a qualified buyer and the transaction will be subject to adequate covenants, then it doesn't make sense for the authorized person to have to go back to the board to execute the contract.

Of course, in many cases it's not so clear-cut. What if the offer is $2,500 below asking price? I would suggest that the authorized personnel be allowed to make an informed determination and move ahead without further board approval. The staff member who has been working intimately with this property from the beginning of the relationship is in the best position to evaluate questions such as these: Is this the buyer's best and highest offer? Is this buyer going to be good for the property? Is it likely that the organization will receive another better offer? If so, how long will it take to obtain another offer, and how much will the carrying costs be until that time? In many cases, waiting a few weeks or months will quickly eat up more than $2,500 in carrying costs—or risk losing the property.

What if the offer is $10,000 below asking price? Then I would suggest a different set of questions and considerations for the organization. How much is saving the property worth to the organization? Are there alternative ways to save the property that will cost less? Will the organization's membership consider the transaction a preservation victory and be willing to subsidize the loss? Does this decision need to be made by the full board? Should it be made by a board committee? Must the committee meet in person to make its decision, or can it decide by teleconference or by e-mail? Or can the decision be made by staff in individual consultation with committee members?

Whether the threshold for these considerations is $2,500, $10,000, or $25,000, an organization needs to have a clear policy about the limits of authority granted to its personnel and to its properties (or executive) committee. Real estate decisions are time-sensitive. Most real estate offers have time limits, and even when they don't, you don't want to give an owner of an endangered property or a potential buyer too much time to reconsider. The longer a real estate transaction is allowed to go without clear resolution, the more likely it is to fail. When an important property is about to be lost and its owner is willing to give the organization a last opportunity to save it, the matter may not wait for board members to come home from their summer vacations at the beach.

So for discussion purposes, here is a theoretical hierarchy of parameters to define the authority of the staff and the committee. The dollar amounts can be changed, depending on the local real estate market and the organization's willingness to take risks. Every organization will have its own "red flags" for decision-making.

1. No board or committee authority is required:

   • for an authorized staff person (or, where appropriate, volunteer) to obtain an option for $2,500 or less on a significant, endangered property.

   • for an authorized staff person to negotiate the sale of a property with appropriate covenants where the organization will not lose more than $2,500—relying on the staff person to use his or her judgment about whether better offers are likely, whether the buyer will do a good job, whether the significance of the property merits the loss, and so on.

   • for an authorized staff person to negotiate modest changes in the covenants that will still ensure the fundamental protection of the property.

   • for an authorized staff person to accept the donation of a preservation easement when it meets the organization's general requirements for easements and there are no apparent complications (no thorny appraisal, ownership, or easement provisions, etc.).

2. Under the following circumstances, the organization requires consultation by the staff with executive or property committee mem-

bers. The staff person is then authorized to proceed with an affirmative "sense of the committee." If committee members aren't in agreement, then the committee must meet in person or by teleconference to confirm the transaction. If the committee can't agree, then the matter goes to the board.

   • The authorized staff person may accept the donation of an endangered historic property when he or she is confident that the property will not entail large carrying costs or be unusually difficult to sell.

   • The authorized staff person may negotiate the sale of a property with appropriate covenants where the organization may lose up to $10,000 in cases where the property is owned by the organization and has been for sale for an extended time or where the property is highly significant and imminently threatened.

3. The entire board of directors must be consulted:

   • when the organization is contemplating the outright purchase of a historic property at market value.

   • when the organization is contemplating relocating a historic structure. (Moving structures usually requires substantial investment and may generate controversy or concern. If a moved structure is slow to sell and requires significant subsidy, then the staff and/or a board committee will not want to "go out on a limb" alone. This hypothetical parameter would not apply to decisions where the organization has an option on a structure to be moved by a purchaser.)

   • when the organization is considering undertaking a substantial stabilization or rehabilitation of a structure without having a buyer in place. Again, getting the buy-in of the full board of directors may be wise in case the project lingers and carrying costs escalate.

These examples don't reflect an inclusive list of circumstances for defining the staff's or a committee's authority. And the extent that authority is delegated is likely to change over time, especially after the staff has developed experience with property and trust with the board. However, the board ultimately holds fiscal responsibility for the organization, so even if the board has delegated substantial authority to the staff, it should insist on comprehensive, accurate, and timely reporting.

One of the most important responsibilities of the board of directors of an organization that relies heavily on its staff is to make sure that the board is getting good information about the organization's activities and transactions. If the key staff for properties were suddenly incapacitated, how vulnerable would the organization be? Including property work in a preservation organization's activities increases its reliance on staff (whether paid or unpaid).

Along with the delegation of authority goes the need for accountability. If the board is not getting satisfactory information or adequate performance from its staff or its committee, then the board must actively address the situation. Getting into property work increases the stakes for an organization. Poor performance in this realm can't be tolerated as casually as it might in others. In too many cases, I have witnessed a board delegate to its staff the authority for property work without requiring adequate reporting and accountability, resulting in significant financial strains for the organization. In more than one case, I have seen organizations close down because the board wasn't sufficiently monitoring the staff's work. If the board of directors is surprised when an organization runs out of money, something is wrong!

However, the staff or board committee shouldn't be expected to accomplish the impossible or to predict the future. National and international forces (such as an increase in interest rates or a drop in the stock market) or local events (such as a natural disaster or the closing of a major local industry) can radically change the real estate market. Nevertheless, the staff or board committee should be expected to revamp strategies for properties as external circumstances change. For example, if interest rates rise, can the organization provide favorable short-term financing for a property in order to get it sold?

Another key role for board members is to serve as ambassadors for the organization (and its staff). Whether or not a board member privately feels completely supportive of the organization's work with specific properties, he or she should be publicly loyal. The organization doesn't need board members who complain that the property "really isn't that important" or is "too expensive." The gift of hindsight doesn't grant a board member unfettered license to second-guess the organization's property work in public. Those kinds of conversations, where appropriate, should occur in open discussion within the organization. Backbiting, private e-mail discussions, and unnecessary "executive sessions" can destroy trust within an organization. When endangered properties are at stake, all players should commit to forthright discussions focused on achieving salutary results. The board, its committees, and the staff must operate as a team—or risk failure.

Board members of a preservation organization that works with real estate can be invaluable in leading it to owners of important historic properties who need assistance. Gifts of real estate can help to sustain an organization financially and, if the real estate is historic, advance its mission. For example, a board member might persuade an elderly neighbor or family member to donate his or her home (whether historic or not) to the organization when moving to a retirement home. The proceeds of the sale might then be split between operating needs and endowment, allowing the gift to aid the organization in both the present and the future.

Personnel matters for an organization working with real estate are not limited to the relationship between the staff and the board. Neither are they unique to such an organization, although real estate may necessitate a more disciplined approach to personnel because of the higher stakes. Mediocre performance may not be tolerable when the interest clock is ticking on a large line of credit.

A nonprofit preservation organization is much like a small business, yet it's not an actual business. A preservation nonprofit should strive to be both "businesslike" and mission-driven. Many of the properties that a nonprofit preservation organization will be working with are properties that the business community has passed over. The organization shouldn't necessarily expect to make a "businesslike" profit, but it should adopt a "businesslike" approach to the use of its human and financial resources. Is the staff sufficiently focused on results? Are the details being handled? Are there ways to use volunteers successfully to save time for the paid staff and to reduce costs? For example, can volunteers show the property to potential purchasers visiting the property for the first time, saving the paid staff for the follow-up visit? Can volunteers help secure a property and keep it clean? Is the organization using its $25-per-hour staff to do $10-per-hour tasks? The organization needs to use its personnel (paid and unpaid) well and be clear about its performance expectations. And it should hold its each member of the organization accountable for his or her performance.

What qualifications do I look for when I'm hiring professionals to work with endangered properties? Rather than hiring someone who knows the workings of historic preservation (National Register nominations, Section 106 reviews, paint research, etc.), architecture, and architectural history, I lean toward hiring persons with experience and training in property-related fields (such as real estate professionals, lawyers, planners, contractors, etc.) who have a passion for preservation and a temperament that's compatible with a sales job in a nonprofit organization. If the person doesn't already hold a real estate broker's license, he or she is assigned to get one as quickly as possible after being hired. This hiring formula is predicated on the reiterated premise that preservation is fundamentally about real estate. As much as I value professionals with training in historic preservation, architecture, or architectural history, our organization can obtain those services when needed. We can also rely on those professionals to help keep us true to our mission. To do real estate work, we need professionals with real estate training and experience.

Then, once we've hired professionals, we try to pay them appropriately. If an employee does an excellent job, the organization has a strong interest in keeping him or her in place. Having turnover can be very expensive and disruptive, especially when complex real estate projects are at stake. Good nonprofit employees can certainly make more money in the private sector, but they are unlikely to have the same rich, diverse, and gratifying experiences in for-profit work. However, rewarding experiences may not be sufficient compensation for employment. One still has to pay the mortgage, save for retirement, and buy groceries.

All too often, I've seen nonprofit groups be "penny-wise and pound-foolish" in their approaches to personnel. Many times I've been called by a board member of an organization with an opening for an executive director and been asked to help identify potential candidates. When I ask about salary, I get a sheepish response about not being able to pay as well as they'd like. I encourage them to go back to the drawing board and work on increasing the salary, because the organization is likely to get what it pays for. They will most likely be able to hire a mediocre candidate, a dreamer (there are scores of fine people who think they'd like to work in historic preservation), or a young inexperienced star. In either case, it's highly likely that the organization's new director will burn out or be lured away.

I also ask whether the staff person will have to raise his or her own salary, and the answer is usually yes. That's another recipe for burnout. If the staff member is expected to execute programs and simultaneously raise money for overhead (including his or her own salary), the path usually leads to a dead end. Another staff killer is unrealistic programmatic expectations, where the organization hopes to do more than its budget reasonably permits.

It can be a vicious cycle. Staff comes and goes, every two or three years. Without continuity of leadership, donors lose faith. The organization has to reconsider its programs and priorities, and personnel lapses result in lost time for orientation and adjustment. Planned gifts aren't made, because relationships aren't built.

Working with real estate may provide a key advantage to preservation organizations considering how to break out of this cycle. I feel immensely fortunate that for the first six years of my career, our small start-up nonprofit preservation organization only worked with real estate. The organization didn't have members, newsletters, conferences, awards, or the other usual programs of many historic preservation organizations. Without apology, we did real estate—period. Our focus on real estate gave us several advantages. We concentrated on a program that generated public interest and financial support. Most donors will respond more favorably to an organization's saving an important endangered resource in the community than to its having a successful conference. Our donors generously gave us funds to do preservation; they weren't rewarded with newsletters, tours, and so on. We were also focused on a program that could generate larger financial rewards. A single gift of real estate could provide a year's operating support in those start-up years. We focused on historic preservation—and not the trappings!

After several years, the organization reached a level of financial strength that allowed us to take on the more time-consuming, less revenue-generating programs of education, technical support, and advocacy. Let me be clear: these programs are important. Nevertheless, I would pose a question to a preservation organization struggling to rise beyond barely being able to hire an executive director at an insufficient salary: might it make sense to tighten the organization's goals to focus only on working to preserve buildings and sites, with a long-term goal of adding further programs as funding and financial stability are available? Such a decision dictates revising staff qualifications, budget requirements, and board responsibilities.

When one looks around the field of successful historic preservation organizations in the United States, the case for organizational continuity is abundantly clear. The most successful groups around the country are generally those that have retained professional leadership for the long term. And if those groups have dedicated attention to planned giving programs, they will become even more successful in the future.

Operating a successful nonprofit organization (in historic preservation or elsewhere) is quite a challenge. Books, articles, and consultants on the subject abound, and the best organizational development resources may exist outside the preservation circle. Board/staff imbalances and personnel challenges are not unique to preservation nonprofits. A little "group therapy" with the leadership of other nonprofit groups in the community may be beneficial for both board and staff. There's nothing like knowing you're not alone!

What Is a Nonprofit?

Nonprofit organizations are complex entities, reflecting the personalities of their founders, their directors, and, where applicable, their staff. Like families, they may operate smoothly, providing tremendous service to constituents, or they may be utterly dysfunctional, concerned with internal conflict and personality politics. They may be constantly struggling with finances or affluent with endowment support. Nonprofit preservation organizations in America cover a spectrum from highly regimented nonprofit tax-exempt corporations to loose confederations of interested citizens. Having a preservation nonprofit that operates successfully over a period of decades is a rare achievement.

Incorporating a nonprofit historic preservation organization takes only a few hours, generally requiring the registration of an organizational charter and bylaws with the appropriate local or state authorities. The documents are largely made up of legal boilerplate, and almost any lawyer can generate them quickly. More important is creating an effective board of directors and adopting a viable mission.

A nonprofit corporation is governed by a board of directors, which bears legal and financial responsibility for the actions of the organization. Being nonprofit does not mean that the organization can't make money on transactions; rather, it signifies that no private individuals profit directly from the organization's activities. There are no stockholders. The organization may hire staff and pay competitive salaries, but those salaries are subject to scrutiny by governmental officials and the public. Property owners may benefit from the work of the nonprofit (such as through the adoption of tax incentives advocated by the organization or by the increase of property values resulting from the organization's work), but board members who so benefit must be careful to avoid conflicts of interest, whether real or perceived.

Following incorporation, a nonprofit needs to apply to the Internal Revenue Service for 501(c)(3) status, through which contributions to the organization are tax-deductible. Getting tax-exempt status is a tedious process taking months and sometimes years. The Internal Revenue Service requires a multiyear plan for the organization, including details about its mission, directors, planned activities, and projected budgets. Once 501(c)(3) status is received, donors may contribute (money, stocks, property, etc.) to the organization and deduct the value of their gifts on their federal income taxes. Upon receipt of 501(c)(3) status, nonprofits may receive other advantages such as local property tax exemptions and sales tax refunds from state and local governments. Private foundations as well as most state and local governments will not grant funds to a nonprofit organization unless it is 501(c)(3).

Having 501(c)(3) status provides many benefits, but it also places limitations. The finances of the organization are open to public scrutiny. Legislative advocacy is limited to a modest percentage of the organization's budget and program. Many aspects of the organization's operations must be annually reported to the IRS on a Form 990 that parallels an individual's Form 1040. However, for all its limitations, the benefits of 501(c)(3) status usually far outweigh the costs and inconveniences, especially in the field of historic preservation, where the preservation of historic buildings and sites is an expensive and long-term proposition.

Many historic preservation organizations have operated for years without staff, often boasting of what they have achieved without "bureaucracy." Yet very few organizations can achieve sustained effectiveness without reaching a point where paid employees execute the day-to-day responsibilities. Since the 1960s, especially as more women enter the workforce, volunteers who can commit several hours every week have become rare.

When a historic preservation organization becomes large enough to hire staff, achieving organizational balance between directors and staff is difficult. Generally the board is responsible for setting policy and for overseeing the organization's financial health (both budget administration and fundraising), and the staff is charged with implementing the policy. Organizations that take full advantage of the talents of both the board and the staff are rare. The line between the responsibilities of the board and staff is often a source of internal conflict. Many nonprofit executives have left organizations because of conflicts with boards over disagreements about the roles of board and staff. A multitude of organizational development consultants have found employment trying to sort out board/staff relationships in nonprofit preservation organizations (and other nonprofits as well).

The National Trust for Historic Preservation has published a number of titles in its "Information" series about the creation, growth, and management of nonprofit preservation organizations. A complete set of the Organizational Development booklets is available through the National Trust's website, www.nationaltrust.org.

ELEVEN

A Case Study: Armstrong Apartments in Gastonia

OUR WORK is seldom easy. Tackling an eminently endangered difficult property may require stitching together a plethora of preservation tools and may entail frequent course corrections. Just when it seems the project is on track, some element derails, threatening to throw the whole project into the ditch. Saving a historic property turns into a constant quest for solutions. The challenge is to keep your eye on the goal, preserving an important historic resource, and not get diverted or discouraged by the frequent changes in fortune. And, as emphasized in previous chapters, success will often be brought about by expertise and gumption rather than by having a big bank account. This chapter describes one of PNC's more challenging transactions.

The Armstrong Hotel Apartments in Gastonia were built in the early 1920s as accommodations for teachers for Central Elementary School, Gastonia's proud new school across the street. Most of the teachers who resided there were single younger women, trained at one of the state's normal schools and new to the booming textile town. A three-story hotel with efficiency units faced Second Avenue, while around the corner a series of townhouses and flats lined Marietta Street.

In late 2000, Preservation North Carolina received a distress call from the director of the Gastonia Downtown Development Corporation. The Armstrong Hotel Apartments were going to be torn down by its owners. The apartments had been rented out through the years, but a decision had been made not to invest any further in their maintenance. As units were vacated, they were simply closed up, until most of the apartments were empty. The owners' insurance carrier had given notice that coverage would be dropped. Demolition was an easy and logical solution for the owners; the property's land value far exceeded its building value.

The director of the Gastonia Downtown Development Corporation was already quite familiar with the work of Preservation North Carolina. PNC was working with other buildings in the downtown Gastonia area, and the two groups had worked as partners in saving three prominent downtown landmarks. So Preservation North Carolina could rely on the downtown coordinator as a reliable source for the necessary information about the property, its ownership, contacts with the owners, its tax value, and other helpful information.

PNC had recently worked to find a new owner for nearby Central Elementary School. A couple of years earlier, when the school's demolition had seemed probable, PNC had obtained an option on the property from the local school board. A sympathetic developer from Winston-Salem who had long been a friend of PNC had expressed considerable interest in acquiring the school for reuse as affordable housing, but the timing of the project was going to be a problem. The developer needed more time than the school board was willing to give. Instead, a new local charter school stepped forward to acquire the property and undertook a remarkably quick and cost-effective renovation of the building. The charter school's enrollment soared in its new downtown location.

Like PNC, the developer recalled the Armstrong Apartments Hotel from his visits to the school. The downtown coordinator showed him the building, and he was indeed interested in acquiring it, if he could convert it into a mix of affordable and market-rate housing. But again timing presented an obstacle. The owners needed to either demolish the building or dispose of the property immediately. The developer, on the other hand, would have to apply for the housing tax credits, a once-a-year application process through the North Carolina Housing Finance Agency. At a minimum, it would be eight months before the developer would know whether he could receive the credits he needed to undertake the project. If the timing impasse could be bridged, then there was hope for the building.

The owners felt like they could not give the project more time, but they were willing to consider a bargain sale of the property. The entire property appraised for $560,000 (mainly land value), but they were willing to sell it to a nonprofit group at $450,000 if the transaction could take place quickly.

Simply buying the property and waiting for the developer to go through the state's application process was not a workable alternative for PNC. PNC didn't have sufficient funds available for the purchase, and the property was of questionable significance for a statewide group to commit substantial resources. The Gastonia Downtown Development Corporation also didn't have the resources to buy it.

Examining the property through the lens of PNC's criteria for involvement portended a difficult decision:

1. Endangered? Absolutely.

2. Significant? The building was certainly interesting, and it had great value to a yet-to-be-nominated downtown historic district. However, the property didn't rise to outstanding significance.

3. Could it be acquired? Yes, but only if the purchase took place immediately.

4. Could it be sold? Most likely. Time would tell.

5. Were there local supporters who would help? Certainly.

Everyone wanted the project to happen, and losing a historic building because of a timing issue seemed to be a shame. How could the transaction be structured to work? Creative people went to work. Within a few weeks, several key commitments were made. A nearby bank was willing to finance the property with no down payment if PNC would purchase it. (The appraisal on the property was high enough that with the bargain sale PNC was deemed to have sufficient equity in the property.) The developer was willing to pay the monthly mortgage payments for one year, and he agreed that if he did not purchase the property, he would turn over his files about the project to PNC. A third-party buyer was willing to purchase a corner of the property for $180,000 (its full appraised value) where there was a nonhistoric building; its sale would reduce PNC's debt load to $270,000. The city would "lease" the property for a year so that it could be placed under the city's insurance policy, and the city would take care of grounds maintenance for a year.

Everything seemed to be in order. PNC's staff agreed to take the package to the organization's board of directors. The project would require PNC to take on a debt of $270,000, line up all the legal agreements, and purchase the property. Because the project had been on such a fast track, PNC's board hadn't been well prepared to make its decision. The board was hearing about the project for the first time, and PNC had already borrowed more than $2 million to acquire other properties. The discussion, appropriately, was intense. The arrangements made thus far sounded good, but they weren't enough. The board concluded that at the end of a year PNC might be left holding the bag. The board agreed for PNC to undertake the project only on the condition that a backup plan was in place in case the developer didn't acquire the property.

So the downtown coordinator went to work and lined up a backup buyer. If the out-of-town developer failed, then a local businessman would acquire it for rehabilitation for rental housing. That purchase agreement had no contingencies. PNC's executive committee agreed that the backup plan was sufficient and authorized the purchase. Quickly the various agreements were committed to writing, and the property was purchased by PNC. The purchase was ballyhooed in the local press as a step forward for the revitalization of downtown Gastonia, though not without some skepticism. The residences would be the first for downtown Gastonia.

The first hint of trouble came when the rumor circulated that a board member of the housing finance agency who lived in Gastonia opposed the project. He favored new suburban development for affordable housing, not rehabilitation in the downtown area. The agency's decision would ostensibly be based on its criteria, professionally applied, but having a hostile local board member would hurt. Not all of the agency's criteria could be objectively measured. So city officials asked local legislators to let the agency know of their support for the project.

Months later, the agency's judgment came: the project would not be funded. However, its rating was good enough for the developer to consider the option of reapplying in the next round, which would take another year. This change in the game plan would require numerous contracts to be amended to reflect the year's delay. All the parties seemed amenable to extending their commitment to the project

The Armstrong Hotel Apartments in Gastonia (also known as the Marietta Street Apartments) were purchased by Preservation North Carolina in a bargain sale in 2001. The quest for a buyer has taken more than six years and demonstrates the many twists and turns that direct real estate involvement can take.

for a year. However, the building was starting to exhibit the problems of long-term vacancy. Vagrants were becoming a problem, and because there was no electricity to operate a sump pump, water was collecting in the basement. News about the project in the press was turning negative; it was becoming another example of a downtown failure.

Another year passed. A new and refined proposal was submitted to the housing finance agency. Legislators were again asked to express their support. But again the project wasn't funded, only narrowly missing the necessary scoring for funding. The developer decided not to try again. Meanwhile, the cast of characters involved with the project was changing. Our friend at the bank had moved on, and the new city executive was less enthusiastic. The downtown coordinator had left the agency, and no replacement had yet been hired. The staff handling the project at PNC had left. And the building was deteriorating more and more.

We moved to the next step in our game plan: the backup buyer. I realized to my great chagrin that though the backup buyer had verbally agreed to the year's extension, the written contract had not been amended to reflect the year's delay. The contract had therefore expired, so we could not compel the buyer to purchase the building. Nevertheless, he was still interested in the project and willing to pursue it. Since he had never worked with the historic rehabilitation tax credits, we were starting from scratch. We had received helpful materials from the previous developer, such as market information and design plans, but our new prospect envisioned a simpler and less expensive renovation. We worked through issue after issue in meeting after meeting. Could the chimneys be taken down? Could the slate roof be removed? Could the city provide any additional incentives?

Like the building, Preservation North Carolina's position was deteriorating. The clock was running on the loan, and the developer was no longer paying our monthly payments. We had an interested potential buyer, but no contract to seal the deal.

And then a vagrant started a fire in the building. Fortunately, the fire department was able to contain the damage to a couple of rooms, and the city agreed to board the building up. But the bigger damage was in the project's dynamics. The fire turned up the heat. The press pondered whether the building should just be torn down. City council members wondered whether enough was enough. The bank threatened not to renew the loan to PNC at the end of its term. PNC's board and staff now understood clearly that the project could turn into a real albatross.

The potential buyer remained interested, but he wanted PNC to reduce the purchase price to reflect the fire's casualty. We maintained that the fire had done little permanent harm, mainly doing surface damage to an unsympathetic 1950s kitchen and bathroom that would have been removed anyway in the rehabilitation process. Fortunately for PNC, the prospective purchaser insisted that PNC have an insurance adjuster look at the building. We agreed to do so, while insisting that we would not reduce the purchase price. Since the property had been sold to PNC in a bargain sale at substantially less than appraised value and we knew that the general housing market in Gastonia was strengthening, we felt that we could find another buyer if need be. To our great surprise, the adjuster determined that the fire had done $22,000 in damage, and a settlement check was forthcoming. Although the check should technically have been applied to the loan balance, the bank allowed us to use the insurance proceeds to make monthly payments.

Meanwhile, several of the banks in the area had established a new bank pool for downtown Gastonia, and our potential buyer submitted his package for financing. Since the pool had not yet made any loans, its process was in flux. We couldn't get clear answers about criteria and timing for a decision. When one of the bankers asked why anyone would want to live in downtown Gastonia, we knew that we were in trouble. The loan was denied, and our buyer decided to end his quest for the Armstrong Hotel Apartments.

A local downtown advocate who had been coaching him through the process then stepped forward as a potential purchaser. (I have often said "Third time's the charm," though sometimes it's the fourth or fifth.) We had trouble nailing down a contract with her for several months, until she persuaded several other partners to join her in the project. Fortunately, by the time we were working out the details of a new contract, we had several fresh faces at the negotiating table, representing the partnership and PNC. These new parties were enthusiastic about the project and not weighed down by old baggage (which by now was hefty).

An agreement was reached with the new partnership that reflected several compromises. The partners agreed to pay half of the holding costs for the project during their examination period, and PNC agreed to defer any payment in excess of the original loan amount until after the rehabilitation was completed. One of the most important provisions of the contract was that the new partners would provide copies of all due diligence materials, such as environmental studies, architectural plans, market studies, cost estimates, pro formas, and so on, if they decided not to purchase the property after doing their due diligence. That way, if PNC had to look for another purchaser, it would be armed with extensive information. The partners also sought to represent PNC in negotiations with the city about its continuing role as insurer and provider of maintenance. Local citizens who were making a personal financial commitment to the project would be better able to persuade the city to continue its involvement.

Just days before the contract was signed, two new interested and highly qualified potential purchasers inquired about buying the property! It's amazing how often that happens.

PNC's role did not end with the signing of the contract. It never does. For example, PNC provided the partnership with names of qualified contractors and other vendors. PNC's staff took the first version of the partnership's rehabilitation plans to the local State Historic Preservation Office for an informal review. By acting as an intermediary, PNC was able to work more comfortably with the state's staff to find solutions at the outset to problems presented by the building. The partnership worked with the city to increase its incentives for downtown residential renovation.

However, after extensive exploration of the property, the partnership decided not to go to closing. A few days later, I was relating the saga to a colleague one day over dinner. To my surprise and delight, he asked me to send him information about the project. Thanks to our earlier sales agreements requiring that materials be turned over to PNC, we had a wealth of information to provide to interested new prospects. Shortly, we had the property under contract for the fourth time. (Important lesson: many of our most important sales grow out of casual conversations over food or drink.) Again, the contract called for the buyers to make the mortgage payments.

When I selected the Armstrong Hotel Apartments as a case study, I thought that surely it would be sold and under renovation by the time this book went to print. But, alas, I was wrong. We've moved the project the closest ever to fruition. The renovation plan has been approved by the National Park Service for tax credit purposes. The City of Gastonia has agreed to transfer a vacant lot across the street from the project so that additional apartment or condo units could be built later. The buyers had hoped to close the transaction by December 31, but when the date arrived, their investors still had concerns.

Now the buyers are asking PNC to remain in the deal as partners in the project in order to close the financing gap. Our continued involvement may be what it takes. It's risky, but even riskier is losing momentum on this project and having the city's incentives retracted. The market for the housing envisioned by the project is better than ever, and it seems that downtown Gastonia is about to "turn the corner," so there may even be an upside to staying financially involved. We can also use our marketing skills to help launch housing in downtown Gastonia.

If the Armstrong Hotel Apartments finally closes soon, more than five years after its purchase by Preservation North Carolina, PNC will probably be able to conclude the project without losing money. PNC made no down payment to buy the property. Between the buyers' payments and the fire settlement, the loan payments were covered by external sources, and the city's help with insurance and security was invaluable. PNC has paid dearly, though, in staff time and board angst. Since the loan payments have significantly reduced the principal balance during the last five years, the projected purchase price will at least partially reimburse PNC for its personnel expenses.

Has this project been worth it? Yes. If we succeed, Gastonia is getting its first downtown housing, and this rehabilitation project will catalyze others. Gastonia has a new set of downtown advocates: the new buyers, their lenders, city officials (who are pleased with the ultimate success), new residents, and others. PNC's staff has certainly learned new skills and made new contacts in this process. And finally, an important historic property will have been saved from destruction.

Perhaps it's appropriate that this case study isn't yet resolved. As noted previously, outright acquisition of real estate is risky. These projects require repeatedly going back to the drawing board to make them work. They take patience and persistence. And, as is so often the case, real estate expertise and preservation tenacity have proven more important in saving the Armstrong Hotel Apartments than having money in a "revolving fund."

TWELVE

When Success Is Elusive

DEALING WITH DISASTERS AND NEAR-MISSES

SOMETIMES IT JUST doesn't work out. Time runs out, and a preservation solution can't be found. Or a buyer doesn't proceed with the expected renovation. Or lightning strikes. It happens!

A responsible preservation organization is undeterred by "failure" (however defined) and resolutely and persistently goes back to the drawing board as many times as necessary. Strategies change and are refined, but the goal remains the same: achieving preservation and maintaining constructive relationships within the community. That advice is easier to give than to follow. Some of Preservation North Carolina's best successes came only after failure seemed imminent, and we've often been glad that we bit our tongues.

One of the advantages of working with a property on an option basis is that an organization is not obligated if success seems impossible. When the organization owns the property, walking away is not a possibility when no buyer (or other solution) materializes. With an option, the organization can assess its choices, including the possibility of moving on to another project. Yet even if the option has expired, as long as the property's integrity is still intact, it's possible that a buyer can be found at the last hour and the transaction can be salvaged.

Key to delayed success is maintaining a positive relationship with the owner through thick and thin. Even if efforts fail and the subject property is destroyed, one should not burn bridges with the property owner, because he or she is likely to own other properties or have influence with other property owners (or donors) in the community. In North Carolina, I'm constantly amazed by who is kin to whom and where longtime friendships and relationships emerge. You may find that the preservation villain in one community is—literally!—the brother or sister of a generous preservation benefactor in another.

A preservation organization that is directly involved in real estate must of necessity stay focused on achieving substantive preservation outcomes. Such an organization is less likely to lob a bombshell at a delinquent property owner, since it realizes that it might have to work again with that property owner (or a related one). For example, if the organization doesn't maintain a cooperative relationship with a school board down to the bitter end, it will have a problem when the next school issue arises. Furthermore, other school boards will eventually hear about the matter from the board's point of view, and the organization will have trouble trying to save other schools. Another example: a bank will be hesitant to work with an organization that has recently tarnished the reputation and goodwill of another bank.

Achieving preservation outcomes often require unrelenting patience and persistence. With Shady

Shady Oaks in Warren County had to be remarketed by Preservation North Carolina several times before it was finally renovated. When PNC first became involved with Shady Oaks, the remarkable Federal-style house was being used to store tobacco, and its woodwork was reputedly being considered for acquisition by an out-of-state decorative arts museum.

Oaks in Warren County, one of Preservation North Carolina's first properties, we had to guide the property through four sales before it was finally restored—and a fifth sale before it was fully rehabilitated for full-time occupancy. Built in 1812, Shady Oaks is a tripartite Federal-style house with unusually fine interior woodwork; when PNC first optioned it, the house had long been vacant and was used to store tobacco. The local scuttlebutt was that an out-of-state decorative arts museum had made an offer to acquire and remove the woodwork. PNC obtained an option on the house with fifteen acres of land and marketed its availability for restoration.

The biggest challenge to its sale was Warren County's poverty. The house was clearly restorable, but buyers had to judge whether they could get their money out of the property after restoration.

We were elated when a couple wanting to retire to North Carolina bought it. Unfortunately, almost a year later, those buyers changed their minds about restoring the property after a regional landfill was constructed in the county (an event that, coincidentally, begat the environmental justice movement in North Carolina). So Preservation North Carolina obtained a new option on the property and went back to work to find new buyers. Buyer Number Two's enthusiasm for restoration was subsequently deflated when interest rates soared and the nation faced an economic downturn. PNC obtained an option yet again. A very capable third buyer was found, but unfortunately he was beset by a terminal illness. After another round of marketing by PNC, a fourth owner was found who completed the restoration but didn't move into the house. Nearly ten years elapsed during this process, and naysayers could point to our lack of success. Nevertheless, each buyer took the property one step closer to the goal and bought additional time for the historic resource. Buyers Number Five, dedicated preservationists, saw the house (this time, listed by a Realtor) on a PNC tour, acquired it, added an addition for the installation of a full kitchen and additional bathrooms, and moved to Shady Oaks as permanent residents. In the end, the property is a regional showpiece, and it has been beautifully maintained by these most recent owners, who have been exemplary citizens in the community. The decade of revolving-door ownership has now been forgotten.

We have worked with numerous other houses in Warren County. One particularly fine house, the John Watson House, combines a Federal-era cottage with an ornate Italianate front addition by locally prominent architect-builder Jacob Holt. However, the wings of the Italianate section had severely damaged floor systems. To address years of roof leaks, the eccentric longtime owner had simply closed the doors into the wings. Out of sight, out of mind. We were delighted to find an ideal young couple to buy the property. Both were professionals

McMullan Building,
Elizabeth City

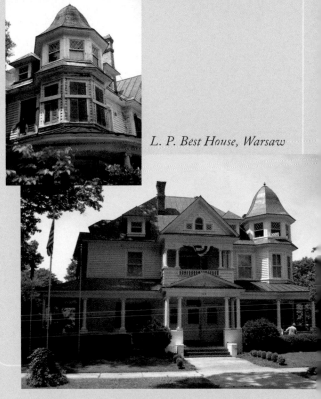

L. P. Best House, Warsaw

D. F. King House, Eden

John Watson House, Warren County

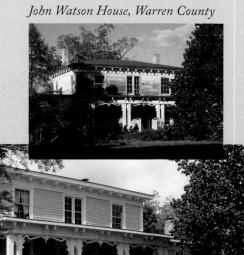

*Properties Acquired and Resold
by Preservation North Carolina*

*Mitchell–Ward House,
Perquimans County*

*Robideau House,
Franklin County*

*Edenton Peanut
Mill*

Lentz Hotel, Mount Pleasant

Shook–Smathers House, Clyde

*High Rock Plantation,
Rockingham County*

Properties Donated to Preservation North Carolina for Resale

McCullough Gold Mill, Jamestown

D. A. Barnes House, Murfreesboro

Loray Mill, Gastonia

Swindell Cash Store, Bath

Grainger High School, Kinston

Pittman–Cobb House, Edgecombe County

Edenton Cotton Mill and Mill Village

Phillips Street—before

King Street—before

Cotton mill during renovation

Phillips Street—after

New infill house

King Street—after

McMullan Street

Glencoe

Glencoe Road—before

House #19 ("The Leaner")—before   *House #20—before*   *House #23—before*

Glencoe Mill

Glencoe Road—after

House #19 ("The Leaner")—after   *House #20—after*   *House #23—after*

Glencoe streetscape—after

Williams House, Raleigh

Vardell House, Blowing Rock

Sargent House, Mount Airy

Wilkinson–Dozier House, Edgecombe County

Kress Building, Greensboro

Wheless House, Louisburg

Dallas High School, Dallas

Baker Sanitarium, Lumberton

Wilrik Hotel, Sanford

Rhode Island Mill, Eden

*Historic Buildings Preserved for Use as
Offices for Preservation North Carolina*

Bretsch House, Raleigh

Caveness House, Raleigh

Bishop's House, Raleigh

Briggs Building, Raleigh

Shell Station, Winston-Salem

Edenton Cotton Mill Office, Edenton

Banker's House, Shelby

Banker's House, Shelby

El Nido, Shelby (documentary photo)

Bellamy Mansion, Wilmington

Bellamy Mansion Slave Quarters, Wilmington

Ayr Mount, Hillsborough

Lithograph of Coolmore Plantation, E.G. Lind Architect (1858)

Coolmore Plantation, Edgecombe County

Coolmore Plantation, Edgecombe County

trained in architectural history, and they relished the house's significance. They weren't daunted by the house's serious structural problems.

Despite our best efforts to assess the buyers' ability to complete the project, they didn't have the necessary financial resources. Apparently their pride prohibited them from letting us help find another purchaser for the property. Instead, they went into default on their loan. The attorney for the lender declined to give us an option that would enable us to remarket the property. So we decided to market the property anyway, sending potential buyers directly to the attorney. Our covenants would still apply, so we had a vested interest in the property. An interested couple saw our ad, contacted us about the property, learned about its status, and made an acceptable offer to the attorney handling the property. The new buyer took on the property's restoration as a family affair, involving their children and friends.

The John Watson House is now an outstanding family-owned bed-and-breakfast inn, bringing visitors and business to Warren County. The husband left his job with a telecommunications corporation in the Research Triangle Park to become the town administrator for Warrenton, the county seat. As with many other properties that have been sold by Preservation North Carolina, the buyers have invested thoroughly in their new community, bringing it new blood, talent, and energy.

Finding these buyers did not financially benefit Preservation North Carolina. We paid for the ad for the John Watson House out of our own pocket, and we never received any compensation for our time and efforts to remarket the house. However, our persistent focus on making sure that the endangered property was preserved led to a happy conclusion that has benefited the organization far more than the cost of the advertising. The restored property and its remarkable owners are great ambassadors for the cause of historic preservation—and Preservation North Carolina.

Don't give up until the resource is gone. Numerous properties have been saved at the eleventh hour. The collapse of the Caswell Motor Building's rear wall prompted the Town of Yanceyville to hold

condemnation hearings, but we still found a buyer. The building's loss would have created a hole in the streetscape on the historic courthouse square. With a loan from an anonymous community benefactor, we saved the former First Baptist Church in Gastonia the day before demolition was to begin.

Of course, we have our share of stories about historic properties that haven't yet been saved—or, worse, ones that have indeed been lost. I think it's useful in those circumstances to do a candid post-mortem evaluation of how we might have been successful, without chastising ourselves. After all, we can't achieve a success every time. It's difficult to

Foreclosure ended the efforts of Preservation North Carolina's first buyers to restore the John Watson House in Warren County. PNC then helped find new buyers who completed the daunting job. Its previous owner had allowed water damage to continue in closed-off sections of the important antebellum house.

Preservation North Carolina was unable to find a purchaser to save the deteriorating 1954 Eduardo Catalano House in Raleigh. The high costs of buying the property and repairing the unusual roof made its renovation economically infeasible. However, efforts to save the remarkable house received national publicity and garnered renewed interest in Raleigh's endangered Modernist architecture.

overcome feelings of failure when a property is lost, but it is important for future efforts for the preservation team to engage in a frank discussion about what might have been done differently.

You may conclude that you should have done things differently, and you can learn from those mistakes. Sometimes you realize that all the king's horses and all the king's men could not have saved the property. The local real estate market may have been too weak. Alternatively, the market pressures may simply have been too strong for the historic property to survive. The structure may have had too many problems. It may not have had sufficient "curb appeal" to attract a buyer. The time frame for

finding a solution may have been too limited. These realizations, if frankly acknowledged, can be valuable in charting future courses of action.

Saving historic properties from destruction is a matter of buying time. Persistence is important. Many times the strategy of not giving up until the property is lost is appropriate, but it's important to stay focused on the preservation goal and not let personal frustrations get in the way. A few harsh words in a public moment of disappointment may make you feel better, but such utterances are sure to haunt the organization in its next effort to save an important property—this one or the next.

THIRTEEN

Protection without Ownership

USING EASEMENTS TO PROTECT PROPERTIES THAT ARE NOT FOR SALE

*A*PRESERVATION ORGANIZATION doesn't have to acquire real estate to gain control over its future. Preservation easements are an effective tool for assuring the long-term preservation of significant historic properties that are in sympathetic ownership in a community. Easements have emerged as a very useful legal tool for protecting land and historic properties. Since under specific conditions a property owner may qualify for tax incentives for the gift of an easement, an organization might be able to parlay an easement program into a revenue source. The rules for easement deductions are complex, and once again skilled personnel and conscientious counsel are required.

An easement is a legal agreement between a property owner and a qualified preservation organization or public agency, in which the property owner (the grantor/donor) promises to protect the property's historic integrity without inappropriate alterations, additions, or demolition, and the organization or public agency (the recipient/donor) is granted the right to enforce the covenants of the easement and to monitor the property. The owner retains the right and duty to manage and care for the property, pays taxes on it, can continue to use it just as before, and may sell or lease it or pass it on to heirs.

The easement is a legal document that restricts the use of privately owned property. Usually a permanent restriction, it is written in deed form and is filed with the county register of deeds, thereafter running with the title to the land and affecting each succeeding owner just as it does the original grantor. The easement is simply a legal agreement between the property owner and a preservation organization into which the parties enter for the mutual benefits of historic preservation, continued private ownership, and possible tax advantages or other compensation to the owner. The organization takes on the responsibility and legal right to enforce the easement. If a future owner or someone else violates the easement (for example, by erecting a building the easement does not allow), the organization has the authority—and obligation—to require that the violation be corrected and may resort to legal means if necessary.

A preservation easement may be very similar in its terms and conditions to the preservation covenants that the organization places on its properties upon sale, but it differs in origin. The preservation organization must own a property in order to place covenants in its deed. The organization doesn't have to own the property in order for an easement to be placed on it; the owner of the property voluntarily places the restrictions on the property.

Easements are flexible tools. The easement should protect the historic resources on the property, but it can be custom-designed to meet the personal and financial needs of the landowner. Historic preservation easements are intended to protect the architectural and historical integrity of a structure by imposing limitations on the types of alterations that may be made. In some cases, the owner may choose to protect only the exterior of the building. A preservation easement may also be designed to protect a building's interior and important elements of the landscape surrounding a structure, such as trees, outbuildings, or associated archaeological remains. The easement may be drafted to restrict or prohibit future subdivision of land. The extent of the restrictions placed on the property is decided together by the parties to the agreement.

The duration of the easement is the choice of the landowner and the recipient and must be decided at the time of negotiation. However, if the landowner wishes to claim any income or estate tax deduction, the easement must be granted in perpetuity. In most cases, the owner will prefer a perpetual easement. Because the preservation easement generally is entered into for the preservation and protection of a cultural resource, it is not designed to allow for quick and simple alterations to its terms. After the easement has been recorded, it may be altered only by mutual agreement of the parties. However, when the donor wishes to take an income or estate tax deduction, the easement must provide that it may be terminated or substantially altered only with the approval of a court of law, upon a showing that the original purpose is no longer attainable. In practice, easements are rarely altered.

An easement seldom significantly restricts the owner's current use and enjoyment of the property. Most landowners will continue to use their property just as before, but with the granting of the easement, the future of the property is no longer left to chance. The land and structures are protected, and the protection will usually run in perpetuity.

An owner considering granting an easement may benefit from savings in estate taxes, income taxes, and property taxes. If the IRS's rules for granting an easement are followed, a property owner may deduct the value of the easement as a charitable deduction from his or her federal income tax. Assume the property owner has his property appraised without an easement at $200,000. He then has the property appraised with the easement in force and it is now worth $150,000, perhaps because the parcel can't be subdivided. The $50,000 difference is the value of the easement gift for tax purposes. For property taxes, the county tax assessor must take into account the reduction in value caused by the easement and should tax the property at its restricted value, not at its highest and best use as if development were unrestricted.

Since the easement appraisal process is highly susceptible to tax fraud, in 2006 Congress added complex new qualification rules for the tax deductibility of preservation easements. Most of these new provisions are directed at easements in urban neighborhoods. In this legislation, Congress sought to close loopholes that have allowed deductions for easements that brought little public benefit or for easements given to nonprofit organizations with little capacity or intention of enforcing them. These new regulations make it more important than ever that a nonprofit preservation organization know the rules and communicate them well.

The Internal Revenue Service has added a number of new qualification requirements for appraisers and instituted sizable fines for both donors and appraisers for overvaluation of an easement's value. As with any charitable donation of an asset, the donor is responsible for the appraisal, and the charity should be circumspect in any involvement with the appraisal process. The financial incentive for the donation of an easement can legitimately be significant, but the prudent preservation organization will advise an owner to follow the IRS's rules carefully.

Most preservation easements can be divided into two sections: affirmative rights given to the organization, and covenants (i.e., promises) made by the property owner concerning the future use of the land. Affirmative rights might, for example, give the organization the right to bring researchers to the property with the consent of the landowner. Covenants concerning the future use of the property can be "positive" (requiring the landowner to take an action) or "negative" (preventing the landowner from taking an action).

The federal and state governments provide tax

incentives only for easements given for certain qualified purposes. To qualify as a charitable contribution, and thus to earn federal and state income tax
reductions, the easement must be perpetual, must
be made to a qualified donee (such as a nonprofit
preservation organization or a public agency) with
the resources and commitment to manage and enforce the easement's restrictions, and must meet one
or more of the conservation purposes set out in the
federal tax code:

- Preservation of historically important land
  or buildings (generally, the property must be
  listed on the National Register of Historic
  Places)

- Preservation of land for outdoor recreation or
  education

- Protection of relatively natural habitats of fish,
  wildlife, or plants

- Preservation of open space pursuant to a
  clearly delineated governmental conservation
  policy

Only the owner of the land or building may decide to grant an easement. In the end, the decision
to give an easement is a personal one made by the
property owner alone, but the owner should always
consult competent legal and tax counsels to assure
that his or her wishes are successfully translated
into the provisions of the easement agreement and
to assure that every advantage is taken of all possible tax benefits.

The easement may be granted to a qualified preservation organization, either private nonprofit or
governmental. The property owner chooses the best
recipient to administer the intended preservation
project. Many statewide and local preservation organizations, as well as the National Trust for Historic Preservation, accept easements. Governmental agencies, such as State Historic Preservation
Offices or local historic preservation commissions,
may also accept easements. In choosing, an owner
should consider the size and location of the property, the kind of protection contemplated, and the
stability and sophistication of the prospective recip-

ient. Many owners may prefer making an easement
donation to a nonprofit organization rather than a
governmental unit because of concerns about future
enforcement. The prospect of receiving an enforcement letter from the attorney general's office about a
minor infraction of an easement may be daunting.

There are some costs for the donor. Generally,
the donor of the easement pays the title search, land
survey, appraisal, accounting fees, and legal fees for
preparing the easement. Some organizations charge
a fee for accepting easements. These fees, deductible for the owner, are justified because the organization receiving the easement will incur costs in
the transaction of receiving the easement and, more
significantly, in providing for long-term monitoring
and enforcement costs. An easement might include
a modest administration fee to be paid when future
changes in ownership take place.

Easements are most effective as a financial incentive for property owners where land values are high
relative to building values. That ratio occurs where
there are mounting development pressures on a
property. Examples include a historic structure that
is considerably smaller than its neighbors (for example, the small historic building among tall downtown commercial buildings), a historic structure on
land that has a high development value (such as a
historic house adjacent to a flourishing commercial
district), or a building sited on substantial acreage
with development potential. Anywhere a historic
parcel could be subdivided and the resulting lots
easily sold for a substantial price, an easement will
have value as a donation. (The new rules for easements passed in 2006 place limits on deductions for
easements on land in designated historic districts.)

Owners of numerous properties have donated
easements to Preservation North Carolina and received significant tax deductions. Owners of houses
sitting on several acres of land in mountain resorts
have placed easements on their properties in order
to assure that the properties won't be subdivided
into multiple lots. Their donations clearly reduce
the market value of their real estate, but the owners
have benefited through the charitable deductions
and property tax savings described above. An owner's heirs may also benefit financially at his or her

death, since the property will be assessed at a lower value for estate purposes. Rarely will the owner ever fully recoup the loss of value for the donation through tax incentives, but for the preservation-minded owner, the satisfaction of knowing that the property will be protected may suffice.

In 2006, Congress passed legislation to encourage higher standards of practice for groups working with historic easements. These changes marked the first major reforms in the law relating to tax deductions for historic preservation easements in a quarter century. Among other things, the new reforms prohibit tax deductions for easements that protect only front façades, without safeguarding the entire exterior of a property. The legislation also increases overvaluation penalties for donors, imposes new overvaluation penalties for appraisers, and requires new qualification standards for appraisals and appraisers. These reforms will encourage higher standards of practice for easement-holding organizations, easement promoters, and appraisers. They also underscore the need for a preservation organization and its personnel to remain up-to-date about

changes in easement laws and regulations, especially when a tax deduction is being considered.

An easement can truly be critical to the long-term preservation of a property. The nephew of Henry Kamphoefner, North Carolina State University School of Design's founding dean, donated a preservation easement to Preservation North Carolina on the Modernist house inherited from his uncle. The small house designed by Dean Kamphoefner and George Matsumoto in 1948 is noted for its architectural excellence in the design community. Sited on a large country club lot, the property was deemed by an appraiser to be more valuable without the house than with it, despite the house's prominence. The first purchaser of the property was enamored of the house and comfortable with the easement. Sadly, he died unexpectedly shortly after his purchase. The real estate agent working for the decedent's estate declared that he was not interested in the terms of the easement; his job was to get the best price for the estate. He asserted that the easement had no validity. A firmly worded letter from PNC threatening to report him for malpractice

The 1949 Henry Kamphoefner House is a prominent Modernist landmark for Raleigh. Without the preservation easement donated to Preservation North Carolina by the nephew of its builder, it would almost certainly have been torn down for its lot overlooking a prestigious country club.

Salem College in Winston-Salem placed a preservation easement on the nationally significant Single Sisters House during its campaign for restoration funding.

to the licensing board for real estate professionals caught his attention, and he went to work to find a sympathetic purchaser. Without the protection of the easement, the house would almost certainly have been lost.

The dilemma of the Kamphoefner House also points out the need for the preservation organization to be vigilant in its monitoring of easements. Besides resulting in the potential loss of important historic resources, a failure to monitor and enforce preservation easements might lead to an action against the organization by the Internal Revenue Service, which has a stake in making sure that the public benefits financed through the tax incentives provided by easements are tangible. The monitoring and enforcement of covenants and easements is a major long-term obligation for a preservation or-

ganization working with real estate. Organizations that require a fee for easement monitoring should consider placing a substantial portion of that fee into an endowment or other restricted account to finance future monitoring requirements.

Not all donations of preservation easements will necessarily result in charitable deductions for property owners. In some cases, an owner may not be willing to include all the provisions required by the Internal Revenue Service, or the property may not meet all of the criteria for deductibility. In others, the prospective financial value of the easement may not be sufficient to justify the appraisal and legal costs of taking the deduction. (For example, a preservation easement on a house in a residential historic district is likely to have no value for deduction purposes. Its highest and best use is as a historic house in a historic district.) However, even these easements may be helpful to a property owner in reducing future property tax assessments and estate tax appraisals. Or the owner may be donating the easement purely for reasons of the heart rather than the wallet.

When no charitable deduction is being contemplated, the organization may choose to be more flexible about the terms of an easement agreement, and it may decide to institute lower fees or waive fees altogether. Although the monitoring obligations for those easements are still a liability to the organization, the goodwill of the property owners may in some cases be more important than a fee. Over the long haul, the owner's contributions to the cause or the importance of protecting the historic resource may exceed the value of any fee to be charged.

Finally, easements may be useful protective tools for properties that are being reviewed for a public project's environmental impact or during rezoning decisions. For example, if the construction of a highway is going to unleash new development pressures on a historic property, a preservation easement given to a nonprofit organization might be stipulated as part of a Memorandum of Agreement between agencies under the National Historic Preservation Act. By protecting the historic resource from a newly created threat, the easement would allow the project to proceed without having an adverse impact on historic resources. Similarly, if the rezoning of surrounding property were to place a historic property in jeopardy, a local government might consider requiring a preservation easement to be placed on the property as a condition of the zoning change.

Preservation easements are an invaluable tool in the preservation arsenal. By agreeing to accept preservation easements, an organization can help ensure the long-term protection of historic properties without ever owning them. It allows a reluctant organization to be involved directly in real estate, and it may even bring revenue to its coffers. However, in order for a preservation easement to provide long-term protection, the preservation organization accepting it must commit itself to a long-term obligation to monitoring and enforcement. Yet isn't the long-term protection of historic resources what preservation is all about?

FOURTEEN

How to Deal with Institutions

PRESERVATIONISTS OFTEN LAMENT that churches, schools, colleges, and hospitals are "the worst." What is it about these institutions that make them the bane of ardent preservationists?

For starters, an institution is made up of numerous layers, none of which is apt to take public responsibility for its actions. When a church plans to demolish its historic chapel, the pastor defers to the church governing board, which defers to the congregation, which in turn defers to the pastor and the governing board. Around and around it goes.

Furthermore, historic preservation is not as important to an institution as its own mission. For a school, educating students is more important than preserving the community's history. For a hospital, saving sick babies takes precedence over saving a historic house.

Preservationists will enthusiastically maintain that you can do both: preserve heritage and meet other objectives. For example, preservation and education are not mutually exclusive; indeed, they can be compatible and mutually reinforcing goals. Restoring a historic school building for continued educational use can be good for the community and for students. Preservationists can rally dozens of arguments to renovate a school: construction savings, improved educational performance, neighborhood walkability, environmental advantages, reduced op-

erating costs, lifetime maintenance savings, child safety, community support, alumni connections, infrastructure cost savings, and so on. But all too often, the institution isn't listening. Minds have been made up. So the answer goes like this: "As much as we'd like to use this building for continued school use, we can't because of [fill in the blank: the state's guidelines, the school board's acreage requirements, building code issues, the asbestos, the lead paint, the terrazzo floors in the hallway, the third floor, no elevator . . .]." To each objection, the knowledgeable preservationist can righteously reply with facts, but to whom? The school superintendent turns to the school board, which points to the rules of the state's education department, which says that it is only adopting the rules promulgated by a national association (which is sustained by fees from school boards). And, again, around it goes.

It's hard to turn an institution around. A savvy preservation group can use its real estate expertise and its community contacts to bring about preservation victories. Institutions often have little or no knowledge about matters of historic real estate, so preservationists can often provide a real service to them by offering to help with solving preservation problems. In working with an institution, one challenge is to be patient and persistent in equal doses. Another challenge is to retain workable relationships with institutional leaders, even when you want to scream, rant, and rave. When bridges have been burned, preservation victories become unlikely.

People sometimes lose their ethical compasses and common sense when they are acting on behalf of an institution. I have witnessed some remarkable displays of audacity. A school board member told an overflow audience that the public really doesn't have any role in making decisions about school renovation versus replacement. (He was not reelected.) An architect told a school board how much it would cost to renovate an existing school building, even though he had done no work to determine that cost. (PNC helped finance an alternative cost study that found that the publicly stated costs were simply fictional. The school has been renovated.) A minister told me that his church had no moral responsibility when one of its members broke the law while acting on behalf of the church. (A judge disagreed. The threatened house was saved.) Note that in each of these cases, a preservation victory was achieved! Also worth noting: after passionately advocating a preservation position, I bit my tongue, taking care not to burn any bridges. You may still need to work with the "perpetrator" the next day.

Preservationists can indeed build sufficient political will within an institution or within its community to achieve bold preservation victories. And when they can't, they may still be able to achieve a good preservation result. At Preservation North Carolina, we strongly advocate that in most cases, the best use for a historic school building is continued school use. But in more than three dozen cases, we have worked to find new owners and adaptive uses for vacated school buildings. North Carolina school buildings have been adapted for elegant condominiums, affordable housing, offices, churches, city halls, and many more uses. Usually these adaptive projects have cost substantially less than the school boards projected for continued use.

Perhaps my favorite reuse of a vacated historic school has been the rehabilitation of Central Elementary School in Gastonia for use as a charter school. The school was renovated for much less money than the school board projected in justifying its abandonment. Parents, neighbors, and students were all engaged in revitalizing the school, and the community pride in the school is evident. Indeed, local school boards would do well to consider how to engage the public in the repair and maintenance of public schools. Citizens truly care about where they themselves went to school—and where their children now go.

With little risk, a preservation group could set up a properties program to deal almost exclusively with surplus institutional buildings. Many communities have surplus historic school buildings, campus buildings, city or county buildings, hospitals, and sacred places in need of new uses and new investment. In many cases, these institutions would happily work in a constructive relationship with a preservation group to dispose of surplus properties. Preservationists can help redeem important community institutions from public relations downfalls, but it may require taking the high road more than once!

A school board's decision to close a historic school has the potential to result in the building falling into irreparable decay. The structure's decline may have adverse affects on the neighborhood, as well as the public's opinion of the school board. No preservationist wants his or her community to reap the consequences of poor or uninformed decisions. Our job may be finding a buyer to renovate the vacated school building for a suitable new use.

Vacated institutional buildings seldom have friends within the institution. They are usually ignored. The institution has moved on to the next chapter and would rather not look back. Often preservationists are considered obstructionists unless we step forward with a solution. We can say, let us find a way to put the old hospital into productive use. Let us help figure out a new use for the old school. Let us help find the money to take care of that structural problem.

The challenge in working to preserve institutional buildings is to strike that delicate balance between being patient and being assertive. Unlike a private property owner who can sign an option on site, an institutional owner of historic real estate must go through its channels. Patience is necessary. The owner's attorney must determine who within the institution has the authority to dispose of surplus real estate. The board? The officers? The management staff? Is the institution bound by specific rules for disposition of real estate? Some school boards may be required by law to first offer the property to other agencies before it can be sold. Are there governing provisions in the institution's charter or bylaws? For a governmental unit, is there statutory authority? Can the real estate be sold? A property may long ago have been given to the institution for an express purpose, and it may revert to the donor's heirs if put to another use.

Patience, however, must be accompanied by assertion. If the process of determining whether a disposition adheres to the rules gets bogged down, a gentle push may be needed. The most effective push may come from within the institution, such as from one of its board members. You can't let up easily.

Creativity must also be in good supply. If the attorney determines that the institution can't sell the property, can it lease it long-term? If the institution can't sign an option, can it sign a contract with broad contingencies, thereby allowing the contract to be voided if the preservation groups can't find a buyer or achieve another solution? If a school board must convey a surplus property to the county, will the county then sell it to the preservation organization?

In 1980, the Hickory Board of Education was ready to sign the contract for the demolition of the historic Claremont High School, a large 1920s Classical Revival structure. The school had been vacated when the community's schools were consolidated a decade earlier. Windows were broken out; part of the roof had collapsed into the building. On a stormy weeknight, three people approached the podium to entreat the board to delay demolition while preservation alternatives were considered. Two of them came from out of town, urged to attend by a preservation-minded school board member. The third was a local preservation mover-and-shaker—a remarkable lady. All three were associated with Preservation North Carolina. Our then-tiny organization, with its real estate focus, was able to connect positively with the school

A delay in its demolition, requested by Preservation North Carolina, helped buy time for the 1925 Claremont High School in Hickory, which was renovated as the Catawba Valley Arts and Sciences Center.

board. We weren't chastising them. We weren't asking them to do unreasonable things. We acknowledged that the school board needed to take action to determine the fate of the building. But would the school board give us six months to explore alternatives to demolition? If we couldn't find a solution in six months, we would move on. They agreed to do so. The next day, a big headline in the local newspaper proclaimed the board's action and started the six-month countdown.

The first impediment encountered was that the property had been given to the school board with a stipulation that it must be used for educational purposes. If it went out of educational use, it would then revert to a local church. That stipulation immediately complicated the picture; not just one, but two institutions could govern the fate of Claremont School. Would the school board be willing to give up a large tract of real estate in an established neighborhood? Would the church then be willing to sell the property for preservation purposes? So the preservation strategy was quickly refined. What local educational institutions were looking for space? The local art museum wanted more space, as did a local children's science center. The donor's language was reexamined. Did the educational uses necessarily have to be under the auspices of the school system? No. Our local preservation advocate went to work, talking to board members of various community groups and potential donors. Even my own skepticism about the feasibility of renovating the school for a new space for private nonprofit organizations faded. In due time, a remarkable transformation took place.

With a stunning amount of private financial support, the historic Claremont High School was masterfully converted into the Catawba Valley Arts and Science Center. The gymnasium was renovated as gallery space for the local arts museum. The auditorium became performance space for the local symphony and oratorio society; they rehearse in the renovated band practice room. The local science center took over much of the classroom space. Local meeting rooms were constructed in former classrooms. The once-abandoned building became a hub of local cultural and educational activities, as well as a tourist destination. After a decade, the project was such a success that the city built its new central library on the former ball field adjacent to the school, adding another compatible component to the property.

As is often the case, Preservation North Carolina's role was to buy time for a solution to be found. Hundreds of other people participated in finding the solution. Indeed, PNC's role in saving the building faded out of sight as so many others joined the effort to save it—and that's fine. This project has helped PNC and other preservationists save dozens more school buildings around the state, by serving as a model of school reuse and as an exemplary community cultural center. And now, because of this project, school boards throughout North Carolina are less likely to view their vacated schools only as liabilities.

A preservation battle with another major community institution in Hickory yielded yet another preservation victory. The local hospital was located adjacent to a historic downtown neighborhood, and the hospital and local preservationists had scuffled many times about the hospital's expansion and its parking. After years of sparring at rezoning hearings, the parties and the city agreed to a plan limiting the hospital's expansion in the neighborhood. When the hospital acquired the historic Fox-Ingold House, a corner property beyond its expansion boundaries, for renovation as its hospitality house, the neighbors were distrustful. So a compromise was reached. The hospital would renovate the house and deed the property to Preservation North Carolina. PNC would then lease the house for fifty years to the hospital's auxiliary, which is fully responsible for its upkeep and operation. Its ownership by a preservation organization provided assurance to the neighborhood that the house won't be demolished in the dead of night or after a few years by its big institutional neighbor.

In nearby Gastonia, the preservation of the former First Baptist Church, a prominent downtown 1920s Italianate church, occurred despite a seemingly nefarious deal between two institutions. The church, having lost many members through the years, decided that it would follow its members to the suburbs. The city, whose city hall was located across the street from the church, wanted to use the church site for downtown redevelopment and contracted to buy the property. Numerous ideas were advanced for the church's preservation, but the property's high sales price defeated one after another. The city announced a deadline for bids for preserving the property and started preparing the building for demolition, taking out its pews and light fixtures. Demonstrating the worst of institutional behavior, the church and the city both publicly bemoaned the necessity of demolition and pointed fingers at each other. The church maintained that its hands were clean, because the city was undertaking the demolition. The city claimed clean hands too, since the contract with the church called for the building's demolition; the church wanted to salvage architectural ornament for its new building. A prominent elected official pulled me into his office and privately berated me for publicly pursuing the building's preservation while also working to save another important building in the community. In his opinion, we should only be advocating one preservation project at a time. I respectfully disagreed.

On Saturday before the planned Tuesday demolition, I received an extraordinary telephone call at home from a longtime Gastonia preservationist (and member of PNC's board). A citizen of the community was willing to anonymously advance the money to PNC to buy the property: approximately $750,000. After a quick series of weekend telephone calls to members of PNC's executive committee for their blessings (the benefactor was offering a loan of unspecified length and with uncertain terms, not a donation), I drove to Gastonia at the crack of dawn on Monday, stealthily picked up a check for deposit, and proudly and nervously executed a bid for the property. You can only imagine the lift in my step that morning! And you can also imagine how badly the stunned local newspapers wanted to know where the money was coming from. (Gloating is not allowed under these circumstances. Again: you can't afford to burn bridges with institutions, since they may own other buildings of significance.)

As with the Claremont School in Hickory, PNC was there to buy time, but it was the local citizenry of Gastonia that saved the building. After numerous brainstorming meetings and the vetting of dozens of ideas, the church was adaptively used in a remarkable partnership between St. Mark's AME Zion Church and the United Arts Council of Gaston County. With a new name, Unity Place, the facility is used for both arts and sacred uses. The rest of the story underscores the power of preservation. One of the community's most prominent architectural landmarks was saved. The former church parking lot was sold to a bank, which built an architecturally compatible new regional banking facility next door (the first major construction project in downtown Gastonia in years). A large "new" performing arts facility with fine acoustics was created in the sanctuary. A new partnership based on racial diversity was established. The city received

All-American City designation, in large part because of Unity Place. Eventually the donor's identity was revealed, and he was lauded. The elected official who objected to PNC's stance was defeated in the next election and replaced by a more preservation-minded candidate. And as in Hickory, so many local people have been engaged in preserving and using the facility that PNC's role in saving it is now only a distant memory. And again, that's fine.

In these cases, Preservation North Carolina acted as a vehicle to accomplish local preservation undertakings. Each situation required having a preservation organization in place that regularly deals with real estate (thereby knowing how to undertake the needed transactions) and that is willing to take the necessary risks to act quickly. If you think through the potential consequences, PNC's making the bid on the church in Gastonia was a huge risk. One could easily argue that it was foolish. We were borrowing money, on terms yet to be determined. Even with advantageous terms, many pitfalls awaited. What if PNC bought the property and couldn't find a suitable use? What if PNC had to default on the loan? If the members of the executive committee had said, "We need to have a board meeting to decide" or "We need a feasibility study," the church would have been lost. The transaction required an enormous amount of faith in the mission, and trust between the parties. We knew the benefactor, and he knew us. The preexisting trust between the benefactor and PNC was essential. Trust between PNC's staff and board members—and among the board members themselves—was also crucial. We had to act first, and figure out the strategy second.

And though we initially disagreed with the City of Gastonia about the fate of the church building, the city had to be treated with public respect. The city's leaders didn't see the wisdom of preserving the church, but as any preacher will tell you, sometimes converts are your best advocates. Little more than a year later, the City of Gastonia asked PNC to help save another downtown property just around the corner from the church: the Armstrong Hotel Apartments, vacant 1920s apartments (featured as a case study in chapter 11). The preservation collaboration between the City of Gastonia

The Bank of Maxton was rehabilitated with private charitable funds as Town Hall for the Town of Maxton. In an unusual arrangement, the building is owned by Preservation North Carolina and leased to the town for ninety-nine years, because the donor wanted to ensure its preservation.

and Preservation North Carolina has required significant investments of time and money from both partners. If the church situation had ended differently, the apartments (and the opportunity to encourage downtown living) would surely have been lost.

Part of the challenge of working with institutions is keeping your eye on the preservation goal and not being diverted by personality and personal differences. One of the most visible preservation stories in Preservation North Carolina's annals has been the preservation of the historic Chancellor's House at the University of North Carolina at Greensboro

(UNCG). As mentioned in chapter 5, Preservation North Carolina raised the funds necessary to relocate and renovate this prominent campus landmark for continued university use, and PNC executed the work under its control. It was abundantly clear that the university's leadership wished that we would go away and let demolition quietly proceed. Through the many meetings about the project, all sides showed personal restraint and never let the situation plummet into petty bickering. All also showed restraint in what was said to the press. To save the building, preservationists had to maintain a workable relationship with the university, which had total control over the building's fate. The institution's sole ability to control the real estate is typical when trying to collaborate with institutions to achieve preservation successes. So a poisoned relationship with the institution's officials is usually the kiss of death for the buildings.

Sometimes institutional victories come out of opportunity rather than conflict. The historic Bank of Maxton, a wedge-shaped building with a clock tower in the heart of tiny Maxton, was the town's most prominent icon. Through the years, the building had fallen far from its original place of community prominence. Sitting empty, it was last used as a Laundromat, until a creative town manager and small group of concerned citizens came up with a bold idea. They went to a wealthy former citizen of Maxton and asked her to consider renovating the building for use as the town hall. She pondered the idea, but she didn't trust the town to be a good steward through good times and bad. So the local citizens came up with a creative idea: deed the property to Preservation North Carolina, have the donor give her gift to PNC, and the town could lease its town hall long-term from PNC. Several advantages accompanied the concept. The building could be privately renovated for less money, since public bid rules would not apply, and the long-term preservation and maintenance of the structure could be assured. All parties agreed to the strategy, and the donor made an outstanding gift of legacy to her hometown. So, Preservation North Carolina now owns the town hall for the Town of Maxton—a remarkable collaboration between a local government and a preservation organization.

Fortunately, most of the institutionally owned buildings that Preservation North Carolina has worked with have not involved last-minute drama or long-term ownership commitments. They have helped solve a problem for both the institution and preservationists. PNC has found purchasers for surplus hospital buildings, churches that were disbanding, and numerous vacated school buildings. To solve a long-standing Section 106 (environmental review) impasse with the U.S. Army Corps of Engineers, the North Carolina Historic Preservation Office engaged Preservation North Carolina

The Mason House in Chatham County long sat vacant after its acquisition for a dam project by the U.S. Army Corps of Engineers. In order to fulfill its Section 106 obligations under a Memorandum of Agreement with the State Historic Preservation Office, the federal agency provided the funds for PNC to renovate the house and lease it to private tenants.

to lease a historic property that the Corps had long ago acquired as part of a dam project (the Mason House in Chatham County), renovate it with Corps funds, and sublease it to private caretakers. The creative arrangement helped preserve a needy house and resolve an institutional deadlock.

Several years after the State of North Carolina was given Ivy Hill in Halifax County, a fine amalgamation of Georgian and Greek Revival structures on a beautiful rural site adjacent to a state park, Preservation North Carolina helped solve a problem for the state by finding a private purchaser to buy and restore it under protective covenants. The state didn't have a use for the property, nor did it have the funds for its upkeep. The process played out quickly, and PNC had to choose among several offers from individuals wanting to buy the property.

Patience and persistence have been required in efforts to find a preservation solution for another state-owned property, the Stonewall Jackson Training School near Concord. The historic portion of the school's campus, a set of handsome brick turn-of-the-century cottages that had been built by counties and private donors, was abandoned over a period of decades. The first negotiations to al-

low PNC to market the properties for private reuse took place in 1989. The sale of the property is still pending, eighteen years later. If the environmental review coordinator for the North Carolina Historic Preservation Office, a local preservation advocate, and interested developers had not persisted to keep the project alive through the years, the campus would surely have been lost. The disposition of the property has involved multiple state agencies, with continually changing staff and priorities. Every time it felt like the project was about to be consummated, a key person would be transferred to another agency, a new administration would take office, or a property survey would turn up a previously unknown easement. Although the campus is a testament to how historic structures can stand up to the elements, they have deteriorated significantly while awaiting a final resolution. Their rehabilitation, if and when it occurs, will be an inspiration.

Preservation work with institutions may not only involve buying properties from the institution; it may require buying properties for the institution. On several occasions, Preservation North Carolina has optioned or purchased important historic properties from private owners and controlled them until a governmental agency could appropri-

When the owner of the significant William R. Davie House in Halifax wouldn't sell the property to the State of North Carolina at its appraised value, Preservation North Carolina purchased it at its asking price and resold it to the state at its appraised price. Private contributions from interested individuals subsidized the difference, allowing it to become a museum.

ate the funds for their purchase. For example, PNC bought the remarkably intact 1897 E. A. Poe House in Fayetteville and held it until the adjacent state-owned Museum of the Cape Fear could obtain the funds for its acquisition. In another case, PNC worked with the State of North Carolina to acquire the historically significant William Davie House in Halifax to add it to the State Historic Site there. Here a little creativity was required. The property appraised for less than the owner would take. Since it is difficult for the state to acquire a property at more than its appraised value, Preservation North Carolina agreed to buy the property at the owner's higher value and sell it to the state at the appraised value. A dedicated preservation advocate helped raise the necessary funds to reimburse Preservation North Carolina for the difference in price. Unfortunately, however, the State of North Carolina will not agree to protective covenants on properties it acquires, so these properties are protected only by the goodwill of the people.

Surplus institutional properties may offer opportunities bolder than a building-by-building approach to preservation. In 2000, a PNC board member approached me about the idea of getting the State of North Carolina to sell nearly six blocks

of real estate near the heart of downtown Raleigh. At first the idea seemed inconceivable. For decades, the historically significant houses of the Blount Street area had served as state offices. Surrounding the twenty-seven historic houses are surface parking lots and the state's motor pool. A powerful state senator latched on to the idea of returning these state-owned historic homes, as well as the adjacent land, to private ownership. Companion House and Senate bills were introduced in 2001 in the North Carolina General Assembly. Under these bills, state-owned properties within the area would be sold to private owners when the properties are deemed no longer needed for state purposes. In the original bills, the historic houses would be restricted to residential uses, such as private homes and bed-and-breakfast inns. Land in the area would be sold for mixed uses by private negotiation so that appropriate plans and designs for new construction could be assured. All sales would be subject to protective covenants. The City of Raleigh and Wake County came out in support of the proposal, and the mayor appointed a task force to advocate for the bill's passage. The Senate bill passed quickly and unanimously, but the House bill was stymied in committee. At the end of the legislative

Preservation North Carolina initiated legislation that directed the State Property Office to sell state-owned properties (such as the Lewis-Smith House) in the Blount Street Historic District with protective covenants. The private reuse of the poorly maintained historic houses and construction of sympathetic infill will transform the area into a vibrant downtown community.

The Fox-Ingold House in Hickory was renovated and given to Preservation North Carolina by Frye Memorial Hospital and then leased back for fifty years to the hospital's auxiliary. The arrangement assured nearby neighborhood residents that the hospital wouldn't demolish the corner house for future institutional use.

session, a compromise bill was passed to have the project studied by the North Carolina Capital Planning Commission, a joint executive and legislative board. After the commission endorsed the proposal unanimously, the bill was reintroduced in 2003 and passed days before legislative adjournment.

The concept of getting local and state governments to dispose of surplus historic properties, one by one or block by block, is a sound one. The arguments for the state's disposition of the Blount Street properties read like a case statement for preservation:

The rising interest in downtown residential living makes this the ideal time for the state to offer the historic houses for sale with preservation covenants so that they may be restored to resi-

dential uses. *The passage of these bills will result in the moving of state offices to more efficient structures, the private-sector preservation of important historic houses, and the residential repopulation of the area. These properties will return to local property tax rolls.* This plan allows vital heritage to be reclaimed and makes economic sense for taxpayers as it would return these stately houses to private owners committed to preserving and enhancing the neighborhood. Extremely valuable urban land that is poorly used for surface parking lots, a noxious bus parking lot, and a motor pool will be put to better use. Bringing residents back to the Blount Street area will attract neighborhood services that add vitality to downtown, to Raleigh, and to our state's cultural heritage.

This proposal will result in significant savings

for the state. In addition to the infusion of cash from the sale of these underused properties, the state's maintenance responsibilities will be reduced. As long as historic Blount Street remains in state ownership, the maintenance costs will continue to escalate despite shrinking state budgets for repair and renovation; the costs for any future capital improvements in the area will also escalate. Various state officials have long complained that these houses are not efficient for offices. In some cases, agencies in these houses are separated by several blocks from their files, and related branches are spread among several buildings. Security and personnel safety are also thorny issues. The precedent for the state's selling property that it doesn't use or uses poorly may be useful in other parts of the state.

The time is right to launch the revitalization of historic Blount Street. The legislature had a recent commission study issues related to Smart Growth. The private revitalization of the Blount Street area offers an opportunity for the state to initiate a model for Smart Growth, with new construction integrated among historic houses, all in an area within walking distance of services, amenities, and public transportation.

The plans developed by the State Property Office for the property's disposition have been first-rate and bode well for an outstanding revitalization project. The master developer selected for the project plans to take ownership in phases, starting in 2007. Ground will soon be broken. By law, the property will be sold subject to covenants. This project promises to be a landmark preservation success, bringing hundreds of new residents into downtown Raleigh and revitalizing one of the city's premier historic streets.

Preservationists can offer tremendous benefit to institutions, such as local or state governments, churches, hospitals, and schools, if they use their knowledge of history, architecture, rehabilitation, and real estate in a supportive way, rather than pontificating or jeering from the sidelines. Often, by offering to help, a preservation group can position itself so that it can help control the fate of endangered historic properties without capital expenditures.

Working to save institutional properties is all about building working relationships and offering constructive expertise. Seldom is a preservation organization going to have a large enough bank account or line of credit for money alone to prevail.

FIFTEEN

Complex and Challenging Projects

CREATING A MARKET FOR UNUSUAL PROPERTIES

SOMETIMES WORKING ON a property-by-property basis isn't enough to achieve an organization's preservation goals and aspirations. A preservation organization might seek to revitalize a precarious neighborhood for a diverse mix of residents, or it might seek to demonstrate how preservation can help reuse buildings that once served a now-departed industry.

These goals can be best served by a preservation organization that takes an active role in shaping the real estate market through its own programs and property engagement. However, having previous experience in working with real estate on a property-by-property basis is wise before attempting a bigger project. (In contemporary lingo: "Don't try this at home without parental supervision.") The same principles apply, but the risks and the potential benefits are both far greater.

For nearly a decade, Preservation North Carolina has been working with former industrial properties on a special project basis. Each of these projects has taken years of direct involvement and investment. PNC's investment of money has been overshadowed by its investment of staff time. Having knowledgeable, dedicated, ambitious employees and limited staff turnover has been crucial to the projects' success.

The buildup to undertake large special projects has been incremental.

Small. At the beginning, Preservation North Carolina's Endangered Properties Program worked to find buyers for rural and small-town historic houses. These abandoned properties were often deemed to have little or no value in the marketplace. Yet when PNC advertised these properties, hundreds of potential buyers emerged to inspect each one, and PNC often found itself having to choose between competing offers. These properties have brought new blood, new energy, and new investment to previously moribund communities. The economic impact is unmistakable; numerous properties that sold for $25,000–50,000 before restoration are now on the private market for hundreds of thousands of dollars . . . or more. Individual houses in rural towns bring with them institutional risk in the range of only a few thousand dollars, making them good prospects for a properties program that is just getting started.

Bigger. As PNC got comfortable with working with property, it set its sights a little higher. In the early 1980s, Preservation North Carolina targeted endangered historic downtown buildings, working in close collaboration with the North Carolina Main Street Center. Leading by example, PNC instigated some of the first major downtown rehabilitation projects in several Main Street communities. In the mid-1980s, its work with the historic Egyptian Revival–style Masonic Temple in downtown Shelby resulted in one of the state's first examples of downtown residential development. Folks were incredulous that so many people wanted to live downtown, and the project's immediate success in attracting residents was broadcast statewide.

Bigger still. Success with downtown projects gave the organization the confidence to work with more demanding projects: schools. In the late 1980s, Preservation North Carolina shifted its focus to the adaptive use of historic school buildings. Public school buildings were being vacated as infeasible for continued use throughout the state. Rather than seeing them destroyed, PNC developed a comprehensive program for encouraging their rehabilitation for new uses. The Endangered Properties Program has placed numerous school buildings into new ownership, resulting in a wide variety of new uses, both private and public. PNC's work with schools has had numerous community benefits. Neighborhoods have not experienced the decline resulting from having a vacant "white elephant" in their midst. Local tax bases have been enhanced. The public's investment in school buildings has not been wasted, as many school boards now have active interest from private buyers for vacated schools. Many historic schools now have new public uses, such as city halls and arts centers. A number of historically African American schools have assumed new lives as community centers. Hundreds of units of affordable housing have been developed in former school buildings. More recently, former public school buildings are serving new educational purposes as charter schools and private religious schools. Many private developers and local governments now view former school buildings as opportunities rather than millstones.

Very large and very challenging. Most recently Preservation North Carolina has been working to preserve the state's historic industrial buildings (such as mills, warehouses, and mill villages). Due to changes in the global economy, North Carolina's industrial landscape dramatically changed in the 1990s, leaving behind dozens of giant turn-of-the-century historic factories. These buildings present

both challenges and opportunities to a local community. A large vacant mill can be a cancer if it remains empty and unused. Surrounding neighborhoods and commercial districts will deteriorate, and crime will increase. The building itself will be subject to vandalism, vagrancy, and arson. Businesses and individuals looking for relocation opportunities will perceive the town as dying, feeding the downward spiral. Alternatively, when renovated for new adaptive uses or for new industrial or business uses, a large old factory or mill can provide an economic boost. Used as an incubator or business development center, it offers inexpensive space for new job development. Used for mixed uses, an old building may attract tourists and stimulate new economic growth, creating housing and new businesses without sprawl.

To date, Preservation North Carolina has undertaken several important industrial heritage projects. These challenging projects are much larger than any previously undertaken by PNC, and they will result in much greater community benefits.

EDENTON MILL AND MILL VILLAGE

PNC's first industrial heritage project has been the Edenton Cotton Mill and mill village, perhaps eastern North Carolina's most intact historic textile site. The property is along scenic Queen Anne Creek, just across the railroad tracks from a National Register historic district in a picturesque town of 5,100. In the fall of 1995, Unifi, Inc., a large textile manufacturer based in Greensboro, announced that it would be closing the century-old mill. So Preservation NC asked Unifi to consider donating the forty-four-acre complex, comprising fifty-seven (mostly vacant) mill houses and 117,000 square feet of vacant mill buildings. Be careful what you ask for—you may get it! Unifi agreed to make the donation, under the condition that the closing take place by the end of the year (for tax purposes).

Heartburn accompanied euphoria. Two weeks before Christmas 1995, PNC's board of directors held an emergency board meeting in Edenton to decide whether to accept the donation. For more than two hours, the board discussed dozens of "what ifs." In the end, the preservation vision of revitalizing a mill and mill village as a demonstration project prevailed over the numerous concerns about potential liabilities. The vote was unanimous to accept the donation. The directors recognized that if all else failed, the forty-four acres on which the property stood would have enough value to bail the organization out. The property was worth more than $1 million as raw land. We certainly didn't want the historic complex to return to raw land, but the land value provided a financial haven in a worst-case scenario.

Borrowing against the value of the property, PNC immediately obtained a $150,000 line of credit from a sympathetic bank (BB&T) to pay for the necessary costs of staffing the project, holding the property, and preparing it for reuse. Interest costs would initially be paid by funds from the line of credit. At the outset, PNC hired the mill's superintendent, who had been laid off in the mill closure. Though he had no preservation training, his knowledge of the property was invaluable in the transition. While we developed the beginnings of a plan for the property, he kept it in stable condition. After a few months, he accepted a job running another textile mill. The time was right for PNC to move toward a staff that had preservation sensibilities and real estate expertise.

Preservation North Carolina first looked for a developer to purchase the entire property for rehabilitation, but we couldn't readily find one. The project was too risky for developers seeking a reliable return on investment. Since there were no comparable real estate transactions, no one really knew whether a mill village in a small, isolated town would be attractive to buyers from near or far. So PNC decided that we would develop the property ourselves.

If PNC itself was going to develop the property, a critical milestone would be getting the town's approval to subdivide the property. We contracted with a preservation-minded developer with a planning background to do a preliminary master plan. He focused on infrastructure issues, such as utilities and street dedication, and on determining property boundaries in preparation for subdivision. His plan included fundamental details such as where utility easements should be established and where driveways would go. An architect from Slovakia, on leave to study with Preservation North Carolina for three months, provided great assistance. Meanwhile, a group of graduate students from the University of North Carolina's Department of City and Regional Planning mapped, inventoried, and documented the buildings on the property. They also contemplated other planning aspects for the project, convening small focus groups to get input. They considered issues such as what covenant provisions should be used, which missing houses should be replaced by infill, if and how the vacant sites along the waterfront should be developed, who would constitute the market for the mill houses, and how cutting-edge New Urbanist principles could be incorporated into the existing mill village. The results fed into the planning process. Within six months of the donation, a subdivision plan was ready to be submitted to the town.

When we publicly revealed our final plans for the project, everyone had an opinion! Our proposal that properties be sold only for owner-occupancy drew praise and disbelief. We reasoned that without protection, the small houses in the mill village would lend themselves to eventual slumlord rentals. The exteriors would have to be renovated within two years of purchase. We placed strict limits on the size of additions so that the small houses wouldn't grow into big houses, in the event the project were a success. Where the mill originally provided employees with space for vegetable gardens behind the houses, we created an area under easement where no construction could take place, no fences could be erected, and no plantings could be installed without approval. The easement would mandate that the former garden area would remain open and unobstructed. This concept was a tip of the hat to the area's original use as a garden, but it also provided a protected green space in the middle of every block, an amenity for the modern backyard dweller. Some folks liked it; others said it would never work.

The protective covenants and design review would

Unifi, Inc., of Greensboro donated the Edenton Cotton Mill and mill village to Preservation North Carolina after the mill was shuttered in 1995. The gift of forty-four acres included fifty-seven (mostly vacant) houses, the mill, office, and several vacant lots. The project resulted in a remarkable transformation of the area.

be our strictest ever. Even though a mill house is not individually an architectural treasure, its place in context is extremely important. We were determined to reach a balance that made the village a practical place to live, while maintaining its historic integrity for the long term. If the fourteen houses on Phillips Street are identical now and their significance comes from the repetition, the challenge is to guarantee that there are still fourteen identical houses 50 or 100 years from now. Covenants on houses in the village dictate that all roofs must be standing-seam tin, painted silver. Porch balustrades are forbidden, unless clear documentary evidence can be provided to prove that a house had a balustrade. Even porch lights and street numbers are regulated. Rather than mandating color, a tricky domain of property owner's choice, we set a standard of reflectivity for color. Since the houses had been

painted in light colors for many years, our standard would allow property owners to choose their own colors, so long as they were light. Any paint dealer could provide an owner with information on a color's reflectivity. No prior approval was necessary.

We were absolutely convinced that having a good plan would be vital to finding buyers willing to invest in this unprecedented project. However, some folks don't recognize planning as forward movement for a project. The question on the street in Edenton was "Why haven't you sold any houses?" Before we even had legal authority to sell houses, some local wags were citing the lack of sales as proof that the project would fail.

Invariably, as a neighborhood is revitalized, concerns about affordability surface. Indeed, one of the first rumors to spread through Edenton after our acquisition of the property was that we were going to kick out the former mill employees who still lived there. The rumor preposterously posited that PNC planned to sell the entire parcel for clearance for the development of new condominiums! One local citizen called me and unleashed a torrent of criticism about what greedy elitists we were. When she finished her tirade, I calmly told her about our plans.

While the planning process was under way, we fashioned plans for a "model house." We asked several designers, including the architect from Slovakia, an architect on PNC's board of directors, an interior designer on PNC's board of advisors, and a local interior designer, to propose layouts for a representative mill house. Everyone agreed that a small addition connecting the house to its original kitchen outbuilding would be a good way to adapt the house for modern use. Using a local contractor who directed a prodigious measure of volunteer help, Preservation North Carolina renovated the exterior of the house, framed in the connecting addition, and cleaned up the interior. No mechanical systems and no new interior walls were installed. The various floor-plan drawings proposed by the designers were mounted on the walls, a few homey touches (such as plants and throw rugs) were added, and the front door was opened to lookers. We piggybacked on the activities of other Edenton organizations, such as the local arts council and local historic house tour, to attract visitors to our "model house." The response was amazing; more than 5,000 people are estimated to have gone through the house. Most were surprised at how the higher ceilings made the small house feel more spacious than it looked from the outside. Others commented on the substantial building materials (real wood!) and the home's detailing (such as moldings, baseboards, and mantels). The house was a hit.

Having a model house served many purposes. It provided tangible progress in the village. It attracted publicity. It engaged interested volunteers. The process also allowed PNC to work through design issues for new construction before having to answer similar design questions from property owners. We could be our own "guinea pig." It also gave us a clearer picture of how much renovation

would cost—information we could share with prospective buyers.

In order to expedite the sales process, we initially offered ten houses for sale by sealed bid. The bids would be opened on a summer afternoon, six months after the property was initially donated. This strategy served several ulterior motives. First and foremost, it bought time for us to complete our plan and get the property subdivided. Rather than having to set asking prices for fifty-seven houses, clean them out, and prepare them for showing, we could narrow the choices down to ten—ten that were in decent shape for marketing. The bid process gave us feedback about buyer's preferences and concerns. We received significant publicity in the press, as reporters played up the drama of whether we would receive any offers. Of course, as one would expect, no proposals were received until the final days before the bid opening. Bids continued to arrive on the afternoon of the opening, and when the dust settled, we had acceptable bids for four houses.

Significantly, the bid process gave us a sense for the market value for the houses. When the property was appraised for Unifi's donation, the smaller mill houses were valued at $2,500–4,500. After looking throughout the state and region, the appraiser could find no comparable sales for small mill houses in an area under revitalization. We thought the values were too low. The bids proved us right; there would indeed be a market for small houses in a protected residential area. The offers for the small houses came in at around $20,000–30,000. Once again, the project hit the headlines, and others came to take a look at this curious preservation project.

The bids for these four houses provided the comparable sales data needed for buyers to get financing for their purchase and renovation. BB&T, the same bank that provided PNC with a line of credit to undertake the project, set up a special loan package for mill village purchasers. The package combined the construction financing and permanent mortgage into a lending package that was easy to explain, and the bank dedicated a loan officer to the project. Over the next two years, forty-seven houses would be sold for renovation for owner-occupied residential use.

Eighteen of the houses were still occupied by former mill employees. Most were older, and several had lived in the village for decades. Generally their homes were in better condition than the surrounding vacant houses, so we offered the existing residents a choice of buying their homes at a discounted price or continuing to rent them at a favorable price. For those who chose to buy, we sold them their homes at the same price as the comparable vacant and uninhabitable houses, so they received the benefit of their own improvements and care through the years. Selling homes to first-time home buyers in their seventies was a heartwarming experience. A decade later, we continue to rent a few houses to former mill employees.

The diversity of buyers for the houses in the mill village is noticeable. White, black; straight, gay; young, old; local, distant; first home, second home—we have a real mix. That diversity reflects the range of house types. The original sales prices ranged from $17,000 to $100,000; house sizes stretch from 800 square feet to about 3,000. With the exception of our very first house (a house at the edge of the village that we sold with special financing to jumpstart the process), our earliest buyers were not from Edenton. It took a while for local people to believe that the project would succeed; they saw the mill village as a dilapidated area on the wrong side of the tracks. That experience has been witnessed many other times.

In Edenton, we quickly recognized that the renovation of the mill buildings would follow, not precede, the revitalization of the mill village. The mill village would have to establish the market, house by house. Until the market values were sufficiently high, renovation of the mill would not happen.

Fortunately, the mill was sited at the back corner of the mill village, farthest from downtown and larger roads. Rather than being greeted by a large empty building, prospects first saw the houses—and the construction activity. The mill's windows had been bricked in many years ago. This preservation lapse ultimately worked to our advantage; the bricked-in windows created a continuous anonymous brick wall that became a neutral backdrop. If the mill had still had its windows, they would surely have been broken out over time, and that would have been a severe liability for the project.

We first agreed to give the mill to a fledging nonprofit arts and humanities institute for renovation, under the condition that they demonstrate their ability to raise the necessary funds for the project. The ambitious project would have been a wonderful benefit for the community, but unfortunately it never gained any real traction. Almost immediately after that deal fell through, the mill gained the attention of two different groups of investors. One offer came from a developer we had worked with before. His offer anticipated Preservation North Carolina's being a partner in the development, financing a substantial part of the mill's value, and agreeing to subordinate its financing. (If PNC subordinated its note on the property to other lenders, PNC would be the last to be paid in the event the project went awry.) The developer wasn't committing enough of his own resources to the project for us to feel comfortable. The second offer came from a mix of local investors and out-of-town professionals that had been convened by Preservation North Carolina. Unfortunately, the chemistry wasn't right. Three years after the initial gift, at our organization's sixtieth anniversary gala event at the Executive Mansion in Raleigh, one of the attendees asked me about the mill. I immediately introduced him to an architect who had been involved with one of the earlier efforts, and their ensuing conversation continued through the evening. Within days we were all en route to Edenton to meet at the mill. Soon we signed an option on the mill, and then a contract. In our sale, we financed most of the sales price with a four-year balloon payment, but without subordination provisions. We assumed that when construction was ready to proceed, we would be paid off from the construction loan. As it ended up, we still had to subordinate our interest to that of the construction lender until the first units were sold.

Plans for the mill included a mix of uses, with a preponderance of residential condominiums. The first phase of condos was quickly reserved. After the initial wave of residents moved in, the public approval was validated by a rapid appreciation in

Timeline for Edenton Cotton Mill Project

1995

September	Property donation solicited from Unifi, Inc.
December	Property donated to PNC

1996

February	Offer accepted on first house (at the edge of the village); sale financed by PNC
March	First staff person hired by PNC
April	$150,000 line of credit obtained
	"Model House" opened to the public for Arts Council event
Spring	Master Plan developed with assistance from graduate planning students
Summer	Utility and road work begins
July	Bids for first properties opened
September	Subdivision of property approved by the Town
October	First mill house sold
December	26 mill houses sold or placed under contract

1997

December	38th mill house sold

1998

April	Additional land purchased at edge of village
July	Mill placed under contract for the first time

1999

January	Mill placed under contract for the second time
February	Mill and mill village placed on the National Register of Historic Places
December	48th mill house sold (last unoccupied house)

2000

March	Mill placed under contract for the third (and final) time
May	First vacant lot on additional land sold for infill
October	Mill sold

2002

April	First lot sold within mill village for new infill house

2003

June	54th mill house sold (after 1999, mill houses are available for sale only after they are vacated by long-term tenants)
August	Second vacant lot on additional land sold for infill

2004

September	Last (6th) lot sold for new infill house

2005

Summer	First condominiums in the mill occupied

LOCAL TAX BASE INCREASE

	1996 tax value	2006 tax value
Edenton Mill Village	$610,485	$12,110,659

In 2006, three houses (total assessed value $294,622) are still owned by PNC and not on the tax books. One infill house is still under construction.

	1996 tax value	2006 tax value
Edenton Cotton Mill	$840,845	$4,629,120

The 2006 value reflects ten out of thirty-nine units that are either completed or under construction within the mill. An additional ten units of new construction adjacent to the mill are anticipated. The Town of Edenton projects a tax value of $14,625,000 for the mill, exclusive of the new construction.

---

market prices. Some investors flipped their reservations into a profit of more than $100,000. Years earlier I had been haughtily told by a native, "Edenton doesn't 'do' condos." So much for that advice! The second phase of condos is now under construction, and the success of the project seems inevitable. Both the design and the quality of renovation work have been exceptional.

Fortunately the Edenton project has been an enormous success—beyond anyone's wildest expectations. Our purchasers have done well financially. In 2006, one of the small mill houses sold for an unbelievable $315,000! Its original purchase price would have been less than $30,000.

The community benefits have also been substantial. New jobs abound as dozens of renovation projects progress and tourists visit the site. The Town of Edenton has built a boardwalk through the now-protected cypress swamp on the property as part of an environmental education project. Developers, city officials, and neighborhood advocates from all over the state have come to Edenton to study the project for ideas to use in other textile communities.

The tax base of Edenton and Chowan County, devastated by the loss of the county's largest taxpayer and employer, was restored after less than three years. Between 1996 and 2006, the tax value of the mill village soared from $610,485 to $12,110,659. The mill itself went from $840,845 in 1996 as an industrial property to $4,629,120 in 2006, with only ten out of thirty-nine units completed. The Town of Edenton projects a total tax value for the mill of $14,625,000, exclusive of an additional ten units of new construction that are planned behind the mill.

As every preservationist has witnessed, revitalization often spurs additional investment nearby. It's contagious! Across the street from the mill village, the Edenton Peanut Mill, a historic processing plant that had stood vacant for more than forty years, finally became economically viable for renovation as its environs were transformed. Its tax value went from $45,336 in 1996 to $1,046,939 in 2006, with only three out of its five floors completed.

The turnaround has been remarkable. *Southern Living* and numerous other magazines and newspapers (both in and out of state) have included feature articles about the mill village. I have enjoyed saying to my fellow Southerners: "Think about that for a second! *Southern Living* featured a mill village!" One would not expect to find a mill village in a slick shelter magazine. Imagine our pleasure in seeing the mill village houses included in the local historic house "pilgrimage" and in watching the local tourist trolley traverse the streets of the mill village. In 2003 the National Trust for Historic Preservation designated Edenton as one of its Dozen Distinctive Destinations, in part because of the mill village. In less than a decade, the vacant "mill hill," the shunned side of town, had been reborn.

The impact of the success will long be felt throughout northeastern North Carolina. The net sales proceeds from the project are being used to fund a regional office for PNC to work with endangered historic properties throughout the economically troubled northeastern region. Preservation North Carolina's office is in the former mill office, and our staff there works to save endangered historic properties throughout twenty-three of the state's most historic (and often its poorest) counties. The project has netted significantly more than $1 million for the organization, much of which has been placed in permanent endowment for continued work in the region.

GLENCOE MILL AND MILL VILLAGE

In the summer of 1997, buoyed by the invigorating success of our Edenton project, Preservation North Carolina purchased Glencoe Mill and mill village, one of the state's most significant early textile mills and mill villages. Developed along the Haw River north of Burlington by the prominent Holt family around 1880 and vacated in 1954, the 101-acre Glencoe property consisted of thirty-two vacant houses in varying stages of deterioration and about 85,000 square feet of vacant mill buildings. Glencoe would be a very different project than Edenton, but it would build on the confidence gained and the lessons learned in Edenton.

Physically Glencoe was quite different. The houses in Edenton were mainly examples of early-twentieth-century industrial housing. We know that some of the houses in Edenton were "kits" purchased from Aladdin Homes Company, which shipped the precut materials to Edenton with instructions for their construction on site. Most were modest houses of balloon-frame construction. Built twenty-five years earlier, Glencoe houses reflected a different type of construction altogether. Despite their construction at the peak of Victorian architecture, the houses feature heavy-timber construction, simple Greek Revival details, and brick nogging in the walls. Perhaps the houses were constructed by older craftsmen who still built in "the old way." Their substantial construction enabled them to stand for nearly a half century without maintenance and mostly vacant.

Whereas the Edenton mill village is situated near the center of a picturesque historic town along a tranquil inlet of the Albemarle Sound, Glencoe is more isolated, three miles from the nearest town and sited on a ridge above a rushing river. Yet unlike Edenton, Glencoe is within commuting distance of two large metropolitan areas, each with a population of a million or more. Whereas Edenton's mill was a backdrop, Glencoe's mill was the first thing you saw on arrival. Unfortunately, it had an unsightly addition across the front. As one developer put it, the mill was a "carbuncle" that needed to be removed.

Acquisition of Glencoe also took a different course. Where Edenton was completely donated, Glencoe was a bargain sale. Preservation North Carolina had to buy out the interests of two of Glencoe's three owners. One owner (Sarah Rhyne), an elderly local woman who with her late husband had purchased a share of the property years earlier in order to keep it intact, generously donated her share. The other two owners, out-of-state descendants of the original builders, graciously sold their shares at a price based on an old estate appraisal. For once, an unsympathetic appraisal worked to our advantage. The appraiser had determined the market value of the raw land and then deducted the estimated cost for wholesale demolition and cleanup of Glencoe. The appraised value was low, so the owners could easily have asked for more. They also agreed to finance their sales, so we could start into the project without a big outlay.

From the outset, Glencoe was more challenging than Edenton. For starters, Edenton had been vacated only recently, and Glencoe was a ghost town. When we started work on the project, freeing the houses from years of vegetative growth, we truly did not know how many Glencoe houses would be salvageable. One of the houses had a huge oak resting on its crushed roof; we removed the tree and reframed the roof. Another house had been knocked off its foundation during a hurricane; we hired a house-mover to pick it back up so it could be placed on a new foundation. Fortunately, the houses' heavy-timber construction allowed them to withstand such disasters.

The biggest obstacle to the revival of Glencoe was infrastructure. The property wasn't served by water and sanitary sewer services. It rested on bedrock, so wells and septic systems weren't a realistic option. Additionally, only one of the three streets at Glencoe was state-maintained. One of the streets was impassable except on foot. So before we purchased the property, we explored how much it would cost to connect the property to Burlington's water and sewer systems; the nearest connection was nearly one mile away, on the other side of the river. We also investigated how much it would cost to rebuild the streets and whether the city would accept their dedication. These issues were new considerations for Preservation North Carolina. (In Edenton, we had to address similar questions, but the solutions were simpler.) Without these basic services, Glencoe would die.

The total cost of extending water/sewer to the site and rebuilding the streets would be $1.2 million. The City of Burlington and the County of Alamance quickly agreed to step forward with generous commitments of $125,000 each toward the costs of the water/sewer extension. Wachovia Bank agreed to provide a line of credit of $975,000 to help cover the infrastructure improvements and other startup costs. The Z. Smith Reynolds Foundation recognized the project's environmental merits and provided a $100,000 grant for capital. We calculated that the cumulative sales of the mill buildings, historic houses, and vacant lots in the mill village would barely cover Preservation North Carolina's operating and capital costs for the multiyear project and repay the loan. The comfort zone for the bank and the board would be created by the property's additional seventy acres of undeveloped land. Having developable acreage along the Haw River with

municipal water and sewer services available would carry the project, even if all else failed.

If the board of directors had not been hearing about the Edenton successes while contemplating the Glencoe challenges, I can't imagine that they would have agreed to undertake the Glencoe project. The risks were substantial, as were the unknowns. Yet Glencoe was a magical place, known by many who had sadly watched its decline over several decades. It had been painted and photographed by prominent artists and used as a film location. The preservation spirit of both the board and the staff prevailed. We knew that if Preservation North Carolina didn't take Glencoe on, its days were numbered.

As with Edenton, having a master plan that communicated the promise of the project and laid out a roadmap for infrastructure investment was key. One of our first moves at Glencoe was hosting a charrette, or design workshop, in preparation for developing a master plan. This charrette, which featured noted land planner Randall Arendt and preservation real estate guru Don Rypkema, attracted more than seventy-five design professionals who for two days trudged around the overgrown property, debated and discussed how the property should be developed, had long late-night discussions, and gave us the benefit of their thinking. Consensus was reached on numerous items, making the master plan much easier. Ironically, the local newspaper headline, instead of reporting on the high energy and passion exhibited in the charrette, focused on how Glencoe was going to have problems with parking. With 101 acres and as yet no people, we would surely be able to find good solutions for parking! The concern addressed during the charrette had been how to sufficiently buffer parking from view.

At Glencoe, we originally thought that we could handle the project with existing staff from two of our offices that were an hour away. That was a mistake. We quickly realized that despite the added cost, we had to have full-time staff on site. The site and the construction projects required daily observation, and fortunately for us, many people were coming to look at houses. We hired my teaching assistant from the University of North Carolina's Department of City and Regional Planning. He had done his master's project on Glencoe, and he came to the job with energy, enthusiasm, and familiarity with the project.

The first few years of the Glencoe project had their successes and frustrations. Every time we took away a truckload of trash from the property, someone else would come along and dump more (washing machines, freezers with rotting meat, tires, etc.). The local sheriff's office kindly agreed to keep a watch on the property.

As with Edenton, we decided to undertake the renovation of a "model house." We picked a house that had long ago been condemned by the county for its lead paint, so that we could learn how much it would cost to do the necessary lead abatement. We could also work through the design issues that would face future buyers. We wanted to enclose the back porch of the house and connect it with the freestanding kitchen. The connected outbuilding would add two auxiliary rooms to the house—great spaces for a master bedroom or for a guest room and studio. We had four design review processes that we (and our future buyers) would have to navigate: our own covenants, the state's tax credit review, the county's historic landmarks commission, and the city's historic district commission. (Now only three reviews are required; the county commission has ceded its review to the city commission.) I'm glad we were the guinea pigs for the process.

The proposed windows for the porch enclosure for the model house exposed conflicting philosophies among preservationists, and the responses were initially irreconcilable. The state and Preservation North Carolina favored a more contemporary casement window that was clearly differentiated from the original nine-over-six double-hung sash. The justification was that most viewers would recognize that the windows were clearly new to the house and part of a porch enclosure. The commissions favored double-hung sash that mimicked the original sash. They wanted the addition to blend seamlessly with the old house. Initially all sides stood their ground, which would have made the addition impossible. The compromise was that the

In 1997, Preservation North Carolina purchased Glencoe Mill and mill village (in Alamance County near Burlington and Graham) in a bargain sale. The mill closed in 1954, and many of the thirty-two remaining houses had been vacant for more than four decades. By 2006, all of the houses were sold for private rehabilitation, plans were in place for the industrial buildings, and vacant land had been purchased for a riverside park.

new windows would be double-hung, made of insulated glass with divided lights, and configured as six-over-six. The savvy observer would see that the windows were new and slightly different from the original, but the less observant onlooker would not. Having charted that course with the model house created a precedent that has been observed time and again. (Thankfully the media didn't attend the initial meeting where the windows were being discussed. The deadlock among preservationists with differing design philosophies would have been easy to deride.)

The first public showing of the model house was a remarkable occasion. On a bright Sunday afternoon, cars lined the road for nearly half a mile in both directions as people came out to see Glencoe during the first Open Village. The public's response was reassuring. We quickly found a buyer for the model house, but the sale's closing had to be delayed until the water and sewer installation was completed.

The installation of the water and sewer lines crossing the river was knocked off schedule by Hurricane Floyd, which created an acute demand for utility contractors in devastated areas of the state. Throughout the delay, the interest clock on our loan was running, and we couldn't sell any houses. Buyers couldn't get financing until the installation of water/sewer services were completed. Yet we couldn't in good conscience complain, when others had been flooded out of their homes and businesses.

Unfortunately, by the time the water and sewer were in place and operable, the nation's economy had stalled. Hurricane Floyd and the accelerated demise of the state's textile industry exaggerated the slowdown in North Carolina. In 2000, the first dozen or so houses sold quickly to buyers who had been waiting for the financing to purchase them, but the pace clearly slowed with the economy.

Preservation North Carolina was contacted by *Country Living* to see if we knew of any renovation projects that would meet its requirements for a feature article. After several conversations, our Glencoe project manager had an idea: Preservation North Carolina could build an infill house—a new house on one of the village's vacant lots—and work with *Country Living* to design and accessorize it. By building an infill house, we could demonstrate the qualities of good infill design and encourage the construction of new houses on the handful of vacant lots in the mill village. We went to the board of directors for the authority to borrow the necessary funds ($200,000) to build a new house. Once again, the board swallowed hard, but said yes.

The result would be a new infill house that in most ways replicated the old houses. From a streetscape view, the house is almost identical. But it is slightly wider and taller (to accommodate modern standards), has a two-story ell off the back (the

With both the Edenton and Glencoe projects, Preservation North Carolina commissioned designs for new infill houses on vacant lots in the mill villages. The plans were conveyed along with the lots to buyers for their use. In Glencoe, PNC itself built the first infill house, which was designated the 2002 House of the Year by Country Living.

ells on the old houses are one-story), boasts six-over-six window sash (continuing the precedent from the historic model house), and has several differentiated details (a different foundation, different rafter tails, etc.) that the casual observer will miss. *Country Living* not only chose to do a feature about the new house; it also selected the house as its 2002 House of the Year. The magazine featured it in a fourteen-page color spread, supplemented by an article about Preservation North Carolina's work to save Glencoe. The publicity drove another wave of potential purchasers to Preservation North Carolina's website and to Glencoe.

Once again I enjoyed the delicious irony: a New York–based shelter magazine selected a mill-house "knockoff" as its house of the year! For generations many Southerners looked down on mill villages with prejudiced contempt, and here we were, attracting visitors by the hundreds. We had over 700 paying visitors the first time we opened the new *Country Living* house to the public. When our Glencoe project manager moved out of state with his new wife, we hired the designer of the *Country Living* house as our new manager.

One of our biggest concerns about Glencoe was getting the mill renovated. We sold the "easy" houses first. The more deteriorated houses, especially on Glencoe's back road, would be more challenging. Prospects for purchasing the new house (priced at $259,000 to cover the costs of the house and lot, plus a commission) were hesitant to invest that much money because of the "carbuncle" sitting at the village's entrance. We also needed to refine our thoughts about the future of the vacant land adjacent to the mill village.

We initially tried to interest a state trust fund in acquiring the property's vacant land for a county park. The trust fund was created to acquire culturally and environmentally significant property for public use. We thought it was a natural, and the county agreed. But the trustees of the fund didn't "get it." They turned us down and encouraged us to find a developer for the riverside property. As one of the trustees noted, we "could make a lot more money that way." I realized later that, unlike the environmental groups that had brought land pur-

chase proposals to the trust, we hadn't done our political homework. We hadn't identified an internal advocate who would push the project, and we hadn't applied political pressure from friendly legislators. If a funding process is political in nature, you have to play the game (a valuable lesson for the future). The park option withered because the county, facing decreased tax collections from the fading textile industry, couldn't allocate funds for the land purchase in the foreseeable future.

Soon thereafter, at Preservation North Carolina's annual conference, one of our speakers was a very successful pioneer in Traditional New Development. I encouraged him to visit Glencoe, as he was intrigued by the possibility of integrating new "traditional" construction into the real thing—historic structures. He came to Glencoe and quickly fell in love with the place. He brought in potential partners to renovate the mill, and he wanted to build compatible new housing adjacent to, but not visible from, the historic mill village. He brought nationally famous designers to the site to get their ideas about how such a new development would work. After several meetings, the development team submitted a proposal to PNC for the property's purchase. Thrilled, I informed the board leadership, who gave me their blessings to proceed with drafting a purchase contract.

And then, sadly, for the first time in years, board dynamics fell apart. Though the executive committee and the entire board had each voted on two occasions in favor of proceeding with the contract negotiations along terms outlined by the staff, a couple of new board members asserted that all board members should review and approve the final contract. A "showdown" meeting was called, and an overwhelming majority of the board voted to authorize the staff to conclude the negotiations with no further board review. The contract was concluded, executed by Preservation North Carolina, and sent off to New York for execution by the project's investors—on September 10, 2001. As they say, timing is everything. The uncertainty that followed the events of September 11 killed the project, at least for the near term. Unfortunately, the board dysfunction set the project back a year and, with the interest clock running on more than \$1 million in borrowed funds (for the water/sewer and the new infill house), hurt the organization financially. It also jarred relationships among and between both staff and board members. (Chapter 18 addresses ways of sustaining a functional nonprofit organization, including the delicate subject of board/staff relations.)

It wasn't until the spring of 2003 that the project truly picked up steam again, buoyed by historically low interest rates and hints of economic recovery. By the end of 2006, all of the thirty-two extant houses had been sold for owner-occupied renovation; five new infill houses had been constructed; the mill was under contract for sale for redevelopment as residential condominiums; and funding had been obtained from a different state trust fund for part of the vacant land to be purchased for a county-owned park.

Glencoe's community benefits have already been substantial, bringing economic development to the economically distressed north side of Burlington. The county's tax base has quickly expanded. Even in its current condition, Glencoe is one of Alamance County's most visited tourist sites, presaging its future potential as a major cultural attraction. After a decade, the completion of the Glencoe project may result in nearly \$500,000 being returned to Preservation North Carolina for its endangered properties fund and its endowment.

LORAY MILL

Late in 1998, while the Edenton houses were selling like hotcakes and while the Glencoe plans were coming together, we received another amazing offer of a gift of real estate. In Gastonia, Bridgestone/Firestone generously offered to donate the enormous (660,000 square feet) and tremendously important Loray Mill (site of the famous 1929 labor strike) to Preservation North Carolina. This project would once again stretch the organization in new ways.

Before accepting the donation, we did a "quick and dirty" feasibility study to determine a host of potential uses and to examine the gross costs of ren-

ovation. A quick pro forma was developed to demonstrate how the federal and state rehabilitation tax credits might facilitate the project. The board of directors came to Gastonia to see the gargantuan factory for themselves before agreeing to accept the donation. They climbed up to the top and walked around on the mill's two acres of roof. What does one do with such a large mill in a city that is struggling with mill closures and layoffs? Easy answers were not on hand. The preservation reality was that the huge factory, nationally famous for its strike and an enormous economic development opportunity for a struggling town, would be imploded if Preservation North Carolina declined to accept the donation. The comfort zone for accepting the donation came from two factors: (1) Gastonia lies within the metropolitan area of Charlotte, the state's largest city and an economic powerhouse; (2) the mill's land value exceeded the anticipated cost of demolition. If Preservation North Carolina couldn't make the project work, accepting the donation would not take the organization down.

As with Edenton and Glencoe, Preservation North Carolina's first actions were (1) setting up a line of credit, borrowing against the value of the property, and (2) producing a master plan to provide to potential developers. We commissioned a team of experienced developers to study how the mill might be revived for a mix of potential uses. The study would enable a developer to get a handle on the project more quickly and easily. As has happened before, the developers who did the study became interested in undertaking the project, and they optioned the property. Unfortunately, as with Glencoe, the downturn in the economy slowed down progress at Loray. Falling interest rates and deflating construction prices kept the developers at the table, and in early 2002 they were ready to go public with the project.

A key component of the proposed Loray development would be a long-needed civic center for Gastonia. The developers deemed having a public use within the building critical for several reasons. A lease from a local government entity would help the developers get their financing. Having a public use in the building would attract other related tenants. It would also give the project a higher community profile and more energy, and the public component would certainly enhance its community impact. Rather than simply being a giant housing complex, it would be a public facility. No walls would encircle the property. Loray is so large that the civic center would occupy less than 10 percent of the building's space, but the public use would be significant to the success of the project.

The developers wanted the city and county to lease the space for the civic center for at least five years, so that the rehabilitation tax credits could be used on the project. The total project's impact on the tax base and the increased fees from city-operated utilities would nearly offset the cost of the lease. In other words, the increased city and county revenue would nearly pay for the lease. After numerous meetings with city officials to work through the details, the developers were ready to announce their intentions and start lobbying for the civic center. A press announcement was set, and we were crestfallen when the mayor announced that the city could not even be able to consider the proposal at the time. Only hours earlier, the governor had announced that the state would have to withhold payment of sales tax revenues to local governments or face insolvency. Without this major source of revenue, the city was plunged into economic crisis. Again, timing is everything. The wind was knocked out of the developers' sails. For several months, they watched and waited. The sales tax funds were eventually restored to the city's coffers, but the project's momentum had been halted. Meanwhile, the developers had pushed ahead with other historic rehabilitation projects, and Loray was sidetracked.

Several months later, Dick Moe, the president of the National Trust, was coming to the Charlotte area to be the featured guest at a gala event. He asked if he could do anything to help Preservation North Carolina while he was in the region. I replied that a visit to Gastonia to plug the Loray project would be timely. So we met at the crack of dawn and headed through rush-hour traffic to a breakfast gathering in downtown Gastonia. It was invaluable having someone who was prominent and from out of town say, "This project is important and worth undertaking." Several key Gastonia citizens announced their support for the project shortly after Dick Moe's visit. The publicity surrounding his visit brought an unexpected result: an offer for the property from Georgia developers. The previously interested developers, now busy with other projects, gave Preservation North Carolina their due diligence materials to share with the new development team.

One of the great challenges of preserving Loray Mill has been dealing with the strike of 1929. Some older and influential Gastonia citizens believed that the strike was an embarrassment to the community and that razing Loray Mill would diminish the perceived blight. In its early dealings with Loray Mill, Preservation North Carolina was deferential and downplayed the strike. In time, we realized that these opponents to preserving the mill weren't going to be deferential in return and that we would gain nothing by trying to appease them.

We finally decided that it was time to stand our ground about the history of Loray Mill and the importance of its preservation. The mill's story is fascinating, and what better place to use as a civic and convention center than a building with a colorful past? Loray was the first textile mill in the area to be financed primarily by Northerners, and it was not a financial success at the outset. (These too were blemishes in the eyes of the Old Guard.) Its owner during the 1920s, the Manville-Jenckes Company of Woonsocket, Rhode Island, was plagued with labor problems in both the North and the South. The story of the 1929 strike is full of intrigue and mystery. The strike leaders were Communists. Gastonia's chief of police was murdered. Newspapers from around the world followed the daily progress of the trial, which was less than impartial. The Communists were convicted of murder, and the strike leader escaped to the Soviet Union. After the trial, the union balladeer, Ella May Wiggins, a single mother with several children, was murdered in plain sight, but her murderers were never brought to trial. Eventually the strike leader returned to the United States, recanted his Communist beliefs, and quietly returned to Gastonia to regain his citizenship. Numerous articles and books have been written about the strike and about Ella May Wiggins, who in 1929 was internationally proclaimed a martyr for labor.

As with the preservation of any site that has a controversial history, it is important to recognize the site's value for interpreting the past. When a tangible place is gone, its history is diminished, too. Just as slave quarters tell a tragic but important story about race relations in the South, Loray speaks eloquently about North Carolina's social history, its industrialization, and its labor history. Furthermore, several important political leaders rose to fame because of Loray Mill. Its significance is national in scope. We resolved that hereafter the complex history of Loray Mill would be an asset, not a liability.

Partly because of the lingering shadow of 1929, we were never able to get business interests in Gastonia to seriously consider using Loray Mill as a site for the city's civic center. The chamber of commerce insisted on a new, much more expensive facility that was rejected overwhelmingly by the voters. Meanwhile, in observation of the strike's seventy-fifth anniversary, a Saturday symposium to discuss the strike and its impact on the community was attended by more than 500 citizens.

Once again, Preservation North Carolina's work with historic real estate brought opportunities to broaden preservation. In 2004, at the suggestion of the state's Division of Community Assistance, Gaston County commissioned Preservation North Carolina to do a study about the reuse of industrial buildings in North Carolina. This study, besides bringing in much-needed revenue, allowed PNC to sharpen its expertise about the preservation of mills. In the process of doing the study, we concluded that while mill renovation was financially feasible in the larger cities, where mill reuse was consistently successful, mills were rarely being renovated in the smaller cities and towns. The projects by their nature were large, and without a strong economic market they were too risky. Our dilemma with Loray Mill was illustrative; the mill would be easy to renovate, but its economic viability was marginal, thereby making it risky.

An additional incentive for mill renovation was

going to be necessary to provide any hope for the renovation of hundreds of mills that had been vacated by the demise of the domestic textile and furniture industries. I found a bright graduate student working on joint degrees in business and planning to research programs for mill renovation across the nation. With his results in hand and him at my side (what a learning experience this project would be!), we asked two chairmen of the North Carolina Senate Finance Committee, a Democrat from Gastonia and a Republican from Concord, for their support for a new incentive for mill renovation. They agreed to cosponsor the bill, and sixteen months later the legislature adopted an enhanced tax credit for the renovation of large industrial, utility, and agricultural buildings. This bill became the saving grace for Loray—and many other mills as well.

The Georgia developers plan to purchase Loray Mill in the spring of 2007 for mixed-use development. The largest tenants at the outset will be the city, the county, and a charter school, and most of the building will be residential.

The impact of the redevelopment of Loray Mill will be prodigious. The project will benefit the large surrounding historic mill village, whose future depends largely on the fate of the mill. The 500-home working-class neighborhood has been listed in the National Register of Historic Places, making available rehabilitation tax credits to encourage new investment in West Gastonia. The redevelopment of Loray Mill will add more than $50 million to the local economy through direct construction expenditures, and it will stimulate additional investment indirectly. When the sale is concluded, it will add more than $500,000 to PNC's coffers.

CONCLUSION

These three projects all carried significant community and organizational benefits. They have increased Preservation North Carolina's level of expertise, confidence, and credibility. They've encouraged North Carolinians to preserve a highly endangered set of buildings from its textile heritage, and they've led to the adoption of legislation that will aid in the preservation of dozens of industrial buildings. Each of these projects has significant environmental, economic development, cultural tourism, and housing components. Each adds millions of dollars to the local tax base and preserves complexes of enormous historical importance. Each reduces sprawl. In each case, thousands of dollars will be spent on environmental cleanup.

Perhaps the biggest benefit of these industrial heritage projects, like the downtown revitalization and school reuse projects before them, is their value as examples to numerous communities statewide. Innumerable economic development officials, planners, developers, and interested citizens have visited the mill villages in Edenton and Glencoe to see how historic industrial housing can be revitalized as a community asset. PNC's mill redevelopment projects are being watched by communities across the state because of the large number of factories that have recently been vacated. These projects have produced a remarkable amount of public interest as well as attention in the media, and their impact will be felt throughout the Southeast.

Yet in each case, by taking ownership of these properties Preservation North Carolina accepted significant financial risks. Those risks will bring financial rewards after a decade of stress and challenge. Has the risk been worth it? At a recent PNC board meeting, the board chose "risk-taking" as one of the organization's five core values—and encouraged the staff to identify other large projects where the organization could have a large impact on preservation over a period of several years. I guess that means the answer is yes.

SIXTEEN

Building Relocation: Victory or Defeat?

MOVING STRUCTURES MAY OR
MAY NOT BE GOOD PRESERVATION

THERE ARE few subjects that generate more animated conversation among preservationists than moving buildings. Some are vehement that they'd rather lose a building than move it. Others see relocation as an easy solution to save a building. Personally I'm somewhere in between.

Moving buildings is nothing new in North Carolina. The kitchen in which President Andrew Johnson was born in Raleigh has been moved several times during the last 150 years. In many Tar Heel communities, a century ago when white congregations planned to build new churches, they gave African American worshippers their old sanctuaries for relocation. Vintage photographs of buildings being moved on logs are not unusual. North Carolinians were frugal people.

At Preservation North Carolina, we're frequently offered buildings to be moved, usually when a land developer or landowner wants to get a historic building out of the way with minimal controversy. The choice presented to us: move it or lose it. Another common circumstance is when the owner of a historic building will neither sell the land nor undertake any maintenance measures on the building. Preservationists are then faced with a choice of finding a (rare) regulatory solution, watching the building's slow demise (while hoping for a change of heart or holding out for a more sympathetic next

generation—known indelicately as "waiting for a good funeral"), or moving the building.

The guidelines of the National Register of Historic Places aptly take a strong stand on relocation. A building's National Register designation is removed when it is relocated, and its chances of being relisted in the register are limited. The property owner (or other applicant for listing) must demonstrate that the building had to be moved and that no alternatives were available to save it on site.

The property owner must also demonstrate that the new site is similar to the old site. Generally, a rural building must be resited in a rural context; an urban structure needs to stay in town. The structure should be historically compatible with the new site, if possible retaining its original orientation (e.g., facing north) and providing a comparable setting (e.g., similar yard and tree cover) at the new location. Significant architectural features of the building, such as exterior chimneys or additions, should be retained in the move. Another limitation is that the building must be significant for architectural as well as historical reasons. If its significance is purely historical, it won't be eligible for the National Register on its new site.

There are numerous reasons to start out with a bias against moving a building. Moving destroys at least a tenth of the original fabric. At a minimum, original foundations are lost. Especially with early houses, the cellar and the foundations tell a significant part of the building's story. All too often, chimneys are lost, as are landscape features. Archaeological resources are left behind. Ideally, the building's original site should either be investigated for archaeological resources or protected from future development. Yet usually the reason for moving a building is impending development that will destroy those resources.

The annals of relocation in North Carolina convey some close philosophical calls. Should the building have been relocated? Should it still be eligible for the National Register after its relocation? Was moving preferable to losing the structure?

Years ago, a North Carolina developer failed to get tax credits when he moved a highly endangered large early-twentieth-century house to a nearby site in front of an endangered mansion of the same vintage. The two houses, once neighbors, have been handsomely renovated and now face each other on the same lot. The National Park Service determined that when the houses were built, they would never have faced each other on the same lot. So even though both houses were threatened with imminent destruction, the developer was not able to use preservation tax incentives on either house.

It's a case that gives preservationists pause. Both houses were saved from certain demolition, and the market value of the land dictated their placement. One house remains on its original site. The preservation alternatives for the house that was moved were limited by its large size and its location between railroad tracks and a freeway. But their new relationship is peculiar. Facing each other, the houses don't look or feel right. What's the right course under the circumstances? The dilemma would provide a fit topic for a debating society.

In another case, a fancy Victorian house (the Hayes House in Blowing Rock), the best of its kind in town, had to be moved out of the thriving downtown. Its pending destruction was without question. The closest available lot was four blocks away from the central business district. The house was moved by PNC, sold, and nicely renovated. Listing in the National Register was deemed unlikely because the

house was moved out of the downtown, changing its context considerably. Yet there was no preservation alternative in the downtown. Further, one could argue that the house was originally built in a residential context, but the downtown grew up around it. What's a preservationist to do?

Moving buildings can deliver some incongruous results. But I rarely feel that losing a significant structure to demolition or salvage is preferable to its relocation. If nothing else, at least its materials have been recycled. In the long run, the oddly placed structure might someday fit in better on its new site after its landscape matures and its surroundings evolve. In time, the structure might even take on significance because of its relocation. One thinks of The Lindens, a 1754 house moved from Massachusetts to Washington, DC, in 1934. The story of its move is a significant part of its history. Destruction, on the other hand, is final.

Relocation can sometimes be downright beneficial. When a building's original setting has been completely altered or compromised, relocation may seem merciful. Every preservationist can envision the stranded house sitting in the midst of commercial development or parking lots. It often tells a sad story about the community's development patterns: once there was a great neighborhood, but now it's gone. Usually the stranded house is a candidate for eventual demolition. On occasion, the stranded building has sufficient presence or sits on a large enough lot that it can stand up to its surroundings and defiantly say, "I was here first." The flamboyant Victorian Dodd-Hinsdale House (Second Empire Restaurant) on Hillsborough Street in Raleigh is an example. A lesser house would look pitiful in its setting.

The George Poland House in Raleigh, a 1953 house designed by noted Modernist architect George Matsumoto, couldn't stand up to the commercial development of its surroundings. Built to look out over Crabtree Valley when cattle grazed beside the broad creek, the small house eventually overlooked one of the state's largest shopping malls. A battalion of chain hotels sprouted on the hill above the house. After the death of its owner, the house didn't have a chance. Its site was worth a for-

The George Poland House in Raleigh, designed by prominent Modernist architect George Matsumoto, had to be moved to a new location in northern Durham County, where it has been renovated under protective covenants. Its new site, though in an adjacent county, closely resembles its original setting.

tune commercially. The house was given to PNC for relocation. Don DeFeo of Durham acquired it from PNC and moved it to a site in northern Durham County. Although the site would at first seem to be too distant from its original location, it isn't. The new site bears remarkable similarities to the original 1950s setting for which the house was designed. Sitting on a hill overlooking the Little River not far from the city limits of both Raleigh and Durham, the meticulously restored Poland House is at home in its new setting. This time the house has enough land and protective covenants to protect its site.

The case of the historic Chancellor's House at the University of North Carolina at Greensboro is apropos. Preservation North Carolina moved the house one block in the summer of 2004. The building is still on the same street, on campus, and used by the university. Why did the house have to be moved? It sat on a large piece of land that was too valuable for the university's future development. And frankly, the house looked ill at ease on its original site. Much larger structures surrounded it on three sides. The new buildings, combined with the slope of the lot, made the house look like it was sitting in a hole, and they had created drainage problems for their older neighbor. Even if it could have been renovated on its original site, it would still have had the feel of a stranded building.

Relocation may have been a benefit for the Chancellor's House. The house occupies a smaller lot with less development potential, and it is more prominent, on a higher site close to the university's entrance. As the trees around it mature, the house will look like it was always there, and in time its relocation will be remembered by only a few.

The irony that the Chancellor's House was relocated to a site where a fine historic house was earlier demolished tells a preservation story of its own. Like the Capehart House in Raleigh, relocated in 1979 to a Blount Street site where a house had earlier been removed to make way for parking, the Chancellor's House is evidence that historic preservation is valued more highly now than it was a generation ago, when institutions tore down historic structures willy-nilly. Let's hope those days are gone.

Relocation can provide good infill for vacant lots in older neighborhoods. Too often, when new houses are built in older areas, they don't fit in very well. Relocating an older house to a vacant lot can solve two problems at once. First, it may save a building that would otherwise be lost. Second, it may provide supremely compatible infill. The Capehart House fits in beautifully with its neighbors, and even the most discerning observer wouldn't guess that it's an interloper on Blount Street. There are dozens of similar examples across the state.

The Privott-Goodwin-Sexton House in Edenton has been moved and renovated on the former site of an unattractive convenience store. Its relocation preserved the endangered house, removed a neighborhood nuisance, and improved the streetscape of Edenton's main street.

Even better is when a relocated structure can replace an incongruous blight. In Edenton, the Privott-Goodwin-Sexton House, given to PNC when its move was necessitated by church expansion, was moved in 2004 to the site of an intrusive convenience store on the town's main street. Instead of being demolished, the house eliminated a nuisance and fits into the streetscape beautifully.

Another relocated house serving as exceptional infill is at Glencoe, PNC's mill and mill village project in Alamance County. The superintendent's house at Glencoe burned down nearly a half century ago. Two years ago, three miles away, a similar superintendent's house at another mill was to be used for firefighting practice, an ignominious fate

for a historic house. Built by the same owner within a decade of the missing house at Glencoe and occupied for years by Glencoe's former superintendent, the house seemed destined to be moved to Glencoe. In July 2002, with financial support from a number of local citizens and Holt family members, the Holt-Heritage House was moved to the site of the missing superintendent's house, overlooking the mill village. The early-twentieth-century landscape plans and plant list for the original house have been discovered, and a buyer is restoring the house on its spectacular site above the Haw River.

Relocated properties can sometimes generate new economic investment. In 1982, Preservation North Carolina moved the Bretsch House to the site of an empty service station on a prominent corner in downtown Raleigh. That same day, the Montgomery House was moved by the local preservation organization to a nearby gravel parking lot. Rather than suffering the sad fate of being demolished for church parking lots, the two historic houses shored up a historic area and helped stimulate massive new economic investment in the east side of downtown Raleigh. Twenty years later, the houses look at home in their improved environment. In Asheville, Richmond Hill (the home of Richmond Pearson) was moved in 1984 to avert destruction; it is now one of the state's most elegant inns, attracting both national and international visitors.

Relocated houses have played a critical role in the urban redevelopment of Fourth Ward in Charlotte. In the mid-1970s, urban planners in Charlotte created a local historic district in a former urban renewal area. A handful of historic Victorian houses and early apartment buildings remained in the seedy area, but most of the land was vacant. The plan called for stranded Victorian houses in the downtown area to be moved to Fourth Ward. The remaining land would be used for new residential infill to be built in contemporary style. Planners were using the historic district designation in order to get design control. Fourth Ward generated either admiration or invective from preservationists—and nothing in between.

Today Fourth Ward is a revitalized downtown residential area, nestled in the shadow of skyscrapers and now joined by midrise residential development on its edges. To this day, some preservationists still have mixed feelings about Fourth Ward, but there can be no mistaking its status as a paradigm of successful city planning. One of the interesting future issues for Fourth Ward will be the preservation of its 1970s infill architecture. The future of the relocated Victorian houses will probably be secure, but will the 1970s houses (often small and stark) be respected for their own architectural integrity?

Is moving a building difficult? The answer varies. It depends primarily on how the building sits on its original site (for example, how hard is it to get steel under the house?) and whether there are too many impediments (trees, utility lines, signal lights, bridges, hills, etc.) en route to a new site. Size may or may not be a determining factor. Strangely, the relocation of some very large structures has proved easier than that of some smaller ones. In other cases, moving a small house a considerable distance has proven quite viable.

When is moving a building economically viable? Generally speaking, if the cost of buying a

Rosedale, a prominent plantation house in Beaufort County, long sat vacant on its original site. Because of its large size and the limited number of acceptable sites for relocation, the house had to be carefully dismantled, piece-by-piece, and reassembled on a new site. A generous donation from a descendant of its original owner made the move financially feasible.

Relocation of historic buildings is a preservationist's last resort, though it often builds excitement and garners major publicity. Examples of houses relocated in order to save them from certain destruction are (top-to-bottom, left-to-right): the Capehart House in Raleigh (moved for the construction of a state office building); the Lowe House in Guilford County (moved for a new reservoir); Piney Prospect in Edgecombe County (moved for agricultural reasons); the Hileman House in Cabarrus County (moved out of the way of suburban development); Reedy Fork in Guilford County (another victim of suburban development); and Richmond Hill in Asheville (moved because of an unsympathetic religious institution).

site plus moving the building and setting it on a new foundation with utility connections is competitive with the cost of buying (or constructing) a similar building in comparable condition, it's viable. The full cost of executing the move, including land costs, should be compared to the cost of purchasing a similar building. Say, for example, it costs $50,000 to move a house to a lot that costs $35,000, with the new foundation and utility connections costing an additional $25,000. When the move is complete, then the buyer has the equivalent of a $110,000 house. How does that cost compare to other houses (similar in size and condition) in the neighborhood? If a similar house would cost $200,000 to purchase, then moving would make great economic sense. There's plenty of cushion in case of unexpected costs. On the other hand, if similar houses cost $100,000, then the move may still be financially viable, but the buyer would need to study the situation carefully. Issues to consider include the house's landmark status and how its historical and architectural significance add extra value. Also, give some thought to how quickly the house will look good in the new setting, and how long the new buyer is going to have to live in the house before it is once again easily marketable. It may take a while for the house to look at home on the new site.

The most pressing consideration is how much damage will be done to the building in the course of moving it. If the building doesn't have to be cut apart for the move (more likely if the house is small or if the move is a short distance), then a good house mover should be able to relocate it without doing any significant damage. Many a house with decorative plasterwork has been moved without plaster damage. Indeed, furniture may be left in place during a move. Chimneys may often be moved intact, but they must be relined and repointed before being safely used. A key ingredient for a successful move is having a good mason who can build the new foundation to match the sills of the building so that cracking doesn't occur when the house is set down.

If the move requires going under too many utility lines or overpasses or if the building's weight is prohibitive for the route of the move, the building may have to be cut apart or otherwise dismantled for the move. Most likely, historical or architectural features will be lost in the move, and reassembly costs will increase the project's price tag. Such a move does not necessarily mean that it won't be viable, but it is certainly more challenging.

Vacant for years, Rosedale, an exceptionally fine antebellum plantation house near Washington, NC, had to be totally dismantled in order to be saved. Dozens of lots were considered for its relocation, but in each case small bridges and county roadways en route would not withstand its weight. Nearby major utility lines further constricted the options. So Rosedale was dismantled piece by piece (including its framing and decorative plaster), parts were carefully numbered, and the house was reassembled on a new site by its owners. This variety of move is drastic and expensive, but there appeared to be no alternative to save one of the region's finest antebellum houses. This project would not have been possible without a generous subsidy from a descendant of its original owner.

Ironically, few preservation activities generate more publicity than moving a building. Why do I say "ironically"? Because relocation is a preservationist's alternative of last resort—a retreat after defeat. It's a time of both celebration and sorrow.

So when you see a historic building being moved, gently celebrate its new lease on life. Wish it better fortune this time around. With any luck (and with preservation protections), it will be treasured on its new site for many years to come.

SEVENTEEN

Museums and Stewardship Properties

WHAT TO DO WITH TRULY SPECIAL PLACES

*W*HEN I FIRST started working with endangered properties in the late 1970s, many people thought that the best, if not the only, use for a historic building was as a museum. Repeatedly we had to tell civic clubs, and write in newsletter articles and fundraising letters, that the private use of historic structures was an important and necessary alternative to museum use. We were looking for private buyers to rehabilitate and enjoy the endangered properties because there were already "enough" museums.

The rising generation of preservationists in the 1970s and 1980s often viewed museums with derision. We wanted to broaden the preservation movement to encompass historic districts, downtowns, adaptive use, vernacular architecture, and diversity. Yet the general public continued to associate preservationists with museums and capital-A Architecture. If a property didn't carry the accolades of the oldest, the best, or the last surviving, then it wasn't worth preserving. The preservation pendulum had to shift away from museums in order for the movement to be successful.

Sometimes, though, the best use for an endangered historic property, especially one of exceptional architectural, historical, or social significance, is for public enjoyment. Museums and community centers often serve as the entry point into the preservation movement. Many preservationists first got

enthused about architecture and history at a museum or other public facility. They may have been ten years old at the time, or fifty. To write museums off as antiquated and superfluous is to close the front door to the movement.

Several of the properties saved from destruction by Preservation North Carolina have become museums or community centers. These properties have had exceptional local value: fine architectural treasures, eccentric follies, African American schools, early homes, and others. They have also had local leadership willing to invest time and resources in their preservation.

Sometimes the properties are too significant or too small—or their significance is too fragile—to be sympathetically adapted for modern uses. For example, the sympathetic adaptive use of a rare, tiny, early-eighteenth-century yeoman farmer's house would be almost impossible. The introduction of a modern kitchen, bathroom, or mechanical systems would compromise its historical fabric. While it is possible that such a building might be used as a private accessory structure that doesn't require these modern intrusions (such as a studio or garden house), its use as a public resource may be best.

Several times we have acquired a distinguished property (or obtained a long-term option) while a local group was organizing to acquire the property from us. Sometimes we have been able to get

The Bellamy Mansion in Wilmington (shown here in a 1951 photograph) has been restored as a museum under Preservation North Carolina's aegis. The 1861 architectural landmark stood vacant in the port city for two decades after an arsonist's fire substantially damaged its interior. Museums are an important, though expensive, portal for the preservation movement.

the property donated to Preservation North Carolina. Usually we serve as the fiscal agent for the first charitable contributions (while the new organization is getting its tax-exempt status). When the local entity is ready to accept ownership, we sell the property to the new group and pass along the monetary value of any contributions received.

In a few cases, Preservation North Carolina has accepted the donation of exceptional properties under the condition that we would retain ownership and ensure their preservation. We refer to these as our Stewardship Properties. With the Bellamy Mansion in Wilmington, an antebellum house with

exceptional significance and financial viability for museum use (it's prominently located in a city noted for its heritage tourism trade), we have ourselves restored, opened, and operated the property as a museum. One might view our work with the Bellamy Mansion to be an outgrowth of our endangered properties work. The Bellamy Mansion was badly damaged by fire in 1972, and the nonprofit organization that owned it for two decades had been unable to complete its restoration. By working collaboratively with the group, we were able to assist with fundraising and oversee its restoration.

We have accepted the ownership of other highly

significant properties that we expect eventually to open for a variation of museum or community use. In most cases, the contribution of a substantial endowment for the property has been a necessary part of the package.

We have also accepted the donation of Stewardship Properties that will probably never be opened and operated as museums. Caretakers live in these properties and are contractually charged with taking care of their maintenance and upkeep. They are required to periodically open the properties so the public can see their most important features. By retaining ownership, Preservation North Carolina will be able to protect these exceptional properties and provide public educational benefit without the full cost of museum operations.

Conversely, we have been involved in finding private uses for museum properties that have been financially unable to survive. In several small towns or rural communities with limited resources, we have had to persuade preservation advocates that returning a house museum to private residential use is not necessarily a defeat. These leaders, though disappointed, have saved an important resource for their communities and are acting responsibly by stepping back from their original vision of public use.

Through the years, I've moderated my own at-

The Walnut Cove Colored School in Stokes County, a Rosenwald school, has been handsomely renovated under Preservation North Carolina's covenants as a community center.

titude about museums. They're important resources in the preservation community. They are the portal for preservation. Nevertheless, I'll also stick with our 1970s mantra that not every historic property needs to be a museum. When an exceptionally important property can be acquired, it's appropriate to consider the viability of every available alternative for its continued preservation. As long as the property and its integrity are preserved, then its future use can be changed if today's vision for the property doesn't last forever. If the property isn't preserved, then all bets are off.

EIGHTEEN

Partnerships for Preservation

PARTNERING CAN MAKE LARGER PROJECTS POSSIBLE

*F*OUNDATIONS love collaborative projects. Politicians love to talk about public-private partnerships. Nonprofits extol the virtues of partnering. Yet true partnerships are rare. Collaboration is truly difficult. As with a marriage of two individuals, a partnership requires give-and-take and, at times, a subordination of self-interest in favor of the interest of the partnership. When a partnership works, it can make bigger and better projects possible.

Partnerships don't happen overnight. First, trust between the partners must be built, often necessitating a personal friendship or working relationship between individuals involved in the partnering entities. Unfortunately, a preservation organization that's struggling with its day-to-day programs and finances will often find it difficult to invest the time and energy necessary in building partnership opportunities. A partnership is not about "What can you do for me?" It's about "What can we do together?"

Further, partners must share a common vision and need. The shared goal may be narrow (for example, to create an exhibit or to revitalize a blighted city block), but the effect of partnership can be catalytic. When a preservation organization successfully partners with an entity in another field of interest, the level of community support for preservation increases exponentially, and the preservationists' message reaches new ears.

Work with real estate opens up new opportunities for partnership. Preservationists, city planners, and downtown advocates may share an interest in seeing a derelict building rejuvenated. Nonprofit organizations of many varieties may be interested in sharing office space in a historic building. Land trusts and preservation organizations may find common ground in the preservation of historic properties with developable acreage. Preservationists and local governments may join hands in efforts to find new uses for vacant industrial buildings. Preservationists may find business opportunities with developers or other real estate professionals that are advantageous for all involved.

And those partnerships based on real estate can be powerful tools for preservation and for preservation organizations: opening new doors, making new friends, garnering new publicity, and building new social equity. Many of Preservation North Carolina's most important projects have involved partnerships with other organizations, businesses, or agencies. A brief account of a few of PNC's partnerships demonstrates the many ways in which work to save endangered properties can build diverse new relationships and accomplish more ambitious goals.

• More than two decades ago, recognizing that the ramshackle condition of many of the state's downtowns was an impediment to economic development, North Carolina's Department of Commerce decided to apply for participation in the National Trust for Historic Preservation's new Main Street Program. The department's staff turned to Preservation North Carolina to help identify communities that would benefit from the program. PNC's involvement with the application included writing descriptions and providing photographs. The fledgling partnership promised to aid the cause of preservation, but not necessarily PNC itself.

After North Carolina was selected in the initial round, Preservation North Carolina's board set a goal of acquiring and reselling an endangered building in each of the five designated Main Street towns. That goal brought PNC in contact with a whole new universe of concerned citizens and widened PNC's sphere of influence. Some of the buildings preserved under that goal were among the most dramatic "saves" in PNC's history: Shelby's Masonic Temple, a groundbreaking reuse of a major downtown building for residential condominiums; Salisbury's Hedrick Block, the successful preservation of a pair of buildings in the 100 block of Main Street that were already under demolition; and Washington's Baugham Building, the successful "save" of a fire-gutted downtown commercial landmark. As important as these preservation success stories were, the new relationships built around a common goal were even more important. The primary local advocate for the Shelby project became a longtime PNC supporter and left a generous bequest for PNC in her will. In Salisbury, PNC built a strong and valued friendship with a young downtown advocate who was later elected mayor, appointed to the state Board of Transportation, and hired as a top adviser for a prominent United States Senator.

PNC has worked with a number of buildings in Main Street communities over the last two decades. The Main Street Program has remained a core partner for PNC. The two organizations have partnered on conferences, publications, legislation (including the highly successful state rehabilitation tax credits), architectural designs, and fundraising. Valuable contacts have been shared. The two entities have been able to accomplish far more together than they would have separately.

• Land trusts and preservation organizations involved in real estate are natural partners. Both share an interest in preserving open space, an interest that intersects with historic landscapes. The Triangle Land Conservancy and PNC worked together through an extended process to save Leigh Farm in Durham. The conservancy was primarily interested in preserving the land that buffered New Hope Creek, while PNC's focus was the antebellum farmstead. Weekly meetings led to an expanded partnership including the local Junior League and Durham County, which acquired the property as a park. The acquisition process took nearly two years, but Leigh Farm will be enjoyed for years to come. The personal relationships that accrued from the process have since led to greater collaboration between the conservation and preservation communities statewide, including shared conference sessions and an ambitious proposal to obtain more financial support for land and heritage conservation.

• In downtown Raleigh, when the condition of the highly significant 1874 Briggs Hardware Building (previously mentioned in chapter 5) was becoming a matter of great concern for preservationists and others, a distress call from the executive director of the A. J. Fletcher Foundation led to a creative partnership to save the building. He and I had known each other for many years, and the Fletcher Foundation had on occasion made grants for PNC projects. The vacant four-story Italianate building's situation was dire. In 1996 Hurricane Fran had severely damaged the roof, and its owners had inadequate capital to do the necessary repairs and carry the debt. One option was to wait for foreclosure and then acquire the property, but active water damage threatened to destroy the building's structural viability first. So the Fletcher Foundation and PNC agreed to buy the building as 50/50 partners in a new limited liability partnership, and each organization would move its offices there. PNC would bring the partnership its real estate expertise, and the Fletcher Foundation would bring financial strength. The total project cost was $3.2 million. PNC had a small nest egg from the sale of a previous office, and the Fletcher Foundation agreed to lend PNC $1.2 million, the remainder of PNC's share of the building's purchase and renovation, as a program-related investment. The news about the building's purchase attracted the attention of North Carolina Special Olympics (which became a tenant at a competitive lease rate) and the Raleigh City Museum (which agreed to occupy the ground floor and become a project partner with financing from the Fletcher Foundation). Before construction was complete, the building was fully occupied, bringing more than forty employees into the heart of a struggling downtown Raleigh.

The results have been gratifying, as several other historic buildings in its immediate vicinity have since been renovated. Such a partnership must of necessity be enduring, since the partners now own a building together. Routine meetings of the partners keep them informed about each other's highs and lows, as well as about the building. On occasion, the organizations have worked together on projects of mutual interest. In the long run, the building promises to be a good investment in terms of both money and mission. None of the partners could have undertaken this project by themselves; only collaboration could succeed.

• The effort to save the highly endangered Old Mount Olive High School led Preservation North Carolina into a very different partnership. The building was slated for demolition,

The Old Mount Olive High School in Wayne County was in terrible condition prior to its renovation for affordable housing by a partnership which included Preservation North Carolina. The success of this exemplary preservation project was diminished by problems within the partnership. On balance, though, an important landmark was returned to good use.

and the local government agreed to give PNC a short time to find a solution. PNC found a sympathetic and creative developer to do the project. Many months, numerous meetings, and stacks of legal documents later, the Town of Mount Olive gave the property to PNC, which placed it into a partnership that included the developer and PNC as "managing partners," and a utility company as the equity investor (in exchange for tax credits). The property was beautifully renovated into twelve affordable apartments for elderly residents and a municipal auditorium.

This project, however, exemplifies both the benefits and the hazards of partnerships. Several years after the building was renovated, the limited liability company that owned the building experienced legal and financial problems because of the actions of one of the partners. The problems mushroomed to impinge on all of the partners, requiring many hours and dollars to rectify. Partnerships require careful evaluation of the compatibility and reliability of the partners, both at the inception and throughout the process.

• A promising partnership has recently been established between the City of Goldsboro, the Downtown Goldsboro Development Corporation, Self-Help Credit Union, and PNC. The residential areas of Goldsboro's downtown historic district have not prospered despite a variety of preservation efforts through two decades (including PNC's work with the Weil Houses). The commercial area has witnessed great improvement with its Main Street designation and downtown development corporation, but it hasn't really thrived either. The parties came together to try to find strategies that would encourage the revitalization of the residential district, which would in turn aid the downtown.

Goldsboro grew up around the railroad; its older areas were first established in the 1850s

and then prospered in the late nineteenth and early twentieth centuries. The downtown area declined rapidly as businesses and middle-class residents moved to the suburbs in the 1950s and 1960s. The large surviving Victorian houses first became rental properties and were subdivided into apartments. Continued disinvestment left them empty, and code enforcement resulted in wholesale demolition.

By 2005, the historic district had numerous empty houses and vacant lots. The city's tax base was being eroded with increased public expenses for grass cutting, litter cleanup, policing, and so on, while it received little or no revenue from the vacant lots. Likewise, the continued loss of a residential base was harming downtown revitalization efforts. The mayor and new city manager recognized that bold action was needed.

After a number of brainstorming meetings, a new public/private partnership was quietly launched to revitalize the residential areas around downtown. The City of Goldsboro would pay a modest stipend to owners of condemned houses if they donated them to PNC within a limited time frame. PNC would then market the properties for renovation subject to protective covenants, and Downtown Goldsboro would assist in showing properties to potential purchasers. Further, the city would create a stabilization and acquisition fund at a local bank for PNC to use to secure the acquired properties and make them marketable or to buy foreclosed properties at auction. Interest would be paid by the city, and the principle would be repaid out of the proceeds of sale.

The stipend offered by the city to the property owners made it possible for them to come out ahead by donating their properties to PNC. The payment covered the legal and appraisal costs necessary to make a property donation, allowing a property owner to walk away with a valid charitable deduction and no out-of-pocket costs. If a property owner didn't cooperate, the city would proceed with condemnation. If repairs weren't made, the building would be demolished and a lien would be placed on the property for the demolition cost.

Further, the city agreed to convey the vacant lots that it had acquired in the neighborhood through condemnation proceedings and tax foreclosures to Self-Help Credit Union. Self-Help would construct new multifamily housing that fit into the neighborhood. Duplexes, triplexes, and quadraplexes would be built to match the scale and form of their Victorian neighbors. The variety of housing choices in the neighborhood would help ensure its diversity. Since Self-Help would get the parcels for little or no money, it agreed to upgrade the exterior materials that it used to make sure that the new houses fit in to the historic district. For example, vinyl siding would not be used.

Despite the project's front-end costs, city officials recognized that the city would benefit from a sizable increase in the tax base as new owners renovated the formerly condemned houses and surrounding properties became more valuable. It would also be relieved of the costs of exercising code enforcement and maintaining vacant lots that have been removed from the tax books.

After its first six months, the project is off to a good start; several condemned historic properties have been purchased for renovation, and new construction is pending. A steady stream of potential purchasers are pouring into the downtown area, creating energy and excitement. At PNC, our biggest concern is the need for additional staff time to take advantage of the interest that's been generated. Once again, the need for personnel trumps the need for capital for acquisition and stabilization.

This partnership is bold, and if successful, it may be a model for other communities to emulate. The rudiments of the partnership are worth noting. All the partners knew and respected each other before the project was conceived. Each partner would do what it does best. The goals for each entity were not identical, but they were compatible. None of the partners could have succeeded alone. The beauty of this partnership is that, if successful, it will achieve an important goal for each partner, and each partner will ultimately benefit financially.

• The case study of the Armstrong Hotel Apartments in chapter 11 illustrates another partnership with a local government. The City of Gastonia, which urgently wanted to see the apartments developed as the city's first downtown residential project, agreed to lease the vacant property from PNC in order to provide insurance, grounds maintenance, and mortgage funding. PNC provided a mechanism to hold and market the property until a sympathetic development team could be found. As the case study demonstrates, the partners had to stick together through thick and thin to achieve a successful conclusion.

Partnerships with other preservation organizations and public agencies, such as local commissions and State Historic Preservation Offices, may seem fundamental for preservation organizations. Given the partners' differing preservation philosophies and rivalries, whether real or perceived, these partnerships aren't necessarily easier to sustain. But they can be some of the most valuable for an organization working with buildings.

State Historic Preservation Offices and city preservation offices can provide invaluable technical assistance on numerous preservation-related subjects, allowing the nonprofit organization to focus on the real estate angle. These offices can help identify endangered properties that need attention. Their survey files can provide invaluable historical information and photographs. Their professional staff can assist owners with rehabilitation advice and help the organization with covenant and easement monitoring. Where responsible for reviewing tax incentive applications, these professionals can help shape design solutions for difficult properties where incentives are crucial. These offices can also supply invaluable information about practitioners and artisans who work in preservation.

Preservation organizations with an endangered properties program can be an invaluable partner to a local historic preservation commission (such as a district or landmark commission) when it invokes a demolition delay or prohibition on a threatened building. In North Carolina, a commission may put into place a one-year delay on demolition for historic landmarks or buildings in a historic district. The state law enabling the delay instructs the commission to try during that year to find a preservation solution. Usually the commission does not have the legal authority and financial resources to purchase the property or find another real estate solution. The nonprofit organization, with its expertise and resources, can step in as a partner. Though moving historic buildings is not ideal, many times Preservation North Carolina has been able to relocate buildings whose demolition has been delayed by local preservation commissions.

Partnerships with other preservation organizations can be invaluable. The National Trust for Historic Preservation can provide a wide variety of financial and technical resources to local and statewide organizations working with real estate. Preservation North Carolina has loaned funds and provided expertise to local organizations in the state, and vice versa. In North Carolina, a dozen or more preservation revolving funds have worked together for more than two decades to jointly market properties for sale, recognizing that increased visibility benefits all. This partnership among statewide and local organizations has had the added reward of encouraging other local preservation groups to get involved with property.

Sometimes the assistance of a partner can carry significant symbolic value. When Preservation North Carolina first began its work with the Edenton Cotton Mill and mill village, the Edenton Historical Commission redeemed maturing certificates of deposit and loaned the funds short-term to PNC at

the same interest rate. Although PNC could have gone to a bank for cheaper funds, the loan from the commission represented its support for the project, a pioneering one for the region. Many of the commission's supporters probably had great doubt about the significance of preserving a twentieth-century mill village on the wrong side of the railroad tracks from Edenton's renowned historic district. The loan gave a symbolic "green light" to the local elected officials and bank executives that the project had validity and support among local preservationists. The symbolic importance of the loan outweighed its financial value.

The challenge in partnerships within the preservation community will often derive from the "chemistry" of the disparate personalities who populate the differing roles in preservation. Public agencies are involved in documentation and evaluation of historic resources, and their role in resource protection is generally regulatory. Often their employees are oriented to research and detailed review; they may prefer to stay out of the limelight. When they show up in the press, their role as regulators may be routinely disparaged, whether or not they are doing their jobs well. On the other hand, tight budgets mean that nonprofit agencies must be entrepreneurial in their approach to preservation, looking for revenue sources while pursuing mission-related accomplishments. In their quest for members and funding, they must seek out every opportunity for positive visibility. Nonprofit executive staff may need to be extroverted generalists to survive. Public agency staff may believe that nonprofits compromise their preservation ethics too easily and claim more credit than they deserve. After all, many of the nonprofit's achievements may rely on the behind-the-scenes work of the public agencies. Alternatively, the nonprofit partners may view their public counterparts as rigid, complacent, and disengaged from the realities of the marketplace.

Sustaining a healthy partnership between these fundamentally different cultures is difficult but crucial. Like a family, public and private preservationists depend on each other's work, and recognizing and respecting the differences may be necessary to advance the preservation cause. There are too many outside impediments to successful preservation to have infighting among preservationists!

To sustain a partnership, the partners need to set clear goals and assign explicit roles in attaining those goals. They need to recognize and acknowledge the diverse personalities and institutional cultures that are at the table. The partners must share credit for achievements and responsibility for failures. They need to celebrate their successes and periodically evaluate the health of the partnership. As with marriages, failed communications are the downfall of many partnerships.

If only partnerships in preservation were as prevalent as the talk of partnership! A successful partnership, like a happy marriage, is hard to find and difficult to sustain. But when it works, it's wonderful!

NINETEEN

The People of Preservation

PRESERVATIONISTS AS SOCIAL CAPITAL

*W*HEN WE THINK of historic preservation's benefits to communities, we often think in terms of saving historic buildings that might otherwise be lost. Just as important is the role of preservation in building a community's "social capital." Social capital refers to the connections among individuals—social networks, and the reciprocity and trust that arise from them. According to the World Bank, "social capital is not just the sum of the institutions which underpin a society—it is the glue that holds them together."

Preservation helps build social capital. The people who take on the rescue and restoration challenges of their own historic buildings often then expand their horizons to build new networks and make broader contributions to their adopted communities.

Preservationists are a diverse and remarkable lot. For all their quirky foibles, preservationists are generally people who care deeply about place and about community well-being. That care often translates into an interest in the long term, an iconoclastic stance in the modern climate of instant gratification.

Preservationists don't fit their stereotype. Preservationists are often not motivated by history. A historical society and a preservation organization are not the same, and they often attract different people. Often derided for caring only about the past, preservationists are more likely to talk about future generations than about ancestors. Preservation is largely about leaving a better legacy for the future, not about worshipping the past.

Nor are preservationists necessarily "little old ladies in tennis shoes." Thank goodness for those preservationists who were derided in the 1960s and 1970s as "little old ladies" (whether female or male, old or young, Episcopalian or agnostic) when historic buildings were considered antithetical to modernity and progress and were penalized by the nation's tax laws. They stepped forward at a critical time in many communities to urge a reexamination of community values. The movement they helped spawn is widely diverse and is generally proud of that diversity. Contrary to outdated and sometimes disingenuous criticism, preservationists are not of one age, gender, race, class, sexual orientation, national origin, or faith.

Through the years I've witnessed some remarkably effective preservationists, and others who despite their best efforts can't seem to convert their vision into results. What makes a preservationist effective? Here are a few thoughts.

• *The ability to communicate a vision.* Preservationists are visionaries. They have a vision of how a building—or a community—can look and function in the future, and their challenge

The people of preservation are a diverse lot and often display a remarkable sense of commitment and optimism.

is usually communicating that vision to others who don't share it or to those who have no vision. Only a preservationist can rhapsodize about the "potential" of a building that is run down, abandoned, vandalized, and full of dead pigeons and trash. Others look at it and see no redeeming value. That divergence can be deadly in the public arena unless the preservationist can deliver (1) a preservation rationale other than the building's history or its "potential" beauty, and, most important, (2) a feasible solution.

• *The ability to connect the long-term goals of preservation with a more immediate community need.* Saving a pitiful building or revitalizing a sagging downtown (or neighborhood) or keeping a rural landscape from being developed may unequivocally serve a worthy long-term goal. But, does it meet today's needs—right now? Unfortunately, thinking long-term seldom wins points in the political marketplace. Often the successful preservation rationale has to promise immediate economic or other community benefits. Widespread support for a preservation project is easier to find if the project will produce jobs, stimulate additional investment and community revitalization, increase the tax base, and enhance the community's potential for tourism and other economic development causes. Even better if the project can serve an already identified community need (such as recreation or affordable housing). When preservationists can effectively tie their vision to the goals of other community members, they are much more likely to succeed.

• *The ability to work with real estate.* Finding a feasible solution for a preservation crisis involves real estate. The most effective preservationists are often those who are able to implement their vision through their understanding of preservation as real estate. Some leaders have individually had the financial resources to buy and renovate property. Many communities noted for their preservation successes have had at least one patron, developer, or investor who has privately bought and renovated some of the first properties in the community's turnaround. Other leaders have worked through preservation organizations that have actively worked with real estate. Real estate is the name of the game in successful preservation, and without real estate skills in the local preservation toolbox, continued success may be elusive.

• *The ability to continue forward after defeat.* Sadly, some preservationists are one-timers. They enter into a fray about one property or issue, lose (perhaps because they haven't yet gained the community's confidence or because they don't understand real estate), and go home to salve their wounds, never again to venture out into the preservation arena. Indeed, sometimes their interest is more in the "fight" than in the final result. Successful

preservation is not about fighting. It's about getting others to share the vision, even if only for a defining moment, and having a successful strategy to implement it.

Effective preservationists know that they will win some and lose some. They have to be able to analyze the reasons for their losses and address the next challenge better equipped and more confident than before. They also exert care not to burn bridges.

Preservation is a constantly moving target. The issues and challenges change over time—sometimes slowly and sometimes overnight. Just when you think you've won a preservation victory, the euphoria may be dulled by new developments. Funding doesn't come through as expected for an undertaking. A much-awaited preservation development project goes into foreclosure. The building next door has a fire. Every effective preservationist has horror stories to tell as well as successes. You have to be able to pick yourself up and move on after a defeat.

People also change. Every effective preservationist will also have tales about conversions of former preservation "enemies." Just like Paul on the road to Damascus, sometimes opponents "see the light" and become allies. It may be a great personal challenge for a preservation advocate to embrace a former adversary and march forward together, but the most effective preservationists do.

Through years of unrelenting work for modest pay, I've said that the people of preservation have kept me going. Most preservationists care intensely about their communities. They are visionaries who seek community betterment, even if their own economic interests are not served. One might even dub preservation a "calling." Like most preservationists, I hold to a belief that future generations of North Carolinians will indeed appreciate the legacy that Preservation North Carolina strives to pass on. That conviction motivates me for the next day.

STATE OF NORTH CAROLINA
COUNTY OF _____

OFFER TO PURCHASE AND
PURCHASE CONTRACT

_____ as Buyer, hereby offers to purchase, and the
HISTORIC PRESERVATION FOUNDATION OF NORTH CAROLINA, INC., a nonprofit
corporation organized under the laws of the State of North Carolina, hereafter referred to as "Seller",
upon the execution hereof, agrees to sell and convey, all of that parcel of land as described below, together with improvements located thereon, ("the Property"), upon the following terms and conditions:

1. **REAL PROPERTY:** Located in_____, North Carolina, being known as and more
   particularly described as the_____, located at _____, _____.

2. **OFFER/PURCHASE PRICE:** The purchase price offered is $_____ and shall be paid
   as follows:

   (a) $_____, paid by _____ (cash, bank check or money order) with the
   delivery of this contract, to be held in escrow by The Historic Preservation Foundation of North
   Carolina, Inc., until the sale is closed, at which time it will be credited to the Buyer, or until this
   contract is otherwise terminated and it is disbursed to the Buyer.

   (b) $_____, with the balance of the purchase price to be paid in cash at closing.

3. **SOURCES OF FUNDS FOR PURCHASE AND REHABILITATION:** Attached is a statement from buyer outlining the estimated rehabilitation cost and the sources of funds available for
   the acquisition and rehabilitating of the building.

4. **FINANCING:** Buyers must be able to obtain a _____ loan in the amount of
   $_____ on or before _____.

5. **PROPOSED USE AND SCHEDULE OF WORK:** Attached is a letter from Buyer outlining
   the proposed use and the scope and time frame of the rehabilitation of the property. This attach-
   ment will be the basis for a rehabilitation agreement to be entered between buyer and seller.

6. **PROTECTIVE COVENANTS AND REHABILITATION AGREEMENT:** The Property
   will be sold subject to protective covenants to be placed in the deed and subject to a rehabilitation
   agreement. Attached to this contract is a set of covenants substantially similar to that to be placed

in the deed. Alterations in the attached covenants may be made following further negotiations. Also attached is a rehabilitation agreement to be completed prior to closing.

7. **CONDITIONS:** All of the Standard Provisions as attached hereto shall apply to this Offer and Contract, unless expressly modified by Addendum to this instrument. The following conditions shall apply to this instrument.

8. **CLOSING:** Closing is contingent upon the exercise of an option from the current Owner to the Seller. All parties agree to execute any and all documents and papers necessary in connection with closing and transfer of title on or before _____. The deed is to be made to _____ _____and will be a General Warranty Deed.

9. **POSSESSION:** Possession shall be delivered immediately upon closing.

This offer shall become a binding contract when signed by both Buyer and Seller.

Date of Offer: _____   Date of Acceptance: _____

Buyer: _____   Seller: The Historic Preservation
                                                      Foundation of North Carolina, Inc.

By: _____   by: _____
Print Name   Print Name

_____   _____
Signature   Signature

Address: _____

_____

Phone: _____

Fax: _____

_____

Receipt of Earnest Money Deposit:

I hereby acknowledge receipt of the earnest money herein set forth and agree to hold and distribute the same in accordance with the terms hereof.

                                          The Historic Preservation Foundation of
                                          North Carolina, Inc.

Date: _____   By: _____

Preservation North Carolina
(The Historic Preservation Foundation of North Carolina, Inc.)
220 Fayetteville Street, Ste. 200   PO Box 27644
Raleigh, North Carolina 27611-7644

STANDARD PROVISIONS

OFFER TO PURCHASE
AND PURCHASE CONTRACT

1. **EARNEST MONEY DEPOSIT:** In the event that this offer is not accepted or any conditions hereto are not satisfied, then all earnest money shall be returned to Buyer. In the event of breach of this contract by Seller, upon Buyer's request all earnest moneys shall be returned to buyer. In the event that this offer is accepted and Buyer breaches this contract, then all earnest monies shall be forfeited upon seller's request.

2. **PRORATIONS AND ADJUSTMENTS:** Unless otherwise provided, the following items shall be prorated and either adjusted between the parties or paid at closing: (a) Ad valorem taxes on real property shall be prorated on a calendar year basis through the date of closing. (b) Ad valorem taxes on personal property, if any, for the entire year shall be paid by Seller. (c) Rents, if any, for the Property shall be prorated to the date of closing.

3. **FIRE AND OTHER CASUALTY:** The risk of loss or damage by fire or other casualty prior to closing shall be upon the Seller.

4. **SOILS AND ENVIRONMENTAL CONDITIONS:** Buyer and Seller acknowledge that the property is to be sold in "as is" condition; that no assurances or warranties are given by the Seller as to the condition of the site, including any adverse conditions discoverable by soils studies or other subsurface investigations of the property. Any assessment in the possession of the Seller will be made available to prospective buyers upon request; however any additional studies or investigations to be performed by the Buyer are the sole responsibility of the Buyer; and that the Buyer expressly releases and discharges the Seller from any and all responsibility and liability resulting from surface, soils, ground water or other contamination or adverse environmental condition of the site, whatsoever.

5. **CONDITIONS:**
   (a) The property must be in substantially the same condition at closing as on the date of this offer, reasonable wear and tear excepted.
   (b) All deeds of trust, liens and other charges against the Property not assumed by the Buyer, must be paid and cancelled by the Seller prior to or at closing.
   (c) Title will be delivered at closing by a General Warranty Deed.

6. **NEW LOAN:** Buyer shall be responsible for all costs with respect to any new loan obtained by the Buyer. Seller shall have no obligation to pay any charge in connection therewith unless specifically set forth in this contract.

7. **CLOSING EXPENSES:** Seller agrees to prepare the proper deed. Buyer shall pay for recording the deed and for preparation and recording of all other instruments, if any, incidental to closing.

8. **EVIDENCE OF TITLE:** Seller agrees to use his best efforts to deliver to the Buyer, as soon as

reasonably possible after the acceptance of this offer, copies of all title information in possession of or available to the Seller, including but not limited to title insurance policies, attorney's opinions on title, surveys, covenants, deeds, notes and deeds of trust and easements relating to the Property.

9. **ASSIGNMENTS:** This contract may not be assigned without the written agreement of all parties, but if assigned by agreement, then this contract shall be binding on the assignee and his heirs and successors.

10. **PARTIES:** This contract shall be binding upon and shall inure to the benefit of the parties and their heirs, successors and assigns. As used herein, words in the singular include the plural and the masculine includes the feminine and neuter genders, as appropriate.

11. **SURVIVAL:** If any provision herein contained which by its nature and effect is required to be observed, kept or performed after the closing, it shall survive the closing and remain binding upon and for the benefit of the parties hereto until fully observed, kept or performed.

12. **ENTIRE AGREEMENT:** The Buyer acknowledges that he has inspected the Property. This contract contains the entire agreement of the parties and there are no representations, inducements or other provisions other than those expressed herein in writing.

Author's Note: As with all of the legal documents contained in these appendices, this document is not presented as a "model" document. These documents need to be reviewed and revised on a case-by-case, state-by-state basis by legal counsel. They are not static documents. Preservation North Carolina frequently updates its documents to incorporate new language or to adjust to new legal requirements. Each document is adjusted to reflect the special requirements of the property and the parties to the agreement.

The documents that follow in this book as Appendices B and C are attached to the Offer to Purchase and Purchase Contract as required in paragraph 6 of the contract. They are not included below as part of Appendix A.

PROTECTIVE COVENANTS FOR THE *[PROPERTY NAME]*

WHEREAS, the *[PROPERTY NAME]* located at *[CITY OR TOWN]*, *[COUNTY NAME]* County, North Carolina, hereinafter referred to as the Subject Property, is a building of recognized historical, cultural and architectural significance; and

WHEREAS, the Historic Preservation Foundation of North Carolina, Inc. (hereafter the Foundation) and the Grantee both desire that the historic *[PROPERTY NAME]* be rehabilitated and preserved for the enjoyment and edification of future generations; and

WHEREAS, the Foundation and Grantee both desire that the Subject Property shall retain its historically and architecturally significant features, while being sympathetically adapted and altered, where necessary, to provide for contemporary uses; and

WHEREAS, the Foundation and Grantee both desire that the Subject Property shall not be subdivided in order to preserve its integrity of site; and

WHEREAS, the Foundation is a charitable organization which acquires certain rights pursuant to historic preservation agreements that will insure that structures located within the state of North Carolina of recognized historical and architectural significance are preserved and maintained for the benefit of future generations; and

WHEREAS, the North Carolina General Assembly has enacted the Historic Preservation and Conservation Agreements Act validating restrictions, easements, covenants, conditions or otherwise, appropriate to the preservation of a structure or site historically significant for its architectural, archeological or historical associations.

NOW THEREFORE, the Grantee hereby agrees that the Subject Property shall be and shall permanently remain subject to the following agreement, easements, covenants and restrictions:

1. These covenants shall be administered solely by the Historic Preservation Foundation of North Carolina, Inc., its successors in interest or assigns; and in all subsequent conveyances of Subject Property, the Foundation, its successors in interest or assigns shall be the sole party entitled to administer these covenants. In the event that the Foundation, or its successors in interest by corporate merger cease to exist, then in such event the Foundation shall assign all of its rights and interests in these easements, covenants, and conditions subject to such duties and obligations which it assumes hereby to a nonprofit

corporation of responsibility which exists for substantially the same reasons as the Foundation itself (as described hereinabove); if no such corporation be available for such assignment then, under such circumstances such assignment shall be made to the State of North Carolina which shall be the sole party entitled to administer those covenants.

Rehabilitation and Maintenance

2. The Grantee covenants and agrees to rehabilitate the *[PROPERTY NAME]* according to the terms, conditions, and deadlines of a Rehabilitation Agreement entered into by the parties and signed by authorized officials of the Foundation and, after rehabilitation, to continuously maintain, repair, and administer the Subject Property herein described in accordance with the Secretary of the Interior's Standards for the Treatment of Historic Properties (1992) so as to preserve the historical integrity of features, materials, appearances, workmanship and environment of the Subject Property. Maintenance shall be continuously provided. Said standards are attached hereto and incorporated in these covenants by reference.

Prior Approval Required For Modifications

3. Unless prior written approval by the President or Chairman of the Board of Directors of the Foundation is obtained, no alteration, physical or structural change, or changes in the color, material or surfacing to the exterior of the *[PROPERTY NAME]* shall be made.

4. Unless the plans and exterior designs for such structure or addition have been approved in advance in writing by the President or Chairman of the Board of Directors of the Foundation, no addition or additional structure shall be constructed or permitted to be built upon the Subject Property. The Foundation in reviewing the plans and designs for any addition or additional structure shall consider the following criteria: exterior building materials; height; fenestration; roof shapes, forms, and materials; surface textures; expression of architectural detailing; scale; relationship of any additions to the main structure; general form and proportion of structures; orientation to street; setback; spacing of buildings, defined as the distance between adjacent buildings; lot coverage; use of local or regional architectural traditions; and effect on archeological resources. Contemporary designs for additions or additional structures shall not be discouraged when such alterations and additions do not destroy significant historical, architectural, or cultural material, and such design is compatible with the size, color, material and character of the property and its environment.

5. The Grantee and the Foundation hereby agree that the interior architectural features listed below are elements which contribute to the architectural significance of the *[PROPERTY NAME]*:

> {features to be listed here}

Unless prior written approval by the President or Chairman of the Board of Directors of the Foundation is obtained, no removal, relocation, or alteration of the above mentioned architectural features shall be made.

6. Neither the *[PROPERTY NAME]* nor any part thereof may be removed or demolished without the prior written approval of the President or Chairman of the Board of Directors of the Foundation.

7. No portion of the Subject Property may be subdivided.

8. Express written approval of the Foundation is required for removal of living trees greater than 12 inches in diameter at a point 4 feet above the ground from the Subject Property unless immediate removal is necessary for the protection of any persons coming onto the Subject Property or of the general public; for the prevention or treatment of disease; or for the protection and safety of the *[PROPERTY NAME]* or other permanent improvements on the Subject Property. Any tree of the aforementioned size which must be removed shall be replaced within a reasonable time by a new tree of a substantially similar species. If so requested, the Foundation may approve the use of an alternate species.

Covenant to Obey Public Laws

9. The Grantee shall abide by all federal, state, and local laws and ordinances regulating the rehabilitation, maintenance and use of the Subject Property.

Right of First Refusal

10. In case of any contemplated sale of the Subject Property or any portion thereof by the Grantee or any successor in title thereto, first refusal as to any bona fide offer of purchase must be given to the Foundation, its successors or assigns. If the Foundation so decides to purchase, it shall notify the then owner of its willingness to buy upon the same terms within thirty (30) days of receipt of written notice of such bona fide offer. Failure of the Foundation to notify the then owner of its intention to exercise this right of first refusal within such thirty (30) day period shall free the owner to sell pursuant to the bona fide offer. The Foundation may, in its discretion, waive its right of first refusal in writing, upon written receipt of such bona fide offer. Provided, however, that if there are any outstanding deeds of trust or other encumbrances against the property, any right to repurchase shall be subject to said deeds of trust or encumbrances, and they shall either be satisfied or assumed as part of the purchase price.

Inspection

11. Representatives of the Foundation shall have the right to enter the Subject Property at reasonable times, after giving reasonable notice, for the purpose of inspecting the buildings and grounds to determine if there is compliance by the Grantee with the terms of these covenants.

Public Access

12. Researchers, scholars, and groups especially interested in historic preservation shall have access to view the interior of the rehabilitated property by special appointment at various times and intervals during each year. The general public shall have access to the Subject Property to view the exterior and interior features herein protected at the Grantee's discretion at various times and intervals during each year at times both desirable to the public and convenient with the Grantee. Nothing shall be erected or allowed to grow on the Subject Property which would impair the visibility of the property and the buildings from the street level or other public rights of way.

Hazardous Materials

13. The properties the Foundation seeks to protect may contain certain hazards as a result of outdated building practices or use of certain materials that may contain lead paint, asbestos, or some other hazards that may need to be removed or encapsulated before the buildings are habitable. Addressing these problems is one of the challenges of owning and restoring a historic property. The Foundation does not have the resources to correct these problems and cannot take responsibility for the condition of the properties being sold. The Foundation is not liable in any way for any hazards, defects, or other problems with the properties under covenants.

Extinguishment

14. The Grantee and the Foundation recognize that an unexpected change in the conditions surrounding the Subject Property may make impossible or impractical the continued use of the Subject Property for conservation purposes and necessitate the extinguishment of these Protective Covenants. Such an extinguishment must comply with the following requirements:

(a) The extinguishment must be the result of a final judicial proceeding.

(b) The Foundation shall be entitled to share in the net proceeds resulting from the extinguishment in an amount in accordance with the then applicable regulations of the Internal Revenue Service of the U. S. Department of the Treasury.

(c) The Foundation agrees to apply all of the portion of the net proceeds it receives to the preservation and conservation of other property or buildings having historical or architectural significance to the people of the State of North Carolina.

(d) Net proceeds shall include, without limitation, insurance proceeds, condemnation proceeds or awards, proceeds from a sale in lieu of condemnation, and proceeds from the sale or exchange by Grantee of any portion of the Subject Property after the extinguishment.

Remedies

15. In the event of a violation of covenants contained in Paragraphs 2, 3, 4, 5, and 6 hereof, the Foundation then shall have an option to purchase the Subject Property, provided that it shall give the Grantee written notice of the nature of the violation and the Grantee shall not have corrected same within the ninety (90) days next following the giving of said notice. The purchase of the Subject Property, pursuant to the exercise of the option retained hereby, shall be at a price equal to the then market value of the Subject Property, subject to restrictive covenants, as determined by agreement of the then owner and the Foundation, or, in the absence of such agreement, by a committee of three appraisers, one to be selected by the Foundation, one to be selected by the then owner, and the other to be designated by the two appraisers selected by the Foundation and the owner respectively. Provided, however, that if there are outstanding deeds of trust or other encumbrances against the property, any right to purchase shall be subject to said deeds of trust or encumbrances, and they shall either be satisfied or assumed as part of the purchase price.

16. In the event of a violation of these covenants and restrictions, all legal and equitable remedies, including injunctive relief, specific performance, and damages, shall be available to the Foundation. No failure on the part of the Foundation to enforce any covenant or restriction herein nor the waiver of any right hereunder by the Foundation shall discharge or invalidate such covenant or restriction or any other covenant, condition or restriction hereof, or affect the right of the Foundation to enforce the same in event of a subsequent breach or default.

Transfer Fee

17. Except as otherwise provided herein, there shall be assessed by the Foundation and collected from the purchasers of the Subject Property, or any portion thereof subject to these covenants and restrictions, a transfer fee equal to twenty-five one-hundredths of one percent (0.25%) of the sales price of such property, or any portion thereof, which transfer fee shall be paid to the Foundation and used by the Foundation for the purpose of preserving the historical, architectural, archeological or cultural aspects of real

property. Such fee shall not apply to inter-spousal transfers, transfers by gift, transfers between parents and children, transfers between grandparents and grandchildren, transfers between siblings, transfers between a corporation and any shareholders in the same corporation who own 10 percent (10%) or more of the stock in such corporation and transfers between a limited liability corporation and any member who owns more than ten percent (10%) of such limited liability corporation, transfers by will, bequest, intestate succession or transfers to the Foundation (each of the foregoing hereinafter referred to as an "Exempt Transfer"); *provided, however,* that such fee shall not apply to the first non-exempt transfer of the Subject Property, but shall apply to each non-exempt transfer thereafter. In the event of non-payment of such a transfer fee, the amount due shall bear interest at the rate of 12% (twelve percent) per annum from the date of such transfer, shall, together with accrued interest, constitute a lien on the real property, or any portion thereof, subject to these covenants and restrictions and shall be subject to foreclosure by the Foundation. In the event that the Foundation is required to foreclose on its lien for the collection of the transfer fee, and/or interest thereon, provided for herein, the Foundation shall be entitled to recover all litigation costs and attorney's fees incurred at such foreclosure, which litigation costs and attorney's fees shall be included as part of the lien and recoverable out of proceeds of the foreclosure sale. The Foundation may require the purchaser and/or seller to provide reasonable written proof of the applicable sales price, such as executed closing statements, contracts of sale, copies of deeds, affidavits or such other evidence, and purchaser shall be obligated to provide such information within forty-eight (48) hours after receipt of written request for such information from the Foundation.

Insurance

18. Grantee shall insure the Subject Property against damage by fire or other catastrophe. If the original structure is damaged by fire or other catastrophe to an extent not exceeding fifty percent (50%) of the insurable value of those portions of the building, then insurance proceeds shall be used to rebuild those portions of the Subject Property in accordance with the standards in Exhibit B. The Grantee shall keep the Subject Property insured under a comprehensive general liability policy that names the Foundation as an additional insured and that protects the Grantee and the Foundation against claims for personal injury, death and property damage.

Mortgage Subordination

19. All mortgages and rights in the property of all mortgagees are subject and subordinate at all times to the rights of the Foundation to enforce the purposes of these covenants and restrictions. Grantee will provide a copy of these covenants and restrictions to all mortgagees of the Subject Property and has caused all mortgagees as of the date of this deed to subordinate the priority of their liens to these covenants and restrictions. The subordination provisions as described above relate only to the purposes of these covenants and restrictions, namely the preservation of the historic architecture and landscape of the Subject Property.

Duration of Covenants

20. The Grantee does hereby covenant to carry out the duties specified herein, and these restrictions shall be covenants and restrictions running with the land, which the Grantee, *[HIS OR HER]* heirs, successors, and assigns, covenant and agree, in the event the Subject Property is sold or otherwise disposed of, will be inserted in the deed or other instrument conveying or disposing of the Subject Property.

21. Unless otherwise provided, the covenants and restrictions set forth above shall run in perpetuity.

EXHIBIT B

SECRETARY OF THE INTERIOR'S
STANDARDS FOR THE TREATMENT OF HISTORIC PROPERTIES
(1992)

TREATMENTS

There are Standards for four distinct, but interrelated, approaches to the treatment of historic properties—Preservation, Rehabilitation, Restoration, and Reconstruction. **Preservation** focuses on the maintenance and repair of existing historic materials and retention of a property's form as it has evolved over time. (Protection and Stabilization have now been consolidated under this treatment.) **Rehabilitation** acknowledges the need to alter or add to a historic property to meet continuing or changing uses while retaining the property's historic character. **Restoration** is undertaken to depict a property at a particular period of time in its history, while removing evidence of other periods. **Reconstruction** recreates vanished or non-surviving portions of a property for interpretive purposes.

In summary, the simplification and sharpened focus of these revised sets of treatment standards is intended to assist users in making sound historic preservation decisions. Choosing appropriate treatment for a historic property, whether preservation, rehabilitation, restoration, or reconstruction, is critical. This choice always depends on a variety of factors, including the property's historical significance, physical condition, proposed use, and intended interpretation.

PRESERVATION is defined as the act or process of applying measures necessary to sustain the existing form, integrity, and materials of a historic property. Work, including preliminary measures to protect and stabilize the property, generally focuses upon the ongoing maintenance and repair of historic materials and features rather than extensive replacement and new construction. New exterior additions are not within the scope of this treatment; however, the limited and sensitive upgrading of mechanical, electrical, and plumbing systems and other code-required work to make properties functional is appropriate within a preservation project.

STANDARDS FOR PRESERVATION

1. A property shall be used as it was historically, or be given a new use that maximizes the retention of distinctive materials, features, spaces, and spatial relationships. Where a treatment and use have not been identified, a property shall be protected and, if necessary, stabilized until additional work may be undertaken.

2. The historic character of the property shall be retained and preserved. The replacement of intact or repairable historical materials or alteration of features, spaces, and spatial relationships that characterize a property shall be avoided.

3. Each property shall be recognized as a physical record of its time, place, and use. Work needed to stabilize, consolidate, and conserve existing historic materials and features shall be physically and visually compatible, identifiable upon close inspection, and properly documented for future research.

4. Changes to a property that have acquired historic significance in their own right shall be retained and preserved.

5. Distinctive materials, features, finishes, and construction techniques or examples of craftsmanship that characterize a property shall be preserved.

6. The existing condition of historic features shall be evaluated to determine the appropriate level of intervention needed. Where the severity of deterioration requires repair or limited replacement of a distinctive feature, the new material shall match the old in composition, design, color, and texture.

7. Chemical or physical treatments, if appropriate, shall be undertaken using the gentlest means possible. Treatments that cause damage to historic materials shall not be used.

8. Archeological resources shall be protected and preserved in place. If such resources must be disturbed, mitigation measures shall be undertaken.

PRESERVATION AS A TREATMENT

When the property's distinctive materials, features, and spaces are essentially intact and thus convey the historic significance without extensive repair or replacement; when depiction at a particular period of time is not appropriate; and when a continuing or new use does not require additions or extensive alterations, Preservation may be considered as a treatment. Prior to undertaking work, a documentation plan should be developed.

REHABILITATION is defined as the act or process of making possible a compatible use for a property through repair, alterations, and additions while preserving those portions or features which convey its historical, cultural, or architectural values.

STANDARDS FOR REHABILITATION

1. A property shall be used as it was historically or be given a new use that requires minimal change to its distinctive materials, features, spaces, and spatial relationships.

2. The historic character of a property shall be retained and preserved. The removal of distinctive materials or alteration of features, spaces, and spatial relationships that characterize a property shall be avoided.

3. Each property shall be recognized as a physical record of its time, place, and use. Changes that create a false sense of historical development, such as adding conjectural features or elements from other historic properties, shall not be undertaken.

4. Changes to a property that have acquired historic significance in their own right shall be retained and preserved.

5. Distinctive materials, features, finishes, and construction techniques or examples of craftsmanship that characterize a property shall be preserved.

6. Deteriorated historic features shall be repaired rather than replaced. Where the severity of deterioration requires replacement of a distinctive feature, the new feature shall match the old in design, color, texture, and, where possible, materials. Replacement of missing features shall be substantiated by documentary and physical evidence.

7. Chemical or physical treatments, if appropriate, shall be undertaken using the gentlest means possible. Treatments that cause damage to historic materials shall not be used.

8. Archeological resources shall be protected and preserved in place. If such resources must be disturbed, mitigation measures shall be undertaken.

9. New additions, exterior alterations, or related new construction shall not destroy historic materials, features, and spatial relationships that characterize the property. The new work shall be differentiated from the old and shall be compatible with the historical materials, features, size, scale, and proportion, and massing to protect the integrity of the property and its environment.

10. New additions and adjacent or related new construction shall be undertaken in such a manner that, if removed in the future, the essential form and integrity of the historic property and its environment would be unimpaired.

REHABILITATION AS A TREATMENT

When repair and replacement of deteriorated features are necessary; when alterations or additions to the property are planned for a new or continued use; and when its depiction at a particular period of time is not appropriate, Rehabilitation may be considered as a treatment. Prior to undertaking work, a documentation plan for Rehabilitation should be developed.

RESTORATION is defined as the act or process of accurately depicting the form, features, and character of a property as it appeared at a particular period of time by means of the removal of features from other periods in its history and reconstruction of missing features from the restoration period. The limited and sensitive upgrading of mechanical, electrical, and plumbing systems and other code-required work to make properties functional is appropriate within a restoration project.

STANDARDS FOR RESTORATION

1. A property shall be used as it was historically or be given a new use which reflects the property's restoration period.

2. Materials and features from the restoration period shall be retained and preserved. The removal of materials or alteration of features, spaces, and spatial relationships that characterize the period shall not be undertaken.

3. Each property shall be recognized as a physical record of its time, place, and use. Work needed to stabilize, consolidate, and conserve materials and features from the restoration period shall be physically and visually compatible, identifiable upon close inspection, and properly documented for future research.

4. Materials, features, spaces, and finishes that characterize other historical periods shall be documented prior to their alteration or removal.

5. Distinctive materials, features, finishes, and construction techniques or examples of craftsmanship that characterize the restoration period shall be preserved.

6. Deteriorated features from the restoration period shall be repaired rather than replaced. Where the severity of deterioration requires replacement of a distinctive feature, the new feature shall match the old in design, color, texture, and where possible, materials.

7. Replacement of missing features from the restoration period shall be substantiated by documentary and physical evidence. A false sense of history shall not be created by adding conjectural features, features from other properties, or by combining features that never existed together historically.

8. Chemical or physical treatments, if appropriate, shall be undertaken using the gentlest means possible. Treatments that cause damage to historic materials shall not be used.

9. Archeological resources affected by a project shall be protected and preserved in place. If such resources must be disturbed, mitigation measures shall be undertaken.

10. Designs that were never executed historically shall not be constructed.

RESTORATION AS A TREATMENT

When the property's design, architectural, or historical significance during a particular period of time outweighs the potential loss of extant materials, features, spaces, and finishes that characterize other historical periods; when there is substantial physical and documentary evidence for the work; and when contemporary alterations and additions are not planned, Restoration may be considered as a treatment. Prior to undertaking work, a particular period of time, i.e., the restoration period, should be selected and justified, and a documentation plan for Restoration developed.

RECONSTRUCTION is defined as the act or process of depicting, by means of new construction, the form, features, and detailing of a non-surviving site, landscape, building, structure, or object for the purpose of replicating its appearance at a specific period of time and in its historic location.

STANDARDS FOR RECONSTRUCTION

1. Reconstruction shall be used to depict vanished or non-surviving portions of a property when documentary and physical evidence is available to permit accurate reconstruction with minimal conjecture, and such reconstruction is essential to the public understanding of the property.

2. Reconstruction of a landscape, building, structure, or object in its historic location shall be preceded by a thorough archeological investigation to identify and evaluate those features and artifacts which are essential to an accurate reconstruction. If such resources must be disturbed, mitigation measures shall be undertaken.

3. Reconstruction shall include measures to preserve any remaining historic materials, features, and spatial relationships.

4. Reconstruction shall be based on the accurate duplication of historic features and elements substantiated by documentary or physical evidence rather than on conjectural designs or the availability of different features from other historic properties. A reconstructed property shall re-create the appearance of a non-surviving historic property in materials, design, color, and texture.

5. A reconstruction shall be clearly identified as a contemporary re-creation.

6. Designs that were never executed historically shall not be constructed.

RECONSTRUCTION AS A TREATMENT

When a contemporary depiction is required to understand and interpret a property's historic value (including the re-creation of missing components in a historic district or site); when no other property with the same associative value has survived; and when sufficient historical documentation exists to ensure an accurate reproduction, Reconstruction may be considered as a treatment. Prior to undertaking work, a documentation plan for Reconstruction should be developed.

Author's Note: As with all of the legal documents contained in these appendices, this document is not presented as a "model" document. These documents need to be reviewed and revised on a case-by-case, state-by-state basis by legal counsel. They are not static documents. Preservation North Carolina frequently updates its documents to incorporate new language or to adjust to new legal requirements. Each document is adjusted to reflect the special requirements of the property and the parties to the agreement.

STATE OF NORTH CAROLINA
COUNTY OF _____

REHABILITATION AGREEMENT

THIS AGREEMENT, made and entered into this _____ day of _____ 200_, by and between **THE HISTORIC PRESERVATION FOUNDATION OF NORTH CAROLINA, INC.,** a nonprofit corporation organized under the laws of North Carolina, hereinafter referred to as the "Foundation," and _____ of _____ County, North Carolina, hereinafter referred to as the "Purchaser";

WITNESSETH:

THAT WHEREAS both the Foundation and the Purchaser desire that the historic _____ _____ be preserved in as authentic condition as possible and, at the same time, be altered where necessary to provide modern conveniences for its new owner; and

WHEREAS, the Foundation and the Purchaser on this day have made and entered into a Deed and Protective Covenants, incorporating by reference this Rehabilitation Agreement and the provisions herein;

NOW, THEREFORE, The Purchaser agrees to rehabilitate the historic _____ _____ according to the following terms, conditions, and deadlines, adequate consideration having been acknowledged in the above mentioned Deed:

A. DEADLINES FOR REHABILITATION

(1) By _____, the Purchaser shall provide modern heating, electrical, and plumbing systems, as needed.

(2) By _____, the Purchaser shall complete all interior and exterior work needed to make the original _____ comfortably habitable and to comply with this Rehabilitation Agreement.

(3) Before rehabilitation work is begun, the Purchaser shall photograph all exterior sides of the building, and all interior walls and trim in order to document the appearance, configuration, and condition of said building prior to rehabilitation.

B. GUIDELINES FOR REHABILITATION

(1) General

(a) The Purchaser agrees to adhere to and abide by the Secretary of the Interior's Standards for the Treatment of Historic Properties (1992), a copy of which is attached as "Exhibit A" and which is specifically incorporated herein by reference.

(b) The terms and conditions of this Rehabilitation Agreement may be changed with the approval of both the Foundation and the Purchaser as new and unforeseen circumstances arise. Changes in the terms and conditions of this Rehabilitation Agreement shall be made in writing and signed by both parties.

(c) This Rehabilitation Agreement does not constitute waiver of any rights of the Foundation retained by it in its Deed and Protective Covenants with the Purchaser.

(d) The Purchaser shall give priority to repairs needed to prevent deterioration of the building.

(2) Exterior

(a) The roof shall be repaired as needed with materials sympathetic to the age and design of the house.

(b) Masonry shall be repaired or replaced as needed with the same or comparable material that matches the bond, size, color and texture as the existing material. Mortar used shall match the color and texture of existing mortar.

(c) Doors, windows and decorative trim shall be retained and repaired with materials and in a style compatible with the character of the building.

(d) The Foundation encourages the Purchaser to have paint research undertaken on the exterior of the house and to use original colors.

(e) (Insert additional provisions as needed)

(3) Heating, Air Conditioning, and Insulation

(a) The Purchaser shall choose methods of insulation which will adequately protect and preserve the original fabric of the building. Methods of insulation which have not been tested for possible adverse effects on historic structures shall be strongly discouraged. Under no circumstances shall foam-in-place or loose-fill insulation be installed in the exterior walls of the house.

(b) The Purchaser shall consult the President or Chairman of the Board of Directors of the Foundation about locations and types of any new heating and/or air conditioning systems and duct chases introduced into the building.

(4) Interior

(a) Any interior alteration made by the Purchaser shall insofar as possible respect and preserve the original wood trim (including but not limited to the floors, moldings, mantels, window and door surrounds, and staircase). No removal or alteration of said wood trim shall be made without the written approval of the President or Chairman of the Board of Directors of the Foundation.

(b) The Purchaser shall consult with the President or Chairman of the Board of Directors of the Foundation prior to the addition of any new interior walls or prior to the removal of any existing interior walls.

(c) The Purchaser shall consult with the President or Chairman of the Board of Directors of the Foundation on the location and plans of any new kitchen or bathrooms to be installed.

(d) The Purchaser shall repair existing plaster walls and ceilings as needed. If necessary, the purchaser may replace plaster walls with sheetrock.

(5) Landscaping

(a) The Purchaser shall fully landscape the premises in a manner compatible with the style and period of the house.

(b) The Purchaser shall make the best effort to maintain a clean and neat construction site while rehabilitation of the _____ takes place.

C. ENFORCEMENT

(1) If the _____ shall not be rehabilitated according to the terms, conditions, and deadlines of this Rehabilitation Agreement, then the Foundation shall have an option to repurchase the premises for the lesser of (i) a price equal to the then market value of the premises, subject to restrictive covenants (said price to be determined by the procedure described in Paragraph (2) of this Section) or (ii) the initial purchase price paid by the Purchaser plus the amount spent (exclusive of interest, insurance, and ad valorem taxes) by the Purchaser toward the rehabilitation of said building. This option will expire on _____, or upon the completion of said rehabilitation, whichever occurs first. Provided, however, that if there are any outstanding deeds of trust or other encumbrances against the property, any right to purchase shall be subject to said deeds of trust or encumbrances, and they shall either be satisfied or assumed as part of the purchase price.

(2) The price indicated in clause (i) of Paragraph (1) of this Section shall be determined by agreement of the Purchaser and the Foundation, or in the absence of such agreement, by a committee of three appraisers, one to be selected by the Foundation, one to be selected by the Purchaser, and the other to be designated by the two appraisers selected by the Foundation and the Purchaser respectively.

(3) In the event of a violation of the terms, conditions, and deadlines of this Rehabilitation Agreement, any matters in dispute will be submitted to binding arbitration by a recognized arbitrator in North

Carolina upon which the Purchaser and the Foundation can agree, or in the event of no agreement on a choice of arbitrator, by a committee of three arbitrators with the first designated by the Purchaser, the second by the Foundation, and the third be designated by the two arbitrators selected by the Foundation and the Purchaser respectively. Nothing in this clause shall be construed to deny the Foundation from seeking injunctive relief to prevent the Purchaser from pursuing further activities which might have or tend to harm interests of the Foundation as set forth in this agreement or prevent damage to other legitimate historical and archaeological concerns. No failure on the part of the Foundation to enforce any term herein nor the waiver of any right hereunder by the Foundation shall discharge or invalidate such term or other term, condition or deadline hereof, or affect the right of the Foundation to enforce the same in event of a subsequent breach or default.

IN TESTIMONY WHEREOF, the parties hereto have executed this Rehabilitation Agreement in duplicate the date first set out above.

THE HISTORIC PRESERVATION FOUNDATION
OF NORTH CAROLINA, INC.

BY: _____

WITNESS: _____

_____

WITNESS: _____

EXHIBIT A

SECRETARY OF THE INTERIOR'S
STANDARDS FOR THE TREATMENT OF HISTORIC PROPERTIES
(1992)

TREATMENTS

There are Standards for four distinct, but interrelated, approaches to the treatment of historic properties—Preservation, Rehabilitation, Restoration, and Reconstruction. **Preservation** focuses on the maintenance and repair of existing historic materials and retention of a property's form as it has evolved over time. (Protection and Stabilization have now been consolidated under this treatment.) **Rehabilitation** acknowledges the need to alter or add to a historic property to meet continuing or changing uses while retaining the property's historic character. **Restoration** is undertaken to depict a property at a particular period of time in its history, while removing evidence of other periods. **Reconstruction** recreates vanished or non-surviving portions of a property for interpretive purposes.

In summary, the simplification and sharpened focus of these revised sets of treatment standards is intended to assist users in making sound historic preservation decisions. Choosing appropriate treatment for a historic property, whether preservation, rehabilitation, restoration, or reconstruction, is critical. This choice always depends on a variety of factors, including the property's historical significance, physical condition, proposed use, and intended interpretation.

PRESERVATION is defined as the act or process of applying measures necessary to sustain the existing form, integrity, and materials of a historic property. Work, including preliminary measures to protect and stabilize the property, generally focuses upon the ongoing maintenance and repair of historic materials and features rather than extensive replacement and new construction. New exterior additions are not within the scope of this treatment; however, the limited and sensitive upgrading of mechanical, electrical, and plumbing systems and other code-required work to make properties functional is appropriate within a preservation project.

STANDARDS FOR PRESERVATION

1. A property shall be used as it was historically, or be given a new use that maximizes the retention of distinctive materials, features, spaces, and spatial relationships. Where a treatment and use have not been identified, a property shall be protected and, if necessary, stabilized until additional work may be undertaken.

2. The historic character of the property shall be retained and preserved. The replacement of intact or repairable historical materials or alteration of features, spaces, and spatial relationships that characterize a property shall be avoided.

3. Each property shall be recognized as a physical record of its time, place, and use. Work needed to stabilize, consolidate, and conserve existing historic materials and features shall be physically and visually compatible, identifiable upon close inspection, and properly documented for future research.

4. Changes to a property that have acquired historic significance in their own right shall be retained and preserved.

5. Distinctive materials, features, finishes, and construction techniques or examples of craftsmanship that characterize a property shall be preserved.

6. The existing condition of historic features shall be evaluated to determine the appropriate level of intervention needed. Where the severity of deterioration requires repair or limited replacement of a distinctive feature, the new material shall match the old in composition, design, color, and texture.

7. Chemical or physical treatments, if appropriate, shall be undertaken using the gentlest means possible. Treatments that cause damage to historic materials shall not be used.

8. Archeological resources shall be protected and preserved in place. If such resources must be disturbed, mitigation measures shall be undertaken.

PRESERVATION AS A TREATMENT

When the property's distinctive materials, features, and spaces are essentially intact and thus convey the historic significance without extensive repair or replacement; when depiction at a particular period of time is not appropriate; and when a continuing or new use does not require additions or extensive alterations, Preservation may be considered as a treatment. Prior to undertaking work, a documentation plan should be developed.

REHABILITATION is defined as the act or process of making possible a compatible use for a property through repair, alterations, and additions while preserving those portions or features which convey its historical, cultural, or architectural values.

STANDARDS FOR REHABILITATION

1. A property shall be used as it was historically or be given a new use that requires minimal change to its distinctive materials, features, spaces, and spatial relationships.

2. The historic character of a property shall be retained and preserved. The removal of distinctive materials or alteration of features, spaces, and spatial relationships that characterize a property shall be avoided.

3. Each property shall be recognized as a physical record of its time, place, and use. Changes that create a false sense of historical development, such as adding conjectural features or elements from other historic properties, shall not be undertaken.

4. Changes to a property that have acquired historic significance in their own right shall be retained and preserved.

5. Distinctive materials, features, finishes, and construction techniques or examples of craftsmanship that characterize a property shall be preserved.

6. Deteriorated historic features shall be repaired rather than replaced. Where the severity of deterioration requires replacement of a distinctive feature, the new feature shall match the old in design, color, texture, and, where possible, materials. Replacement of missing features shall be substantiated by documentary and physical evidence.

7. Chemical or physical treatments, if appropriate, shall be undertaken using the gentlest means possible. Treatments that cause damage to historic materials shall not be used.

8. Archeological resources shall be protected and preserved in place. If such resources must be disturbed, mitigation measures shall be undertaken.

9. New additions, exterior alterations, or related new construction shall not destroy historic materials, features, and spatial relationships that characterize the property. The new work shall be differentiated from the old and shall be compatible with the historical materials, features, size, scale, and proportion, and massing to protect the integrity of the property and its environment.

10. New additions and adjacent or related new construction shall be undertaken in such a manner that, if removed in the future, the essential form and integrity of the historic property and its environment would be unimpaired.

REHABILITATION AS A TREATMENT

When repair and replacement of deteriorated features are necessary; when alterations or additions to the property are planned for a new or continued use; and when its depiction at a particular period of time is not appropriate, Rehabilitation may be considered as a treatment. Prior to undertaking work, a documentation plan for Rehabilitation should be developed.

RESTORATION is defined as the act or process of accurately depicting the form, features, and character of a property as it appeared at a particular period of time by means of the removal of features from other periods in its history and reconstruction of missing features from the restoration period. The limited and sensitive upgrading of mechanical, electrical, and plumbing systems and other code-required work to make properties functional is appropriate within a restoration project.

STANDARDS FOR RESTORATION

1. A property shall be used as it was historically or be given a new use which reflects the property's restoration period.

2. Materials and features from the restoration period shall be retained and preserved. The removal of materials or alteration of features, spaces, and spatial relationships that characterize the period shall not be undertaken.

3. Each property shall be recognized as a physical record of its time, place, and use. Work needed to stabilize, consolidate, and conserve materials and features from the restoration period shall be physically and visually compatible, identifiable upon close inspection, and properly documented for future research.

4. Materials, features, spaces, and finishes that characterize other historical periods shall be documented prior to their alteration or removal.

5. Distinctive materials, features, finishes, and construction techniques or examples of craftsmanship that characterize the restoration period shall be preserved.

6. Deteriorated features from the restoration period shall be repaired rather than replaced. Where the severity of deterioration requires replacement of a distinctive feature, the new feature shall match the old in design, color, texture, and where possible, materials.

7. Replacement of missing features from the restoration period shall be substantiated by documentary and physical evidence. A false sense of history shall not be created by adding conjectural features, features from other properties, or by combining features that never existed together historically.

8. Chemical or physical treatments, if appropriate, shall be undertaken using the gentlest means possible. Treatments that cause damage to historic materials shall not be used.

9. Archeological resources affected by a project shall be protected and preserved in place. If such resources must be disturbed, mitigation measures shall be undertaken.

10. Designs that were never executed historically shall not be constructed.

RESTORATION AS A TREATMENT

When the property's design, architectural, or historical significance during a particular period of time outweighs the potential loss of extant materials, features, spaces, and finishes that characterize other historical periods; when there is substantial physical and documentary evidence for the work; and when contemporary alterations and additions are not planned, Restoration may be considered as a treatment. Prior to undertaking work, a particular period of time, i.e., the restoration period, should be selected and justified, and a documentation plan for Restoration developed.

RECONSTRUCTION is defined as the act or process of depicting, by means of new construction, the form, features, and detailing of a non-surviving site, landscape, building, structure, or object for the purpose of replicating its appearance at a specific period of time and in its historic location.

STANDARDS FOR RECONSTRUCTION

1. Reconstruction shall be used to depict vanished or non-surviving portions of a property when documentary and physical evidence is available to permit accurate reconstruction with minimal conjecture, and such reconstruction is essential to the public understanding of the property.

2. Reconstruction of a landscape, building, structure, or object in its historic location shall be preceded by a thorough archeological investigation to identify and evaluate those features and artifacts which are essential to an accurate reconstruction. If such resources must be disturbed, mitigation measures shall be undertaken.

3. Reconstruction shall include measures to preserve any remaining historic materials, features, and spatial relationships.

4. Reconstruction shall be based on the accurate duplication of historic features and elements substantiated by documentary or physical evidence rather than on conjectural designs or the availability of different features from other historic properties. A reconstructed property shall re-create the appearance of a non-surviving historic property in materials, design, color, and texture.

5. A reconstruction shall be clearly identified as a contemporary re-creation.

6. Designs that were never executed historically shall not be constructed.

RECONSTRUCTION AS A TREATMENT

When a contemporary depiction is required to understand and interpret a property's historic value (including the re-creation of missing components in a historic district or site); when no other property with the same associative value has survived; and when sufficient historical documentation exists to ensure an accurate reproduction, Reconstruction may be considered as a treatment. Prior to undertaking work, a documentation plan for Reconstruction should be developed.

Author's Note: As with all of the legal documents contained in these appendices, this document is not presented as a "model" document. These documents need to be reviewed and revised on a case-by-case, state-by-state basis by legal counsel. They are not static documents. Preservation North Carolina frequently updates its documents to incorporate new language or to adjust to new legal requirements. Each document (and especially the Rehabilitation Agreement) is adjusted to reflect the special requirements of the property and the parties to the agreement.

STATE OF NORTH CAROLINA
COUNTY OF _____

WAIVER OF FIRST REFUSAL

THIS WAIVER, made and entered into this _____ day of _____, 200_, is by and between **THE HISTORIC PRESERVATION FOUNDATION OF NORTH CAROLINA, INC.**, a nonprofit corporation organized and existing under the laws of North Carolina, with its principal office in Raleigh, North Carolina ("Foundation") and _____ ("Purchaser").

WHEREAS, the Foundation has heretofore been granted by a deed recorded in Book_____, Page ____ of the _____ County Registry a right of first refusal to purchase the real property therein described;

WHEREAS, the historic _____ is situated on said property, and;

WHEREAS, the Purchaser is aware of and understands the Restrictive Covenants incorporated in the deed herein described, has agreed to abide by said covenants, and shall make any future conveyance subject to said covenants.

NOW, THEREFORE, in consideration of the purchase by Purchaser of the hereinafter described real property subject to restrictive covenants, Foundation does hereby waive in favor of the Purchaser its right of first refusal as established in the aforesaid instrument recorded in Book _____, Page _____, as to the real property described in Exhibit A.

This Waiver constitutes a release of the right of first refusal as to this transaction only, and it is stipulated and agreed that the right of first refusal as set out in the aforesaid instrument recorded in Book _____, Page _____ shall continue to apply in the case of a contemplated sale of the premises or any portion thereof by Purchaser or any successor in title thereto.

IN WITNESS WHEREOF, the Foundation has caused this instrument to be executed in its corporate name by its President this the day and year first above written.

THE HISTORIC PRESERVATION FOUNDATION
OF NORTH CAROLINA, INC.

BY: _____
PURCHASER

BY: _____
[NAME]

STATE OF NORTH CAROLINA
COUNTY OF WAKE

I, _____, a Notary Public of the County and State aforesaid, certify that J. Myrick Howard, personally came before me this day and acknowledged that he is the President of **THE HISTORIC PRESERVATION FOUNDATION OF NORTH CAROLINA, INC.**, a nonprofit North Carolina corporation, and that by authority duly given and as the act of the corporation, the foregoing instrument was signed in its name by him as its President and sealed with its corporate seal.

Witness my hand and Notarial Seal, this the _____ day of _____, 200_.

_____
Notary Public

My Commission Expires: _____

STATE OF NORTH CAROLINA
COUNTY OF _____

I, _____, a Notary Public of the County and State aforesaid, certify that _____, personally came before me this day and acknowledged the due execution of the foregoing instrument.

Witness my hand and Notarial Seal, this the _____ day of _____, 200_.

_____
Notary Public

My Commission Expires: _____

Filed for Registration on the _____ day of _____, 200_, _____ o'clock _____. M. and duly registered in the Office of the Register of Deeds of _____ County, North Carolina, Book _____, page _____.

_____
REGISTER OF DEEDS

_____
BY ASST. OR DEPUTY REG. OF DEEDS

EXHIBIT A

Legal Property Description

Author's Note: As with all of the legal documents contained in these appendices, this document is not presented as a "model" document. These documents need to be reviewed and revised on a case-by-case, state-by-state basis by legal counsel. They are not static documents. Preservation North Carolina frequently updates its documents to incorporate new language or to adjust to new legal requirements. Each document is adjusted to reflect the special requirements of the property and the parties to the agreement.

STATE OF NORTH CAROLINA
COUNTY OF _____

HISTORIC PRESERVATION AGREEMENT

THIS AGREEMENT, made this the _____ day of _____, 20___, by and between _____ _____, of _____ County, North Carolina (hereinafter referred to as the "Grantor"), and **THE HISTORIC PRESERVATION FOUNDATION OF NORTH CAROLINA, INC.,** a nonprofit corporation organized and existing under the laws of the State of North Carolina with its principal office being in Raleigh, North Carolina (hereinafter referred to as the "Foundation");

WITNESSETH:

WHEREAS, the Grantor owns certain real property (hereinafter referred to as the "Subject Property"), a description of which is attached hereto as Exhibit A and incorporated herein by reference; and

WHEREAS, the Subject Property currently has certain permanent improvements consisting of *[BRIEF PROPERTY DESCRIPTION]* hereinafter referred to as *[PROPERTY NAME]*; and

WHEREAS, *[PROPERTY NAME]* located at *[ADDRESS, CITY OR TOWN], [NAME OF COUNTY]* County, North Carolina, is a property of recognized historical and architectural significance; and

WHEREAS, the Foundation and Grantor both desire that the Subject Property shall retain its historically and architecturally significant features, while being sympathetically adapted and altered, where necessary, to provide for contemporary uses; and

WHEREAS, the Foundation and Grantor both desire that the Subject Property shall not be subdivided in order to preserve its integrity of site; and

WHEREAS, the Foundation is a charitable organization which accepts preservation easements on buildings having historical or architectural importance, said easement subjecting such buildings to restrictions that will insure that they are preserved and maintained for the benefit of future generations; and

WHEREAS, the North Carolina General Assembly has enacted the Historic Preservation and Conservation Agreements Act validating restrictions, easements, covenants, conditions, or otherwise, appropriate to the preservation of a structure or site significant for its architecture, archaeology or historical associations.

NOW, THEREFORE, for and in consideration of the Grantor's interest in historic preservation and their support for the Foundation and its purposes, and for and in consideration of the sum of **ONE DOLLAR ($1.00),** the Grantor, for himself, his successors and assigns, hereby covenant and agree to abide by the following restrictions (hereinafter referred to as "covenants"), said covenants to be restrictions of record to attach to the land described in Exhibit A:

1. These covenants shall be administered solely by the Historic Preservation Foundation of North Carolina, Inc., its successors in interest or assigns; and in all subsequent conveyances of Subject Property, the Foundation, its successors in interest or assigns shall be the sole party entitled to administer these covenants. In the event that the Foundation, or its successors in interest by corporate merger cease to exist, then in such event the Foundation shall assign all of its rights and interests in these easements, covenants, and conditions subject to such duties and obligations which it assumes hereby to a nonprofit corporation of responsibility which exists for substantially the same reasons as the Foundation itself (as described hereinabove); if no such corporation be available for such assignment then, under such circumstances such assignment shall be made to the State of North Carolina which shall be the sole party entitled to administer those covenants.

Maintenance
2. The Grantor covenants and agrees to continuously maintain, repair, and administer the *[PROPERTY NAME]* herein described in accordance with the Secretary of the Interior's Standards for the Treatment of Historic Properties (1992) so as to preserve the historical integrity of features, materials, appearances, workmanship and environment of the Subject Property. Maintenance shall be continuously provided. Said standards are attached hereto and incorporated in these covenants by reference.

Prior Approval Required For Modifications
3. Unless prior written approval by the President or Chairman of the Board of Directors of the Foundation is obtained, no alteration, physical or structural change, or changes in the color, material or surfacing to the exterior of the *[PROPERTY NAME]* shall be made.

4. Unless the plans and exterior designs for such structure or addition have been approved in advance in writing by the President or Chairman of the Board of Directors of the Foundation, no addition or additional structure shall be constructed or permitted to be built upon the Subject Property. The Foundation in reviewing the plans and designs for any addition or additional structure shall consider the following criteria: exterior building materials; height; fenestration; roof shapes, forms, and materials; surface textures; expression of architectural detailing; scale; relationship of any additions to the main structure; general form and proportion of structures; orientation to street; setback; spacing of buildings, defined as the distance between adjacent buildings; lot coverage; use of local or regional architectural traditions; and effect on archeological resources. Contemporary designs for additions or additional structures shall not be discouraged when such alterations and additions do not destroy significant historical, architectural, or cultural material, and such design is compatible with the size, color, material and character of the property and its environment.

5. The Grantor and the Foundation hereby agree that the interior architectural features listed below are elements which contribute to the architectural significance of the *[PROPERTY NAME]*

{features to be listed here}

Unless prior written approval by the President or Chairman of the Board of Directors of the Foundation is obtained, no removal, relocation, or alteration of the above mentioned architectural features shall be made.

6. Neither the *[PROPERTY NAME]* nor any part thereof may be removed or demolished without the prior written approval of the President or Chairman of the Board of Directors of the Foundation.

7. No portion of the Subject Property may be subdivided.

8. Express written approval of the Foundation is required for removal of living trees greater than 12 inches in diameter at a point 4 feet above the ground from the Subject Property unless immediate removal is necessary for the protection of any persons coming onto the Subject Property or of the general public; for the prevention or treatment of disease; or for the protection and safety of the *[PROPERTY NAME]* or other permanent improvements on the Subject Property. Any tree of the aforementioned size which must be removed shall be replaced within a reasonable time by a new tree of a substantially similar species. If so requested, the Foundation may approve the use of an alternate species.

Covenant to Obey Public Laws
9. The Grantor shall abide by all federal, state, and local laws and ordinances regulating the rehabilitation, maintenance and use of the Subject Property.

Right of First Refusal
10. In case of any contemplated sale of the Subject Property or any portion thereof by the Grantor or any successor in title thereto, first refusal as to any bona fide offer of purchase must be given to the Foundation, its successors or assigns. If the Foundation so decides to purchase, it shall notify the then owner of its willingness to buy upon the same terms within thirty (30) days of receipt of written notice of such bona fide offer. Failure of the Foundation to notify the then owner of its intention to exercise this right of first refusal within such thirty (30) day period shall free the owner to sell pursuant to the bona fide offer. The Foundation may, in its discretion, waive its right of first refusal in writing, upon written receipt of such bona fide offer. Provided, however, that if there are any outstanding deeds of trust or other encumbrances against the property, any right to repurchase shall be subject to said deeds of trust or encumbrances, and they shall either be satisfied or assumed as part of the purchase price.

Inspection
11. Representatives of the Foundation shall have the right to enter the Subject Property at reasonable times, after giving reasonable notice, for the purpose of inspecting the buildings and grounds to determine if there is compliance by the Grantor with the terms of these covenants.

Public Access
12. Researchers, scholars, and groups especially interested in historic preservation shall have access to view the interior of the rehabilitated property by special appointment at various times and intervals during each year. The general public shall have access to the Subject Property to view the exterior and interior features herein protected at the Grantor's discretion at various times and intervals during each year at times both desirable to the public and convenient with the Grantor. Nothing shall be erected or allowed to grow on the Subject Property which would impair the visibility of the property and the buildings from the street level or other public rights of way.

Hazardous Materials

13. The properties the Foundation seeks to protect may contain certain hazards as a result of outdated building practices or use of certain materials that may contain lead paint, asbestos, or some other hazards that may need to be removed or encapsulated before the buildings are habitable. Addressing these problems is one of the challenges of owning and restoring a historic property. The Foundation does not have the resources to correct these problems and cannot take responsibility for the condition of the properties being sold. The Foundation is not liable in any way for any hazards, defects, or other problems with the properties under covenants.

Extinguishment

14. The Grantor and the Foundation recognize that an unexpected change in the conditions surrounding the Subject Property may make impossible or impractical the continued use of the Subject Property for conservation purposes and necessitate the extinguishment of this Historic Preservation Agreement. Such an extinguishment must comply with the following requirements:

(a) The extinguishment must be the result of a final judicial proceeding.

(b) The Foundation shall be entitled to share in the net proceeds resulting from the extinguishment in an amount in accordance with the then applicable regulations of the Internal Revenue Service of the U. S. Department of the Treasury.

(c) The Foundation agrees to apply all of the portion of the net proceeds it receives to the preservation and conservation of other property or buildings having historical or architectural significance to the people of the State of North Carolina.

(d) Net proceeds shall include, without limitation, insurance proceeds, condemnation proceeds or awards, proceeds from a sale in lieu of condemnation, and proceeds from the sale or exchange by Grantor of any portion of the Subject Property after the extinguishment.

Remedies

15. In the event of a violation of covenants contained in Paragraphs 2, 3, 4, 5, and 6 hereof, the Foundation then shall have an option to purchase the Subject Property, provided that it shall give the Grantor written notice of the nature of the violation and the Grantor shall not have corrected same within the ninety (90) days next following the giving of said notice. The purchase of the Subject Property, pursuant to the exercise of the option retained hereby, shall be at a price equal to the then market value of the Subject Property, subject to restrictive covenants, as determined by agreement of the then owner and the Foundation, or, in the absence of such agreement, by a committee of three appraisers, one to be selected by the Foundation, one to be selected by the then owner, and the other to be designated by the two appraisers selected by the Foundation and the owner respectively. Provided, however, that if there are outstanding deeds of trust or other encumbrances against the property, any right to purchase shall be subject to said deeds of trust or encumbrances, and they shall either be satisfied or assumed as part of the purchase price.

16. In the event of a violation of these covenants and restrictions, all legal and equitable remedies, including injunctive relief, specific performance, and damages, shall be available to the Foundation. No failure on the part of the Foundation to enforce any covenant or restriction herein nor the waiver of any right hereunder by the Foundation shall discharge or invalidate such covenant or restriction or any other

covenant, condition or restriction hereof, or affect the right of the Foundation to enforce the same in event of a subsequent breach or default.

Transfer Fee

17. Except as otherwise provided herein, there shall be assessed by the Foundation and collected from the purchasers of the Subject Property, or any portion thereof subject to these covenants and restrictions, a transfer fee equal to twenty-five one-hundredths of one percent (0.25%) of the sales price of such property, or any portion thereof, which transfer fee shall be paid to the Foundation and used by the Foundation for the purpose of preserving the historical, architectural, archeological or cultural aspects of real property. Such fee shall not apply to inter-spousal transfers, transfers by gift, transfers between parents and children, transfers between grandparents and grandchildren, transfers between siblings, transfers between a corporation and any shareholders in the same corporation who own 10 percent (10%) or more of the stock in such corporation and transfers between a limited liability corporation and any member who owns more than ten percent (10%) of such limited liability corporation, transfers by will, bequest, intestate succession or transfers to the Foundation (each of the foregoing hereinafter referred to as an "Exempt Transfer"); *provided, however*, that such fee shall not apply to the first non-exempt transfer of the Subject Property, but shall apply to each non-exempt transfer thereafter. In the event of non-payment of such a transfer fee, the amount due shall bear interest at the rate of 12% (twelve percent) per annum from the date of such transfer, shall, together with accrued interest, constitute a lien on the real property, or any portion thereof, subject to these covenants and restrictions and shall be subject to foreclosure by the Foundation. In the event that the Foundation is required to foreclose on its lien for the collection of the transfer fee, and/or interest thereon, provided for herein, the Foundation shall be entitled to recover all litigation costs and attorney's fees incurred at such foreclosure, which litigation costs and attorney's fees shall be included as part of the lien and recoverable out of proceeds of the foreclosure sale. The Foundation may require the purchaser and/or seller to provide reasonable written proof of the applicable sales price, such as executed closing statements, contracts of sale, copies of deeds, affidavits or such other evidence, and purchaser shall be obligated to provide such information within forty-eight (48) hours after receipt of written request for such information from the Foundation.

Insurance

18. Grantor shall insure the Subject Property against damage by fire or other catastrophe. If the original structure is damaged by fire or other catastrophe to an extent not exceeding fifty percent (50%) of the insurable value of those portions of the building, then insurance proceeds shall be used to rebuild those portions of the Subject Property in accordance with the standards in Exhibit B. The Grantor shall keep the Subject Property insured under a comprehensive general liability policy that names the Foundation as an additional insured and that protects the Grantor and the Foundation against claims for personal injury, death and property damage.

Mortgage Subordination

19. All mortgages and rights in the property of all mortgagees are subject and subordinate at all times to the rights of the Foundation to enforce the purposes of these covenants and restrictions. Grantor will provide a copy of these covenants and restrictions to all mortgagees of the Subject Property and has caused all mortgagees as of the date of this deed to subordinate the priority of their liens to these covenants and restrictions. The subordination provisions as described above relate only to the purposes of these covenants and restrictions, namely the preservation of the historic architecture and landscape of the Subject Property.

Duration of Covenants

20. The Grantor does hereby covenant to carry out the duties specified herein, and these restrictions shall be covenants and restrictions running with the land, which the Grantor, *[HIS OR HER]* heirs, successors, and assigns, covenant and agree, in the event the Subject Property is sold or otherwise disposed of, will be inserted in the deed or other instrument conveying or disposing of the Subject Property.

21. Unless otherwise provided, the covenants and restrictions set forth above shall run in perpetuity.

IN WITNESS WHEREOF, the Grantor has hereunto set their hands and seals, and the Historic Preservation Foundation of North Carolina, Inc., has caused this instrument to be signed in its corporate name by its duly authorized officer and its seal to be hereunto affixed by the authority of its Board of Directors, the day and year first above written.

[NAME OF GRANTOR]

_____ (Seal)

THE HISTORIC PRESERVATION FOUNDATION
OF NORTH CAROLINA, INC.

BY _____

Corporate Seal

STATE OF NORTH CAROLINA
COUNTY OF _____

I, _____, a Notary Public of the County and State aforesaid, certify that _____
_____ personally came before me this day and acknowledged the due execution of the foregoing instrument.

Witness my hand and official stamp or seal, this _____ day of _____,
200_.

My Commission Expires: _____   _____
                                                 Notary Public

STATE OF NORTH CAROLINA
COUNTY OF _____

I, _____, a Notary Public of the County and State aforesaid, certify that J. Myrick Howard personally came before me this day and acknowledged that he is President of THE HISTORIC PRESERVATION FOUNDATION OF NORTH CAROLINA, INC., a North Carolina corporation, and that by authority duly given and as the act of the corporation, the foregoing instrument was signed in its name by its President, sealed with its corporate seal.

Witness my hand and official stamp or seal, this _____ day of _____, 200_.

My Commission Expires: _____   _____
                                                 Notary Public

EXHIBIT A

Legal Property Description

Author's Note: As with all of the legal documents contained in these appendices, this document is not presented as a "model" document. These documents need to be reviewed and revised on a case-by-case, state-by-state basis by legal counsel. They are not static documents. Preservation North Carolina frequently updates its documents to incorporate new language or to adjust to new legal requirements. Each document is adjusted to reflect the special requirements of the property and the parties to the agreement. Congress and the Internal Revenue Service have recently been issuing new rules about preservation easements, which will require frequent updating of easement documents.

The Exhibit B for the Preservation Easement (Appendix E) is the same document as Exhibit B for the Protective Covenants (Appendix B). See p. 158 for that exhibit.

Index

About the Author

SINCE 1978, Myrick Howard has been executive director of Preservation North Carolina, the state's only statewide private nonprofit preservation organization. The National Park Service has referred to Preservation North Carolina as "the premier statewide preservation organization in the South—if not the nation."

A Durham native, Myrick attended Brown University and the University of North Carolina at Chapel Hill, where he received degrees in city planning and law in 1978. He teaches a graduate seminar on Historic Preservation Planning each year at the University of North Carolina at Chapel Hill. From 2003–2005, he served on the Board of Trustees of the National Trust for Historic Preservation.

Through the years, Myrick has received a number of statewide awards. In 1996, Gov. James B. Hunt, Jr., inducted him into the Order of the Long Leaf Pine, the highest civilian honor in North Carolina, presented for extraordinary service to the state. He lives in a 1911 historic house in Raleigh which he renovated.